Biogr.
CARS.1(ii)

THE LIFE OF LORD CARSON

VOLUME TWO

THE LIFE OF LORD CARSON

by

IAN COLVIN

LONDON
VICTOR GOLLANCZ LTD
14 Henrietta Street Covent Garden
1934

AUTHOR'S NOTE

Thanks are due to Lord Carson for patience under examination and for leaving to the biographer the freedom of his own opinions, even where he disagreed with them ; to his many friends, among them Lady Oxford and Asquith, Lord Lansdowne, Mr. Richard Law and Mr. Eric Long, for information and for leave to quote from correspondence ; to Lady Carson and Miss Goldsmith in the search for papers, and to Lady Craigavon and Sir Thomas Moles, of the *Belfast Telegraph*, for providing the illustrations.

I. C.

Printed in Great Britain by
The Camelot Press Ltd., London and Southampton

CONTENTS

5

6

CONTENTS

7

CONTENTS

ILLUSTRATIONS

CHAPTER I

IRISH HOME RULE

The Act of Union—England and Ireland—Irish prosperity—The Liberals and Home Rule—Mr. Asquith's pledge—Carson gives warning—Nationalist strategy.

WHEN EDWARD MARJORIBANKS, upon a fatal impulse, laid down his pen and left this book unfinished, its subject stood upon the threshold of great events. Sir Edward Carson had arrived at that time of life when a man might look for a little ease from his labours. He had neglected health and recreation in his arduous work of law ; he had made for himself a great name and a great position. He had held high office yet had no ambitions in politics : if he had any thought of a new career it was bounded by a seat on the bench which he held so much in reverence. He was ready to devote himself the more to the law since his family life was saddened by illness and misfortune. At the age of fifty-seven, of a somewhat hypochondriacal habit, he would willingly have turned his back upon Parliament, but for one circumstance, and that decisive. He was asked by his friends the Irish Unionists to lead them in the House of Commons, and he decided, on a point of duty, to accept that invitation.

The cause to which he thus devoted himself was nothing less than to maintain the Act of Union by that time manifestly threatened. To the English politicians who were getting out their tools and rigging up their scaffolding for the demolition of that structure, it was a political question, to be decided on grounds of principle and of expediency. To the Irishman it was something more : a question of life and death.

Most Irishmen, indeed, took sides in such a cause instinctively, as if striking or defending themselves against a blow. Reason was for them superfluous, since instinct consists in the accumulated reasons not of one life alone but of many generations. Carson, himself, was a natural Irishman, with an Irishman's instincts healthily alive, yet he did not act on these alone : knowledge of his country, her stormy history, her turbulent people, actual experience of the danger which threatened, confirmed the swift conclusions.

Great Britain and Ireland together, their people formed one nation ; but whereas on its eastern side the nation was, or seemed to be, one single mass of the same sedimentary rock, solid, united, uniform, coherent, on its western side it was stratified and twisted in layers of apparently different and incongruous material, separate deposits, never united, at open or tacit enmity. At the bottom, and interspersed, some primitive Pictish race, dark, secretive, revengeful, conquered and enslaved, it is said, by a later Celtic invasion of godlike people, and over these again, Norman and English and Scottish settlements, made in historic times still remembered, still heavy with animus, barely tolerated and deeply resented—charged with living volcanic fire.

Alien and native, they were all held together by the adjacent sedimentary mass ; but taken by themselves they had never been one nor could ever unite. On the contrary, they must crack apart, they must come into sharp conflict, they must engage in a turmoil of jarring fragments, with what disastrous consequences Carson clearly foresaw. And what was to him most obvious was this—that such a conglomerate would never be content under any rule of law devised by themselves, at least without a first ferocious settlement of old scores. Government by assent, forbearance in power let loose—for these, as Carson well knew, it was impossible to hope.

The happiness, the possessions, even the lives of his own people, the loyal Minority, those who had upheld the British law, their relatives and their dependants, it was the danger to them that touched him most nearly. He had already held inquests over bleeding bodies ; he had faced a ferocious mob with revolver or blackthorn in hand ; he was aware of the smouldering fire : it had blazed up and scorched his cheek, uncontrollable even under British law ; he had seen and felt it all : he knew.

Carson had taken the wolf by the ears : he had had experience of its strength and its ferocity ; we shall see later all that his heart foreboded and that his mind foresaw coming true. In the meantime it will help the reader to understand this story if we point out how obvious to the Irishman, how dark to the Englishman, these things were.

Those strata, to which we have referred, they were not dead, they were living. Here lies one great difference between Ireland and England—that whereas in England the social divisions are united in one race, one national feeling, one religion, in Ireland the racial, social and religious divisions all coincide and reinforce one another. We shall examine later the special case of Ulster : as to the south of Ireland, the lower classes were, generally speaking, native

Irish—Roman Catholic; the upper classes, again generally speaking, Anglo-Irish—Protestant. The labourers, the peasantry, the village shopkeepers and publicans belonged to the one division ; the large shopkeepers, merchants, officials, professions, gentry and nobility to the other. Thus the racial division was strengthened by a social division and reinforced by a religious division. On the one side were about three-quarters of the population, on the other about one-quarter, and the three-quarters had never reconciled themselves to the position, the possessions, even the presence of the one-quarter.

These things being frankly stated, it is easy to understand the ease with which the majority could be set against the minority in a political quarrel, and the difficulty of confining that quarrel, once started, to constitutional limits. To drive out the invader, to punish the heretic, to spoil the possessor, these three motives concentrated in one object gave to this old feud a strength of which the English Liberal politician had no conception. It was something fundamental which few Irishmen cared to explain and which few Englishmen troubled to understand.

We have said that it was difficult to confine this quarrel to constitutional limits : if history may be allowed its say we might call it impossible. Not even in Celtic times had the Irish ever been a united nation ; since the conquest of Strongbow they had never lost an opportunity of insurrection. There had indeed been one golden age of " glorious independence," between 1782, when the British Parliament conceded to the Irish Parliament its legislative liberty, and 1800, when the Act of Union brought it to an end. For that brief space a Parliament in

Dublin made laws for Ireland, in that short time
Ireland passed through such variegated evils as
made the troubles of the Century of Union which
followed seem mere trifles by comparison.

The Parliament of that golden time, as Carson
well knew, was a Protestant Parliament, a Parliament of the Minority, artificially maintained on a
restricted franchise, and round it seethed and
foamed a constant and shrieking tempest of ani-
mosity, culminating in the fifty-third rebellion of
'98, possibly the most ferocious in the history of
Ireland.

The mere list of the societies, secret or terrorist,
some formed before but most during that time,
which tried to enforce their will upon that Parliament might suffice to suggest the precariousness of
its existence—Right-boys, White-boys, Peep-o'-Day-
boys ; Conventions, Aggregate Bodies, Defenders,
Assassins ; National Congresses, Emancipators,
United Irishmen, Houghers of Men and Houghers
of Cattle, and Standing Feathering Committees—
were a few of the organisations which brought a
gentle pressure to bear on that gallant but pre-
carious assembly. " Armed Associations," says
Martin, " controlled every act of the legislature."
In 1783 an armed convention of the " Irish Volunteers " sat at the Dublin Exchange, and sent their
delegates in uniform to present a Bill which they
had framed for its reform to the Irish House of
Commons. The House stood on its rights, and the
Convention was fortunately dispersed without enforcing its will, as it threatened, upon Parliament
at the point of the bayonet. In 1793 the House of
Commons was burnt down, and the members
narrowly escaped, " amidst the shouts of an

immense and ferocious multitude " before the dome fell in upon the floor.[1] In 1794 an armed mob of " Aggregates " broke into the House as part of a design to over-awe Parliament and force it to pass a " non-importation act " against British produce. While the Irish Legislature stood firm for the Crown and the English connection, the United Irishmen negotiated an alliance with Republican France, and claimed to have nearly three hundred thousand men armed and ready for insurrection.[2]

" The tension and anxiety in some parts of Ireland," says the judicious Lecky, " was intolerable. . . . The whole framework of society, and the moral principles on which it rests, seemed giving way. Habits of systematic opposition to the law were growing up ; outrages sometimes of horrible cruelty were looked upon merely as incidents of war, and savage animosities were forming."

The French Invasion of 1796 was dispersed by unfriendly weather ; the Rebellion of 1798 broke out prematurely and incompletely owing to the vigilance of Government in the confiscation of arms, but was not suppressed before 20,000 lives were lost on the side of the Crown and 50,000 on the side of the rebels. The massacres of Wexford Bridge and Vinegar Hill and the ferocious reprisals by the undisciplined part of an Irish militia suggest human passions roused to the height of madness. The rebels frequently boasted, and the loyalists had reason to fear, that the design was to exterminate the whole Protestant population.

Whether these disasters could have been averted

---

[1] The mob being so ferocious, the belief was general that the House had been set on fire by incendiaries ; the true cause, however, was a flaw in the heating apparatus.

[2] *Ireland before and after the Union,* by R. M. Martin (1868), p. 17.

if the Catholic disabilities had been wholly removed
before they occurred is a question which may be
debated but can never be settled, for religion, as
we have seen, was only one of the several causes of
the division. What remains true is, as Lecky says,
that " Anarchy and bloodshed, religious and class
warfare, great measures almost wholly failing to
produce their expected results, disaffection widening and deepening as grievances were removed,
public opinion more and more degraded and
demoralised, political life turned more and more
into a trade in which the vilest men were exalted."
Such was the state of Ireland which made the Act
of Union seem for well-disposed people on both sides
a blessed relief. Many of the leading Catholics petitioned for the Union, possibly on the consideration
suggested by Montesquieu to Lord Charlemont.
" Were I an Irishman," said the author of *L'Esprit
des Loix*, " I should certainly wish for it, and, as
a general lover of liberty I certainly desire it, and
for this plain reason : an inferior country connected
with one much her superior in force, can never be
certain of the permanent enjoyment of constitutional freedom, unless she has, by her representatives, a proportional share in the legislation of the
superior kingdom."

Sage advice—if only the Irish had had the sagac-
ity to take it ! In the hundred and ten years which
had followed the Act of Union Ireland had become
peaceful and prosperous. The famine, result of a
system of tillage ill-suited to her climate, was far
behind : she had turned to stock-raising and dairy-
farming, and England had become the best market
of her produce. Five years later (speaking in Dublin
on the 1st July, 1915) John Redmond was to

describe this new and happier Ireland when it was already lost. His candour came too late ; but, since his words described the situation as Carson saw it in 1910, they may well be quoted here.

" To-day," said the Irish Nationalist Leader, " the people, broadly speaking, own the soil . . . the labourers live in decent habitations . . . there is absolute freedom in local government and local taxation . . . we have the widest Parliamentary and municipal franchise . . . the congested districts . . . have been transformed . . . farms enlarged . . . decent dwellings provided . . . a new spirit of hope and confidence among the people." And he went on to describe the provision for the housing of the working classes—" far in advance of anything obtained for the town tenants of England," and " the system of old age pensions . . . whereby every old man and woman is . . . free to spend their last days in comparative comfort."

Carson had a heart humane and compassionate : he not only knew but felt that all those material benefits which the people of Ireland enjoyed through this prosperous partnership were put in hazard. Thus in his speech at Birkenhead on the 23rd November, 1910—to go forward a little in our story—we find him occupied with these advantages of the Union which Redmond recognised too late— " local self-government . . . £150,000 a year in relief of taxation . . . a system of education " such as he wished England had . . . every child trained in the religion of its parents (and discharged out of the Imperial taxation) . . . University education . . . land purchase." He even presents the balance sheet between the oppressed country and its op- pressor : the total revenue of Ireland, £8,335,000, her total expenditure, £10,712,507 ; contributed to the Imperial forces, nothing ; received from the British Exchequer towards local expenditure, £2,357,000 a year.

Alas, neither considerations of statesmanship nor pleadings of humanity but hard political bargaining were to decide this question. The British Government, in fact, had been driven into such a predicament that either they or the Union had to fall. There was no other way out.

The Liberals were about to launch an attack upon the Act of Union, by a curious paradox, not because they were strong but because they were weak. When they entered office in 1905, they looked back upon the Home Rule Bills of Mr. Gladstone as disastrous episodes in a past already remote. There were, indeed, one or two members of the Government who were faithful to the Gladstonian tradition, but even the most zealous of them, even John Morley, had written to John Dillon a year before the great victory of 1905, " the longer it is before the Irish question interrupts the swing in our direction, the better for all of us." Some years earlier, Lord Rosebery had put the case with more of statesmanship and less of politics. Before Home Rule could be passed, he had declared, " England as the predominant member of the partnership of the Three Kingdoms will have to be convinced of its justice." And again "if we wanted Home Rule, we must carry conviction to the heart of England." Mr. Asquith was understood to favour that point of view. Liberals, he told his constituents, had to recognise a repugnance " which not even Mr. Gladstone's magnificent courage, unrivalled authority and unquenchable enthusiasm had been able to overcome. . . . The reconciliation of Ireland

Bc

. . . could only be overcome by the methods which will carry with them, step by step, the sanction and sympathy of British opinion."

" Conviction," " sanction," " sympathy "—such words suggest the Liberal Doctrine of " Mandate," which was to be bandied about on every platform for the next four years. Mandate—no student of history would affirm and no Liberal would deny the validity of the claim. The Liberals themselves, in 1914, took the greatest decision in history without any mandate from the people. No government could be carried on unless both the Government and Parliament were prepared on occasion to take such decisions.

Nor is a member of Parliament a mere " delegate " : on any worthy consideration he is armed with representative power. And yet, if there were ever a case where the Mandate might be thought to apply it was here, where two attempts to dissolve the Union had been defeated by decisive votes of Parliament and people.

And there was besides this strange paradox in the Liberal position, that although in theory that Party favoured Home Rule for Ireland, the stronger it found itself the less was it inclined to go forward in that cause. Speaking of the great Liberal victory of 1905, the biographer of John Redmond describes it as " much more overwhelming than the Nationalists had wished." " There had been," Mr. Denis Gwynn continues, " a real hope that the Nationalist Party might once more hold the ' balance of power ' between two opposing parties of more or less equal strength. But their eighty-three votes would henceforward be impotent against the immense Liberal majority. The new situation would require

dexterous diplomacy if the Liberals were to be
kept responsive to the Irish demands."

"Balance of power," "demands "—such terms
illuminate political relations, which by the beginning of 1909 already threatened a crisis. Mr. Redmond demanded a specific promise of Home Rule
in the next Parliament ; the Liberals put him off
with vague and conditional promises, which he
found altogether unsatisfactory. On February 17th,
1909, he sent a note to Mr. Lloyd George reminding
him that they were at a deadlock and asking him to
inform the Prime Minister ; in June the Nationalists voted against the second reading of the
" People's Budget." As the elections approached,
so the Irish Nationalists increased the pressure.
Thus, John Redmond wrote to John Morley on
the 27th November, 1909 :

> " The political conditions in Ireland are such
> that, unless an official declaration on the ques-
> tion of Home Rule be made, not only will it be
> impossible for us to support Liberal candidates
> in England, but we will most unquestionably
> have to ask our friends to vote against them . . .
> as you know very well the opposition of Irish
> voters in Lancashire, Yorkshire, and other places,
> including Scotland, would most certainly mean
> the loss of many seats . . . we must therefore press
> for an official declaration . . . on the lines of
> national self-government, subject to Imperial
> control, in the next Parliament."

These certainly are not such words as one com-
rade might expect from another in the Army of
Progress, nor do they accord with any theory of an

advance only to be made with the " sanction and sympathy " of the British electorate. In their naked brutality, they savour more of blackmail ; but Mr. Asquith was too practical a politician to take offence in a matter of business. The demand for an " official declaration " was made, it will be noted, on the 27th November ; on 1st December a Cabinet meeting was held and Mr. Birrell reported to Mr. Redmond that there had been " complete agreement as to necessity for a declaration . . . without limitation or restriction other than the old tag about the supreme control of the Imperial Parliament " ; on the 10th December following the declaration was made by the Prime Minister in the Albert Hall.

" Ireland," said Mr. Asquith, " was the one undeniable failure of British statesmanship," and the solution could be found only in one way—

" by a policy which while explicitly safeguarding the supremacy and indefectible authority of the Imperial Parliament, will set up in Ireland a system of full self-government in regard to purely Irish affairs.

" There is not and cannot be any question of separation. There is not, and there cannot be, any question of rival or competing supremacies, but subject to those conditions that is the Liberal policy."

Here then was the declaration, complete with the " old tag," as demanded.

It is the classical passage which is held to justify the Liberal claim that they placed the issue of Home Rule fairly before the British electorate. How it was

extracted we have seen, and we have to note also
that it was made half way through the elections,
that Home Rule had not been mentioned before
nor was it mentioned afterwards and that it found
no place in the election addresses and the manifestos of the leaders of the Party.

The Union, it will hardly be denied, was one of
the foundations of the British system of government. If this fundamental issue were to be raised
again, especially after being twice and so decisively
rejected, we should have expected that at least the
main lines of the change proposed would have been
laid before the electorate ; but the declaration left
everything vague except the supremacy of Parliament. Sir Edward Carson, almost alone in these
elections, tried to bring the issue before the electorate, and afterwards described to the House of Commons the difficulties of that attempt.

" I know myself," he said, when arguing this
question in the constituencies, " I asked the question
of an audience : ' Are you prepared to submit the
question of Home Rule to a single Chamber ? '
And a gentleman in the audience very politely said,
' I am.'

" And I said, ' Have you fully considered the
details of the question ? ' He said, ' Yes.'

" I said, ' Very well, is the Home Rule you are
in favour of a Home Rule Bill which will exclude
Irish Members from the English House of Commons ? '—because that is what Mr. Gladstone
proposed in his first Home Rule Bill—and he said
' Yes.'

" And I said, ' Are you in favour of the Second
Home Rule Bill by which they were to be kept in
the House of Commons ? ' and he said ' Yes.' "

There were other questions—financial relations under the Home Rule Bill, the burden upon England, the burden upon Ireland, the share of the National Debt, the contribution from Ireland for Imperial purposes—" all questions of such magnitude that when you are talking of Home Rule, and saying you are in favour of Home Rule, you are giving really no indication to the constituencies nor to the people as to what it is you really mean at all."[1]

On that basis the elections went forward without any further reference to Home Rule ; but even if it could be said that the Declaration made the issue clear the result was far from being a " mandate." The Liberal Party came back only 275 strong against 273 Conservatives and Unionists. There were besides forty members of the Labour Party and eighty-two Irish Nationalists.

This was no " mandate " either against the House of Lords or against the Act of Union. But from the Irish Nationalist point of view it was something better. " The result," says Mr. Gwynn in his *Life of John Redmond*, " was that the Nationalists actually obtained that position of absolute dictatorship which had always been the objective of Nationalist strategy. Parnell's dream of the balance of power at Westminster had once again come true."

[1] 14th April, 1910, *Parl. Deb. Com. 5th Series*, vol. xvi., c. 1479.

CHAPTER II

REDMOND'S TERMS

The tug-o'-war—Mr. Asquith—John Redmond—The Irish Nationalists—
A trial of strength—Carson intervenes—Winston Churchill—The
Irish and the Lords—Mr. Balfour on the bargain.

ON THE 10TH FEBRUARY, 1910, John Redmond, at Dublin, publicly proclaimed his dictatorship. His terms might be expressed in a single
phrase : No guarantees ; no Budget : " I say
plainly that if Mr. Asquith is not in a position to say
that he has such guarantees as are necessary to
enable him to pass the Veto Bill through the House
of Lords this year, and if, in spite of that he intends
. . . to pass the Budget into law . . . that is a policy
that Ireland cannot and will not uphold." On the
27th February Sir Edward Carson accepted the
invitation to lead the Irish Unionist Party. This
close coincidence of dates suggests the opening of a
notable struggle between these two Irishmen—a
tug-o'-war in which Edward Carson pulled against
John Redmond on a rope, tough and a little
slippery, which was Mr. Asquith.

These three men, who were thus to strain their
muscles and their nerves—pull devil, pull baker—
were all lawyers, all men of strong character and
great abilities ; Carson might be trusted to throw
his whole weight into the pull on the one arm as
Redmond on the other of their victim, and Asquith
might be expected to endure until his sinews cracked

under the torture, and not to endure only but to
twist and to turn and to use all means to be free
of his tormentors.

Personally, they were all upon good terms ;
Carson had met Redmond on Circuit in Ireland
and had served as Junior to Asquith in England.
When death had quenched even political animosities Carson spoke of Asquith in terms which suggest
that if they had not been public enemies they might
have been private friends.

Asquith was a Yorkshireman, Nonconformist
bred, Liberal in the grain, who had made his way
up the ladder of party politics by the whole-
hearted application of his considerable talents to
the service of his cause. " His splendid gift of
speech " (Lord Haldane wrote of him with the
nicely tempered malice of an old friend) " recommended him to the official leaders. Moreover he
had fewer views of his own than most of us . . . his
judgement was wise . . . distinctly he would have
office before very long." His gift of speech, indeed,
was Ciceronian, weighty without being dull, and
seeming to say more than it said. There was besides
in his eloquence a certain elusive transparency or
inverted candour which made it peculiarly service-
able to Liberal policy : it combined evasion with
precision in a remarkable degree. Thus when Mr.
Asquith described anything as " unthinkable " he
honestly meant that he was already considering it ;
when he said, " we cannot admit and we will not
admit," the emphasis conveyed the admission ;
when he spoke of " a debt of honour " he meant a
deferment until the Greek Kalends. This notable
gift of speech made him deservedly trusted by the
Liberal Party.

The Liberal Party was at that time divided between Whigs like Sir Edward Grey and Radicals who looked for their spiritual guidance to Mr. Lloyd George. Mr. Asquith had always inclined by temper and inclination to the Whig view, but was uneasily conscious of the Radical power in the constituencies. There was nothing of the Celt in Mr. Asquith's composition ; he did not know Ireland, and was constitutionally incapable of understanding what is called in politics " the Irish question." This indeed was no obstacle to his oratory. If in the matter of Home Rule he had " fewer views of his own than most of us," they were always discreetly chosen and admirably expressed. In 1890 he explained to the Eighty Club that " we should be incurring grave constitutional risks if even in appearance we were to surrender the absolute, the continuous, the unquestionable authority of the Imperial Parliament." He was prepared, however, to recommend a plan which would—" without any difficulty "—satisfy " the legitimate and sincerely felt aspirations of the Irish people." He would make Home Rule safe by giving Home Rule all round. " Home Rule in this larger sense, in my opinion, rests upon the necessities, is demanded by the responsibilities, and is indeed due to the honour of the Imperial Parliament." " Without any difficulty "—O, valour of ignorance !

When, however, " even Mr. Gladstone's eloquence failed to recommend Home Rule to the British electorate," Mr. Asquith followed the lead of Lord Rosebery, and when that lonely star was lost in the dawn of the Liberal morning, he thought it wise to wait upon public opinion. Home Rule, he said, was only to be reached, if at all, by the

policy of "step by step." When on the death
of Sir Henry Campbell-Bannerman, Mr. Asquith
became Prime Minister, he was regarded by the
Irish Nationalists " with much less cordial feelings,"
as " he was believed to be very much under the
influence of the old Liberal Unionist wing." So at
least we are told by the biographer of John Redmond,[1] yet on the other hand there is this illumin-
ating entry in the Diary of Mr. Asquith's colleague,
John Morley : " Talk with Asquith about Ireland :
said he had told Redmond that he would act in
Irish things with me. I said my polar star was the
Irish themselves, as it had been ever since I entered
Parliament." The passage suggests that the Irish
Nationalists possibly read too much into the mind
of Mr. Asquith : we are uncomfortably reminded
of Lord Haldane's remark, " He had fewer views of
his own than most of us." He would follow Lord
Rosebery at one time, at another Lord Morley
according to a " wise judgement " not indeed of
Ireland but of English politics. To be drawn apart
between two Irishmen, as between wild horses, was
in such a case poetic justice.

As for John Redmond, he was, politically speaking, rather an ugly customer for a Liberal statesman
to meet on a dark night. He belonged, it is true, no
more than Carson, to what is called the native
Irish : his ancestry has been traced to a Norman
invasion ; his ancestors had held land and castles in
Wexford for centuries, had lost their territories in
the confiscations of the seventeenth century, were
in fact among those dispossessed Anglo-Irish gentry
who took the Catholic side and cherished a

[1] Denis Gwynn, *Life of John Redmond*, p. 154. Here the author gratefully
acknowledges the debt which he owes to that biography.

hereditary grudge against the Government. John Redmond, himself, educated by the Jesuits at Clongowes, had been dedicated from his youth to this ancestral quarrel ; had learnt early what gratitude to expect from the native Irish ; had stood beside Parnell against a hostile mob at Enniscorthy, had been knocked down and cut about the face, and had been a little comforted by the laconic words of his leader, " Why you are bleeding. Well you have shed your blood for me at all events."

Undeterred, he had entered Parliament as a Parnellite in 1881 and had followed the singular course of remaining faithful to his leader through good and ill report. When the long feud between the two factions came to a formal end in 1900 he was elected Chairman of a United Party as one of the very few among them whom they cared to trust : how far he could trust them we may have occasion to consider in the course of our story. In London he led a life almost monastic. " Like Parnell," says his biographer, " he thought seclusion necessary to the Leader of the Nationalist Party. Long and bitter experience had taught him to distrust the promises of politicians, and to rely entirely upon that attitude of absolute independence which Parnell had practised with such masterly success."

" Absolute independence "—it is a large claim to make for any man : Mr. Redmond was not only leader but servant of a jealous, revengeful and suspicious party. He himself was not altogether one of them either in caste or in race, since in his blood ran the instincts of the gentleman, of the landowner, of an Anglo-Norman ruling class. He had narrowed his mind to a concentration on the cause of Home

Rule ; but he could not but be aware of the element
of Jacobinism, of savagery, in the party which he
served and led. He knew, if he allowed his mind
to range so wide, that he himself, and much that
he held dear, were threatened by the victory of that
cause. He had become by his devotion to it almost
a stranger in Ireland, and was yet at least vaguely
aware that Ireland was outgrowing the dogma of
his Nationalist faith. On the one side, conceal it
from himself as he might, she was undeniably
prospering under the Union, on the other she was
cherishing wild, lawless, insane dreams of a
legendary tribal Ireland in which he had no part.
The keen eye of Tim Healy had noted the change,
at least as early as 29th February, 1908, on which
date he had written : " I think a completely new
political, journalistic and party situation will soon
be created by Sinn Fein." And Redmond, himself,
writing to Douglas Hyde, the President of the
Gaelic League, some nineteen months later,
reminds him that when some years before, "at your
invitation," he went to a meeting of the League
in the Rotunda, Dublin, " to my amazement, I
was received with hisses by a large portion of
your audience." To be received with hisses by
a new party of " Irish Ireland "—it was as unpleasant as it was puzzling to the Irish Nationalist
Leader.

The Irish Nationalist Party rested on the United
Irish League ; the United Irish League was well
organised ; the publican and the gombeen man
were its faithful henchmen, and the priesthood, on
occasion, its powerful allies. The League was
strong, it was tyrannical ; in December 1910 it
drove William O'Brien, Tim Healy and their little

faction out of Parliament ; it was vigilant to suppress any movement which even indirectly threatened to weaken its power. Thus, for example, when
Sir Horace Plunkett organised Raiffeisen Banks
and Co-operative Creameries to rescue the
peasantry from a chronic indebtedness, the Irish
Nationalists savagely attacked both the credit of the
banks and Sir Horace Plunkett.

On the 7th July, 1910, the question came up in
the House of Commons, and Sir Edward Carson
indignantly denounced a tyranny which sought to
crush prosperity lest it might mean independence.
" The real reason," said Carson, " why this Organisation Society is abused . . . is not because it
is a political movement, for that is absolutely
untrue, but because it is looked upon by some
people, and by the hon. gentleman who has just
sat down (Mr. Dillon) as undermining the party
to which he belongs because it turns the minds of
the people to economic and industrial questions,
and away from mere agitation and political conflict. He knows that it occupies the minds of the
people and takes them away from what is called the
Irish Parliamentary Party. . . . The Irish people
co-operate among themselves with a view to better-
ing their condition, entirely apart from politics,
and that is why the Agricultural Organisation
Society has been so much attacked."

The Irish Nationalist Party, as Carson well knew,
was a tyranny which brooked no opposition in
Ireland. In another of his speeches we find him
protesting against a surveillance which threatened
those who belonged to the loyal minority if they
dared to support the Unionist cause or subscribe
to Unionist funds. Such was the Party which John

Redmond led—a party brutal, vindictive, ignorant, arrogant, which demanded of its leader an attitude and an allegiance not altogether easy for a gentleman and a loyal subject to give. Mr. Redmond had to show himself a good hater if he was to keep his position. " We from this county of Wexford," he proclaimed (on the 23rd June, 1907) " send therefore this message to England—we tell her that we Wexford men, to-day, hate her rule just as bitterly as our forefathers did when they shed their blood on this spot. We tell her that we are as much rebels to her rule to-day as our forefathers were in '98."

There were other reasons for that sort of language. The principal paymasters of the Irish Nationalist Party were the Irish of the United States, from whom and their friends in Canada in the course of one tour, in 1910, John Redmond and T. P. O'Connor collected no less than a hundred thousand dollars. These Irish-Americans, organised in their Clan-na-Gael, cherished an enthusiastic Republicanism and a bitter hatred of England. They did not want any constitutional settlement ; they wanted a rough house ; they wanted a dog fight. " Every howl of despair emitted from the Tory Press," said Mr. Dillon, " would bring them tens of thousands more of American dollars." " It was American dollars," said Mr. Devlin, " that enabled Parnell and Davitt to break and destroy Irish landlordism. It was American dollars that would enable John Redmond to destroy foreign rule in Ireland."

" To destroy foreign rule in Ireland "—it was hardly an object which a loyal subject could pursue or a British Prime Minister could approve, yet Mr.

Redmond in his collecting tours had often used such language. " Who will undertake to say," he had demanded of the Irish of Boston, " that the separation of Ireland from England is impossible . . . it did not seem more impossible a few years ago that England would be humbled to the dust, as she had been, by a handful of farmers in South Africa." " There is not an Irishman in America to-day," he had told the Irish of Chicago, " in whose veins good red blood is flowing, who would not rejoice to hear that a German Army was marching in triumph across England from Yarmouth to Milford Haven."

Such were the forces that John Redmond had to obey or to cajole in Ireland and America. On the other hand, we have seen him making a bargain with John Morley to accept " National Self-Government subject to Imperial control." After he had made that bargain and was helping the Liberals to win the first General Election of 1910, "we simply want," he had told the people in Manchester, " to turn the energies and abilities which are to-day dissipated in this horrible racial conflict between England and Ireland to the prosaic work of advancing the national and moral and educational elevation of our own people at home." Sir Edward Carson, in his sardonic way, described these politic transformations. " When," he said to the Irish Nationalists, " you went down into a constituency where there was a narrow margin for the Liberals, you used to tell them, ' after all it is only a gas-and-water bill,' and in Ireland, when you went over to speak there, you used to tell them, ' It is absolute independence.' "

The General Election, however, was over. Mr. Redmond, with " the balance of power " in his hands, was haughty and menacing. In particular, he demanded drastic measures against the House of Lords. We have seen at the beginning of this chapter what he said in public. What he said in private was conveyed, in the form of an ultimatum to the Master of Elibank, then Chief Liberal Whip, on the 24th February, 1910. Unless, this document ran, the Government introduced their veto resolutions " at once " ; unless—if it were to be rejected or hung up in the House of Lords—they " at once ask the King for guarantees " ; unless, in any case, they postponed the introduction of the Budget " until after the foregoing "—" unless we receive these promises we could not support the Liberal candidate in the St. George's in the East election, and would be quite free to give any advice we liked to Irish electors. Further we would feel bound to vote against the Government and oppose them consistently in the House of Commons."

These were humiliating terms, and, to begin with, at all events, Mr. Asquith had the spirit to resent them. The Master of Elibank was instructed by the Cabinet that " they had nothing to say in reply," and on the following day Mr. Asquith reported to the King that " in view of the exorbitant demands of Mr. Redmond and his followers . . . certain Ministers were of opinion that the wisest and most dignified course for Ministers was at once to tender their resignation to your Majesty."

If they had acted upon that wise resolution and " defied the foul fiend," the story here to be written would have been different. But the Cabinet spoke with a divided voice. On the one hand, those very respectable Whigs who believed in a tradition of English government knew that the loss of a hundred

JAMES CRAIG (LORD CRAIGAVON)

seats was a dubious sort of mandate upon which to proceed with a change in the constitution ; they felt besides this insolent dictatorship, these " exorbitant demands," as in the last degree humiliating to a British Government. But on the other hand, there were the Radicals, led by Mr. Lloyd George, eager and willing to make a deal, and ready to denounce any Liberal who went back on it as a traitor to " the Army of Progress." There was so much to gain of office and of legislation by remaining in, so much to lose by going out, that the Government hesitated, and, like a woman, a Government which hesitates is already lost.

We see the wavering issue swiftly decided. On the 25th February, Mr. Asquith was telling the King that rather than surrender he might resign. On the 20th March, at Liverpool, Mr. Redmond proclaimed : " With us this question of the Veto is the supreme issue. With us it means Home Rule for Ireland." On the 5th April, Mr. Asquith moved the resolutions dealing with the relations between the two Houses of Parliament. The Government would take the Resolutions first, then introduce the Parliament Bill, and lastly proceed on the Budget. Except on the question of guarantees, Mr. Redmond had won.

Sir Edward Carson had been watching this struggle with an anxious eye, well knowing what it meant for him and for the people of Ireland. So long as the House of Lords could interpose its veto, the Union was reasonably safe ; no Home Rule Bill could be passed through Parliament without an appeal to the country. With the experience of two such Bills to guide him Carson had reasonable faith in the British people ; but if there was no power to
Ca

refer a Bill to the electorate there was no power to prevent it from being passed. Carson saw as clearly as Redmond that this quarrel with the House of Lords involved the issue of Home Rule for Ireland.

It is no matter for surprise, then, that we find him making a strong fight against both the Resolutions and the Parliament Bill. His fears are indicated by the general lines of his opposition. Thus on 7th April, 1910, supporting an amendment to refer differences on money bills to a conference of the two houses, he pleaded for a reasonable settlement. After all, " constitutions were set up to carry out what is the will of the people at large." To satisfy what was little more than half the population while leaving the other part, nearly as large, " utterly dissatisfied "—surely that could not be the intention of the Government. Let them, therefore, consider " whether we can in any wise modify the extreme views upon both sides," and agree upon an accommodation.

Carson appealed to the moderate man ; but he appealed in vain. The Government, bullied by the Nationalists, played the tyrant with the Opposition. The Resolutions were forced through at the edge of the guillotine, amid the cheers of Irish Nationalists and Radicals, and day by day the temper of the House grew more bitter and more excited. Carson spoke in a different tone when he next took part in the debate.

It was the 14th April, 1910 ; matters had reached a crisis behind the scenes ; that afternoon Mr. Redmond had gone to see Mr. Asquith in his private room ; the House was well aware that close bargaining was going forward over the Budget, the Constitution, the Act of Union, with what result it did not know ; the House was crowded ; the feeling was tense.

The Resolutions then being discussed in Committee dealt with the powers of the House of Lords and the duration of Parliament : they made no confession of the end to which they were being pushed through. To make that purpose clear Mr. Chambers, the member for South Belfast, moved an amendment : to exclude from their scope such Bills as gave powers to subordinate Parliaments within the United Kingdom. The amendment placed Home Rule fairly on the carpet.

Mr. Chambers was answered by Mr. Winston Churchill. That enterprising politician had deserted the Conservative Party some years before ; he had been received with open arms by the Liberals, who knew better how to reward and encourage juvenile talent ; he was then Home Secretary, and his zeal for his new friends aroused the fury of his old. There had, he said, been great changes in English opinion on Home Rule : " the new generation that has grown up in our country is not going to be frightened out of its wits by the nightmares and bugbears of a vanished past."

These words were very much to the taste of the Irish Nationalists : they were no less obnoxious to the Irish Unionists, who, having loved the father, were the more offended by the son. Lord Randolph Churchill's famous battle-cry, " Ulster will fight and Ulster will be right," was bandied about with derision on the one side and defiance on the other.

Sir Edward Carson, who rose to face and quell a turbulent House, had the manner of speaking which marks the great orator. He gave to every word he used a value which belonged less to the word than to the utterance, as if he had charged it with some elemental power in his own nature, so that it became alive and gave forth fire. Weighted and seasoned with an Irish brogue, his invective fell like a heavy lash about the shoulders of the Home Secretary : " I do not think anybody in this Committee supposes for a moment that the Home Secretary will ever be frightened out of *his* existence by the nightmares and bugbears of *his* vanished past."

Mr. Churchill had brought the punishment on himself, for he had suggested that the Conservative Party might themselves bring in a measure of Home Rule. " I have no doubt," Carson retorted, " if the right honourable gentleman had remained a member of the Conservative Party, and had seen any political advantage of any kind to be gained from the introduction of Home Rule, or from opposition to Home Rule, he would have been equally willing to adopt the particular view that suited his particular interests for the moment."

The speaker paused and looked first at the Treasury Bench and then at the Irish Nationalists— all painfully conscious of critical interior negotiations—and proceeded : " Does the right honourable gentleman not see that . . . if the Unionist Party were as corrupt as he seems to think they are—and nobody abuses their former friends so much as those who have fallen out with them—by a mere promise of a Home Rule Bill we could defeat his Resolutions, his Budget, and everything else."

It was true and the House knew it, for the Irish Nationalists found the taxation proposals of the Budget so distasteful, so embarrassing to their position in Ireland, that they would willingly have

thrown over the Government if they could have got
what they wanted from the Opposition. The Conservative Party, however, had not yet begun its
latter-day practice of selling its friends to placate
its enemies.

Then Carson, having thus quelled the House,
proceeded in his favourite way to reduce a transaction to its naked simplicity. Here, he said, was an
illustration of what would happen under Single
Chamber Government :

" The Government go to the country on the
Budget Bill.

" They come back here and find themselves in the
position that they are not able to pass it without the
Irish Members.

" Then, of course, they go to the Irish Members.

" The Irish Members say : ' We will support your
resolution to get rid of the House of Lords,' and
they openly say, ' We do so because we want to be
in a position to pass Home Rule. And that is our
sole reason.' "

If Carson did not know how closely he was describing what was actually happening that very day,
the Irish Nationalists knew, and Patrick O'Brien
blurted out in open confession : " Not our sole
reason."

" ' Our *main* reason ' (Carson corrected himself),
for supporting this resolution."

Carson proceeded to taunt the Irish Nationalists
with the profligacy of their bargain : they were
prepared, he said, in order to advance a step towards Home Rule, to put their country into a state
of bankruptcy.

Turning from the Irish he made appeal to the
prudence of Parliament. " When they came to the

House of Commons were they to leave their common sense outside the doors in the same way as worshippers in Eastern temples leave their boots ? ” They all knew what was going on : “ the whole origin of bringing up this matter, as a preliminary to getting their Budget, has been at the dictation of the Irish Nationalist Members, and solely with a view to improving their position in regard to the great national question of the dismemberment of the Empire.”

“ The dismemberment of the Empire ” : the heavy words rolled through the House like a prophecy of doom.

Then Carson challenged the Government. Facing the front Treasury Bench, he addressed his words directly to the Ministers.

“ You would not dare to-morrow,” he said, “ to put Home Rule as a net issue before the country— and the only issue.”

He waited for a reply : none came, and he proceeded :

“ No, you tried it twice, and you were twice defeated.”

There were cries of denial, but Carson silenced them : “ Once through the action of this House and once through the action of the other House ; but in each case it was emphatically decided by the people that they would have nothing of it.”

On a few who still kept on shouting “ No,” he turned in scorn. “ I know what is in your minds,” he said. “ Whenever there is a Unionist majority, it does not represent the views of the people. It is only when there is a Radical majority that it does.”

He paused again, and again addressed the

Ministers, choosing his last words, slowly, with the
solemnity of an accusation : " You have had it
twice rejected, and now, by your bargaining with
the Irish Nationalists, for the sake of your Budget,
for the sake of remaining in Office, you want to
sneak this Bill through, breaking up the United
Kingdom, without the people having an opportunity of expressing an opinion upon it, which they
have expressed so emphatically upon former occasions."

Sir Edward Carson could hardly have known, as
he used these words, that the bargain had been
struck, and, if we may judge on probabilities, that
very afternoon. There had been minor negotiations
between Mr. Lloyd George and the Irish Nationalists on the Budget itself, with certain minor concessions. But Mr. Redmond had held with a
tenacious grip to his main point, " No veto, no
Budget," as he had put the case in Dublin. " For
that which ' means Home Rule for Ireland,' they
were," he said in Liverpool, " willing to subordinate
everything—any number of Budgets, any conceivable issue that can be raised." And so he had
held on, refusing to grant supplies, so that the
Treasury had fallen into arrears to the extent of
thirty millions sterling and had been forced to
proceed by temporary borrowings. It was a position
not only humiliating but increasingly difficult for
the Government. What was Mr. Asquith to do ?

We have seen that of the three demands made by
Mr. Redmond two already had been granted. There
remained only that one which concerned the King.
Mr. Redmond had stated it in his ultimatum to the
Chief Liberal Whip in these words : " If resolution
rejected or hung up in Lords to at once ask King for

guarantees," and Mr. Asquith had been tempted to resign rather than comply.

It touched his honour nearly ; he had promised the King that he would tender no such advice until " the actual necessity arose," and, although it was not then publicly known, the King had insisted on another General Election to test the will of his people before he would consent to use his Royal Prerogative for the creation of peers to coerce the House of Lords. On the address Mr. Asquith had told the House of Commons that to make such a request before any Bill had been considered would be improper for a Constitutional statesman. He was thus tied to the King and to the House of Commons—yet Mr. Redmond refused to grant supplies.

That morning the Cabinet had considered the question : they had debated a form of words which Mr. Asquith had submitted to them ; that afternoon Mr. Redmond had been received by the Prime Minister in his private room.

What had happened in that interview we can only guess by what followed when Sir Edward Carson sat down. The Prime Minister rose, not to answer him but to announce the formula which had been designed to smooth over these difficulties.

" I do think it right to say that if the House of Lords fail in regard to this or any other resolutions . . ."

Mr. Asquith got no further : Mr. Balfour, rising to a point of order, pointed out that such a statement should not be made when there was no time to discuss it. The two men faced each other across the Treasury Bench " amid a clamour such as can never have been exceeded." " The passion of the contending parties was intense." The Liberals demanded that their leader should be heard ; the Conservatives shouted " Redmond " and " Dollar Dictator."

The Chairman ended the scene by forbidding the Prime Minister to proceed, and when Mr. Asquith found it possible to speak, he said he would make his statement on the motion for the adjournment, " his restrained tones suggesting that he felt deeply the rebuff which he had suffered."

When at last the statement came to be made it was found to be one of those formulas for which Mr. Asquith was justly famous, a masterpiece of lucid and logical equivocation, which held several meanings in every coil of its involutions. To Mr. Redmond it seemed to promise his " guarantees " ; to others it might imply a referendum ; in certain events it promised a resignation or a dissolution : in the latter event, only " under such conditions as will secure that in the new Parliament the judgment of the people as expressed in the election will be carried into law."

When this masterpiece of indeterminate political conveyancing had been delivered the Nationalists cheered with an enthusiasm which suggested that they at least were satisfied, and Mr. Balfour expressed what most decent people felt about the transaction. " The Prime Minister," he said, " has bought the Irish vote for his Budget and has bought it successfully. The price he has paid is the price of the dignity of his office, and of all the great traditions which he, of all men, ought to uphold."

CHAPTER III

THE HOUSE OF LORDS

The Budget and the veto—Death of King Edward—The Conference—Mr.
Balfour declines—Carson takes a hand—Nottingham, December 1910
—Carson as Cassandra—Hedgers and Ditchers.

THE BARGAIN was notorious and manifest, as
described by Tim Healy in a contemporary letter.
" Redmond," he said, " foolishly offered to accept
the Budget if a Bill to restrain the House of Lords
Veto was passed, and the Chancellor gladly took
that *quid pro quo*, which secured the passage of
the Budget." " Redmond," that same shrewd and
close observer added, " will get a sore sell in the end
with his policy."

Redmond, we shall see, had his doubts, but for
the moment he concealed them. " My colleagues,"
he said, " take the view that the abolition of the
Veto means the concession of Home Rule for Ireland. I believe that the declaration of the Prime
Minister is a sufficient guarantee, and this movement will go on now full steam ahead." The very
day, 18th April, 1910, on which he used these words
in the House of Commons, the Irish Nationalists
had met and had come to " the unanimous decision,
without doubt or hesitation, to support, actively
and enthusiastically, within the House and out of
the House, the policy of the Government, as stated
by the Prime Minister." As up till that time they
had refused to allow the Government to collect the

taxes, the Prime Minister was felt to be expressing himself with a more than characteristic candour when he said in the course of the same debate, " there has not been, and there is not at this moment, anything in the nature of an agreement between those who are represented by the hon. Member for Waterford and ourselves."

Sir Edward Carson, as shrewdly as Mr. Healy, considered the case, but feared a different result. It consisted in his view in " the sale of a community of loyal subjects for a block of political support," and he was resolved at all costs and with all weapons to prevent the " nefarious transaction." The general public, however, were still ignorant of these intentions. If they thought on the matter at all, there was, to reassure them, the House of Lords, a stout mediæval fortress, like the Tower of London, with the Union Jack flying at its high flagstaff. As long as that banner streamed above the Thames, the English people could not be expected to believe that the system of government which united the British Isles was in any serious danger. The siege, however, was begun in due form : with Radicals and Irish Nationalists straining at the ropes, those ponderous engines of war, the Veto Resolutions, had been got into position under the walls, and a Bill founded upon them had actually been prepared, when the warlike proceedings were interrupted by the death of King Edward VII.

The King, it was known, deeply disliked the attack on his hereditary Senate ; it was not only, as he held, directed to " the destruction of the House of Lords," it obliquely involved the throne, and he had told the Prime Minister, as already related, that he would not consent to use his Royal

Prerogative for the creation of peers until the Government had secured, by another election, the assent of his people. When His Majesty died there was so strong a revulsion from these political discords that the Government felt it unsafe, even indecent, to proceed with their campaign, without at least an attempt at settlement. And so for six months the politicians occupied themselves with a series of intricate and secret negotiations :

> *Content to keep, while revolution slept,*
> *Their single Chamber where such things are kept.*

So a contemporary poet. " The nation," as the Prime Minister more heroically described it, " witnessed an incident unparalleled in the annals of party warfare . . . the two combatant forces, already in battle array, piled their arms, while the leaders on both sides retired for private conference."

This diversion, as may be supposed, gave the Irish Nationalists a good deal of uneasiness ; but when they complained to the Liberal Ministers that a conference would " damp enthusiasm," the reply was " That there was no enthusiasm in the country at this moment to damp down." Mr. T. P. O'Connor reported to Mr. Redmond on the 6th June, 1910, that he had seen Mr. Lloyd George, Mr. Winston Churchill and Mr. Birrell immediately after the Cabinet.

" B. spoke very freely and he attaches no importance to the Conference—though agreeing that it was necessary to soothe public opinion here. . . . It will be informal and, above all, it will not be *binding.* ' Nobody will bind me,' said he.

" ' Or me,' added C.

" L. G. said that when the Conference fizzled out he proposed to resume the fight immediately.

" Birrell laughed outright at the idea of any wavering ; so did they all.

" Moreover, L. G. said to me to-day, and several times to me before, that he wanted such resolutions as would enable Ireland and Wales to get the measures on which their hearts were set."[1]

As both Mr. Birrell and Mr. Lloyd George were members of the Conference, they might again have " laughed outright " when Mr. Asquith described it as " an honest attempt " to secure a settlement. Yet the Irish Nationalists remained uneasy. On the 5th June, 1910, we find Mr. Dillon writing to Mr. Redmond, " It looks as if we were faced by another attempt to bolt on the part of the Government."

How far were these fears justified ? Mr. Redmond must have known that there were forces on both sides working for a coalition, Conservatives who were nervous about the House of Lords and Liberals who feared another General Election. On the 23rd June, 1910, he made a memorandum, that he had been invited to meet Walter Long and " discuss with him the possibility of settling a Home Rule scheme, to be adopted by consent as part of the settlement of the constitutional crisis." We are not told by Mr. Redmond's biographer how the talk went ; but we can hardly suppose, from what we know of both men, that the result was satisfactory to either. The entry, however, does suggest that there were Unionists who hoped to get Ireland out of the way by some sort of " Home Rule Scheme," and there were Liberals who were also

[1] Denis Gwynn, *Life of John Redmond*, p. 182.

working for a settlement. Mr. J. A. Spender, in his
Life of Lord Oxford and Asquith, says that, " Mr.
Lloyd George, anticipating his later self, was
supposed to be keen on the idea of a ' National
Government ' and Mr. Balfour by no means discouraging." It was even alleged in (*The Times* of
20th March, 1930, in the course of an obituary
article on Lord Balfour), that " a common programme of a Ministry was laid down, Mr. Asquith
being excluded " ; but that Balfour " declined
participation in the intrigue." Mr. Spender says,
however, that " Asquith believed himself to have
been fully informed of all that was going on, and
he was certainly aware that Mr. Lloyd George was
conferring with Mr. Balfour." A man who believed
himself to be " fully informed of all that was going
on " where Mr. Lloyd George was concerned might
be described as an optimist.

The wary historian will not presume to profess
that he is fully informed upon that, or any subject.
What is certain, however, is that Mr. F. E. Smith
and Mr. Lloyd George were working together for
this " common programme of a Ministry." The
settlement of the Constitution, a measure of Home
Rule, a bigger Navy (to satisfy the Conservatives),
such was the main programme of measures ; as for
the men, the choice was to be negotiated. To
that end F. E. Smith sounded Jack Sandars, the
Secretary (and friend) of Mr. A. J. Balfour, and
was told that such a matter could only be considered
by the Principals, whereupon Mr. Lloyd George
invited Mr. Balfour to a *tête-à-tête* breakfast. Mr.
Sandars who had advised his chief to go, " if it
were only to know what mischief might be in the
air," anxiously awaited the result. Upon his return,

Balfour threw himself into his favourite chair by the fireplace in his house in Carlton Gardens, for a while said nothing, and then, when his friend had asked him what he thought of it all, replied that he did not deny the scheme had some attractions ; but that, considering the strong line he had taken—his life's work in fact—in resisting Home Rule, and the pledges he had given to the Loyalists in Ireland, he could take no part in the business. Mr. Lloyd George and his friends must do without him.

There is other evidence. Lord Newton in his *Life of Lord Lansdowne* states that Mr. Balfour was invited to co-operate in passing the Budget, and that he refused. We may, therefore, the more readily believe that he " declined participation in the intrigue." We know also that both Mr. Balfour and Lord Lansdowne stood firm on the question of Ireland, upon which the Conference actually broke down. " To-day's meeting of the Conference," Mr. Asquith reported to the King, on 8th November, 1910, " brought matters to a head. The proposed exclusion from the new machinery for settling deadlocks of Home Rule and other so called organic changes . . . showed an apparently irreconcilable divergence of view."

" At the twenty-first sitting," says Lord Newton, " it was suggested by Mr. Balfour that it might be intimated that the breakdown had taken place over the separate treatment of constitutional questions ; but Mr. Asquith and Mr. Lloyd George objected. The final conclusion was that the announcement would simply be that the negotiations had broken down." According to Liberal doctrine the People must be told everything and decide everything :

on this issue of Ireland, if the Liberals could manage it, they were to be told nothing, and decide nothing.

While these protracted negotiations were drawing to this impotent conclusion, Sir Edward Carson heard something of " the common programme of a Ministry " to which we have referred. His information was that Mr. F. E. Smith, Mr. Winston Churchill and Mr. Lloyd George, not to mention others, were working for some sort of Coalition, in which Home Rule and Welsh Disestablishment were to be conceded on the one side and " Tariff Reform " on the other. Such a Coalition, it was calculated, would raise the two Parties above the risks of a General Election, and above the dangers which threatened them from Labour and the Irish Nationalists. It would give them office with security: it involved merely a sacrifice of principles and of friends.

This move, on the Conservative side, came to the surface in a letter signed " Pacificus " which appeared in *The Times* of 22nd October, 1910. " Unionists," " Pacificus " wrote, " cannot champion Home Rule ; but they might nevertheless submit to it without loss of dignity or self-respect." *The Times* with a balancing article inclined to a settlement on that basis ; the *Morning Post* lapsed from its settled convictions so far as to broach the old cask of " Federal Home Rule " ; the *Daily Telegraph*, the *Globe*, the *Daily Express*, with a unanimity much too marked to be spontaneous, discussed the question on similar lines.

Sir Edward Carson was somewhat troubled by the appearance of these kites over Westminster ; but was reassured to hear from Mr. Balfour that the proposals had no authority from the leaders of the

Party. He thought it worth while, however, to join with other men of his own way of thinking in a statement of faith in the Union, which was circulated for signature between 28th October and 10th November. The " unauthorised scheme of ' Home Rule all round ' which had lately been canvassed in certain newspapers," was in the opinion of the signatories, " equally injurious to the Constitutional Conference and to the Unionist Party " ; they " desired to place on record their emphatic protest against a policy which they held to be opposed to the most vital interests of the Kingdom and the Empire, and they wished to state their conviction that this country must remain a Union governed by one Parliament."

Among the numerous signatures to this manifesto, which was published on the 11th November, were those of Sir Edward Carson, Mr. J. H. M. Campbell, Lord Hugh Cecil, Lord Willoughby de Broke, and Walter Long.

Carson did not stop there : the more he considered it the more clearly he saw that any such weakening would do great harm to the cause for which he was fighting. He expressed this conviction strongly in a letter which was read at a demonstration of Irish Unionists on the 5th November, and he sought an opportunity to nail the Union flag so firmly to the Unionist mast that the busy fingers of intrigue could not undo it.

This occasion he found in the Annual Meeting of the National Union of Conservative and Constitutional Associations, held at Nottingham on the 17th November, 1910. There he moved a resolution exhorting " all Unionists throughout the Kingdom to maintain unimpaired their unalterable opposition

Dc

to the policy of Home Rule " and " not to . . .
adopt a weak and vacillating attitude in . . . any
legislation . . . to the weakening of the Union
between Great Britain and Ireland."

Carson had for his audience not only the Party
in Parliament but the greater Conservative Party
in the country, and he appealed to them confidently, as one who loved them much and knew them
well. He had been, he said, for twenty years in
public life and the whole of that time he had
devoted to the maintenance of the Union " between
your country and mine." He was himself a Liberal
Unionist : " I came into public life and I left my
party because I was determined that our two countries never should be disunited." Then he quoted
the words John Redmond had been using at
Chicago.

" I believe," Redmond had said, " that the
leaders of the Liberals are sincerely friendly to
Home Rule, but, sincere or not, we have the power,
and we will make them toe the line."

It was a quotation which had its maximum effect
in such an audience, and having won the laughter
and the cheers of these good Englishmen, Carson
proceeded to his point. " I saw something in the
papers some time ago," he said, " that our leaders
in the Conference were meditating a surrender of
my rights and the rights of those who think with
me in Ireland. Sir, I denounce that as an infernal
lie."

Englishmen love that plain manner of speech
which they too seldom hear from flattering politicians ; they cheered, and cheered again when
Carson added, " I denounce it (though not in that
language) on the authority of Mr. Balfour himself."

Then Carson asked them not to put any trust in the smooth words of Irish Nationalists in English constituencies ; but remember how these same men had behaved in the South African war, which would have made him blush as an Irishman had he not known that his fellow countrymen were at that time covering themselves with glory on the battlefields of South Africa. Let them remember also Mr. Redmond's message from New Ross in 1907. Carson rolled out the words of the Nationalist Leader, his brogue restoring to them their original tinge of Irish melodrama :

" We from this County of Wexford send therefore this message to England. We tell her that we Wexford men to-day hate her rule just as bitterly as our forefathers did when they shed their blood on this spot. We tell her that we are as much rebels to her rule to-day as our forefathers were in '98."

Then after allowing this remarkable piece of evidence to sink into the minds of his audience, " No, Sir," Carson went on, " let us make an end of these announcements that a section of the Unionist Party is flirting and coquetting with Home Rule. For my own part I would rather, for the rest of my life, stay in the honest Division Lobby of the Opposition than surrender one particle of my principles to obtain the highest office in the land."

This robust appeal was characteristically reinforced by an old Presbyterian Minister from Ulster, Mr. Thompson of Derry, long since gathered to his fathers. " I am," said this worthy, " a Minister of the Gospel of the Lord Jesus Christ, and therefore

I am a man of peace "—here he paused, and added
in a meditative aside—" but not of peace at any
price." Mr. Redmond had threatened to " crush
the handful of Loyalists in Ulster with a strong
hand " ; but they were " English, Irish and Scotch,
a fighting mixture," and Mr. Redmond would find
it " a tough job." " He will require a Division of
30,000 soldiers," said this man of peace. Then the
old minister proceeded to explain how he had once
been a Liberal and had even helped to turn Lord
Claud Hamilton out of Derry. " I believed in Mr.
Gladstone," he went on, " and then Mr. Gladstone
betrayed us "—and then in another aside—" My
Lord Duke, I do not like being betrayed."

The Duke of Portland, it should be explained,
was President Elect of the Party ; Mr. Chaplin was
Chairman of the meeting, and with the permission of the latter Sir Edward Carson again rose to
make an explanation. It had been suggested, he
said, that the question might be solved by the grant
of a separate Parliament to Ulster ; the Irish
Unionist Party had considered that proposal and
asked him to say that Ulster would never be party
to any separate treatment, that Ulster would never
desert those who thought with them in other parts
of Ireland. " If we sink we sink together, but with
God's help we will swim."

Thus while Mr. Redmond was working to keep
the Liberals to their bargain, Sir Edward Carson
was working to keep the Unionists to their faith.
As we have noted of the negotiations, Carson in the
stand he took had the support of Lord Lansdowne
and Mr. Balfour, who had both refused to place
Ireland at the hazard of the Parliament Act. If at
that time any danger threatened the Act of Union

from the Unionist side, it was not from the leaders
of the Unionist Party but from a cabal of Unionist
and Liberal politicians. The temptation was strong
—to be rid of a vexatious faction and an eternal
controversy. The politician hoped to be rid of
eighty hostile votes in the House of Commons ; it
required statesmen to realise that England could
never be free of Ireland, nor throw into the sea the
burden of her destiny.

Whatever the hopes, they were disappointed. On
the 16th November, 1910, Mr. Asquith and Lord
Crewe went to Buckingham Palace, and made
terms with the King. They would submit the Parliament Bill to the House of Lords ; they would appeal
to the country ; they would lay that issue before the
electorate and if they returned with a sufficient
majority the King on his side would use his prerogative to overcome the resistance of the House of Lords.

Ireland was not in the picture. It would have
been better both for Mr. Asquith and his Party if
in those elections of December 1910, they had laid
their policy for Ireland fairly and squarely before
the electorate. As it was their manifestos and
election addresses were silent on the subject. The
Prime Minister himself only mentioned Ireland
when he was heckled on the point by an East Fife
elector, on the 6th December, 1910, and then he
contented himself with a bare reference to the
passage in his speech at the Albert Hall the year
before. Nor did any of his colleagues as much as
mention the issue of Home Rule in their election
addresses. It was left to the Opposition to warn the
country of the intentions of the Government.

In *The Times* of 10th December, 1910, there
appeared this direct challenge :

" 5, Eaton Place, S.W.
" *December 9th.*

" SIR,—The belated statements of Mr. Asquith on the question of Home Rule, coupled with Mr. Redmond's statement yesterday that ' we will have a Home Rule Bill passed before we know where we are,' are a complete confession of the treacherous bargain we Unionists have been asserting. Even at this late hour I now challenge Mr. Asquith to meet me on any platform he may choose and unfold and discuss his Home Rule proposals. Let us have a fight in the open and some fair play.

" Yours faithfully,
" EDWARD CARSON."

On the same day that he wrote this letter Sir Edward Carson, speaking at Macclesfield, tried to goad the Prime Minister out of his silence. Scornfully describing him as " the man with the strong face and the weak knees," Carson put him a series of direct questions :

What would be the fiscal relations between England and Ireland ?

What about the National Debt ?

Was England to go on paying two and a half millions to Ireland without having any voice in the expenditure of that sum ?

Were Irish Members to continue to sit in the House of Commons ?

Was England to continue to advance money to Ireland for the purchase of land by the tenants ?

Here, then, was an opportunity to make an end of all complaints that these questions had never been put before the country ; but Mr. Asquith, although he had described himself as being " in battle array," declined the challenge. " The sole issue of the moment," he said three days later at Bury St. Edmunds, " was the supremacy of the People," and " it was sought to confuse this issue by cate-chising Ministers on the details of the next Home Rule Bill."

There was another note—deep, grave, portentous —in these election speeches, a note of warning. " Mr. Asquith," Carson said at Macclesfield, " was playing with fire if he thought he was going to trifle with the loyal minority, who were as keen for King and Constitution as any Englishman." And at Liverpool, after quoting Mr. Asquith's metaphor about " reverting to a state of war," Carson used words intended to shock Liberals into a sense of reality : " Perhaps," he said, " if the Prime Minister did not look out, there was more real war in it than figurative war. It is my wish, and the wish of those with whom I act, to be law-abiding citizens ; but, by heaven, I tell you this—from what I know of the men of the North of Ireland they will not yield their birthright, not one inch, without a struggle."

Their birthright, their nationality, and, as they believed, their religion, these were things for which Englishmen had often been ready to fight, things which went far deeper than those questions which elections and votes in Parliament are able to settle ; they went down into the primitive nature of man, and we find Carson in those elections of December 1910 passionately and desperately trying to make the depth of these feelings clear. " He was not the kind of Irishman," he said at Birkenhead, " who was always running down England. He believed that the destiny of England depended upon their nation and his clasping hands. . . . The policy to which he was pledged waš that never, so long as he lived, would their countries be divided."

While Carson was thus pleading, in vain, at the knees of the English electorate, the Liberals might have noted, had they but the eyes to see, ominous signs of the coming struggle in Ireland. Mr. Redmond, indeed, had used language little to the Liberal taste in America. " These concessions," he had said at Buffalo, in October, " are only valuable because they strengthened the arm of the Irish people to push on to the great goal of national independence." The Liberal Party managers implored him to use more discretion during the elections, and we find T. P. O'Connor writing to him on the 22nd December, 1910. " The Master (of Elibank) insisted strongly on an attitude of reticence and reserve with regard to the King, and was a little frightened, he said, at one passage in one of your speeches . . . which seemed to lift the veil a little." Redmond, therefore, thought it prudent to concentrate his invective on the House of Lords; but even so the violence of his language might have opened the eyes of the British public to the ferocity of the passions which were being fanned into flame. " The House of Lords," Redmond said at Wexford, " had oppressed and insulted and starved and murdered the Irish race. Its crimes against Ireland cried aloud to heaven for vengeance. . . . Thank God . . . when the future of Irish freedom was still hanging in the balance . . . the Irish Nationalists . . . struck the blow that had precipitated the ruin and destruction of the House of Lords."

The native Irish, whom Mr. Redmond thus incited, had no particular quarrel with the House of Lords; their grudge was against the loyal minority in Ireland, whose faith they hated and whose possessions they coveted. In the south the whole country was consolidated under Nationalist sway by the fierce rally of these elections; William O'Brien and his little party of dissidents were swept away; Tim Healy noted an organised terrorism against which it was in vain to oppose his wit and his eloquence. The feelings of the loyal minority in Dublin were concisely expressed in the message which Carson addressed to them—" Home Rule for us means national bankruptcy and for England national dishonour." They knew it, but they knew also their helplessness. In Ulster, on the other hand, where resistance was possible, men were already thinking of resistance. " Perhaps the time had arrived," Captain Craig said at Lisburn, " when they should change their tactics . . . and spend the money hitherto used in the sister counties in buying arms and ammunition. . . . In a short time the Unionist Clubs would be reorganised, and he would advise all the young men of the countryside to join and to employ some old soldiers to train them in military tactics, and then God help Mr. Birrell and the Nationalists if they came near them ! "

Blissfully unconscious of this approaching need for divine assistance, the Liberals celebrated a victory, narrow but, as they hoped, sufficient. They had been 275 ; they were 272, exactly the same strength as the Unionists who had gone to the polls 273 and returned 272 ; only with the help of the Labour Party, by that time 42, and the Nationalists, 84, could Mr. Asquith reckon on a majority. The election, indeed, from his point of view had been fought in vain, for he was still under the Irish yoke.

The position being exactly as before, the Government could only proceed to break up the Union by first breaking the power of the House of Lords ; but even before the Parliament Bill was passed Ireland cast a slanting shadow across the Parliament of 1911. On the 15th February, the question being raised by amendment on the Address, Sir Edward Carson warned the House of the misfortunes about to fall upon both countries.

He had, he said, asked himself over and over again what possible benefit Home Rule could confer upon Ireland. He could think of none. From the financial point of view it meant embarrassment if not bankruptcy ; but there were worse evils. He touched on the racial hatred that was leaping again into life at the mere rumour of Home Rule ; he described the political intimidation that made it almost impossible in some parts of Ireland for a man to support the Unionist cause. Then he went on to make two prophecies, both of which have since been fulfilled : one that the Irish Parliament would set up a tariff against British goods ; the other that no safeguards would be of any service. " They all knew," he said, " that all these paper safeguards were shams."

These warnings were in vain. The Liberals pressed on with their Parliament Bill, which, if it left the Constitution unreformed, was yet a masterpiece of political contrivance. It disenfranchised the electorate, as far as Home Rule was concerned, and in the name of the People ; it lulled apprehensions by putting the event three years ahead of the Bill ; it disarmed opposition by making the passage of the measure automatic ; and it tied the Irish Nationalist Party to a three years contract of service before they were paid their wages.

King George, following in his father's footsteps, had insisted upon a General Election to test the will of his people before the creation of peers. The result of these elections we have seen, and the House of Lords, not being a party to the arrangement, did not feel itself bound to accept so indeterminate a verdict. The Opposition, therefore, obstinately resisted the Parliament Bill until at last, on 20th July, 1911, Mr. Asquith informed the Conservative leaders that he had the Royal permission to create peers enough to carry the Bill against any opposition. Upon this the House of Lords fell into a new division, of those who thought it better to fight and those who thought it wiser to submit.

On the 11th May there had been a luncheon of peers and commoners to organise resistance, and Lord Curzon, newly arrived from India, had given a strong lead to the assembly. " Let them make their peers," he said, " we will die in the last ditch before we give in." When, therefore, this new division came about, those who stood for resistance were called ditchers and those who inclined to give way were called hedgers.

In the early days of this strange conflict Sir Edward Carson and his little party of Irish Unionists had begged Lord Lansdowne, in the name of the Irish Loyalists, to stick to his guns. Carson took this view not by temperament alone, although he was always a fighter, but by reason. It was not merely that a wholesale creation of peers would greatly weaken and embarrass the Liberal Party, since

Who can deny,
When Peers are born that Liberals must die ?

Carson looked further and saw clearly that such a creation would force the Government to undertake the reformation of the House of Lords as an immediate measure, and would thus provide a young and vigorous Senate which might be trusted to take an independent view of such questions as the Act of Union. This counsel, however, was little to the liking of Lord Lansdowne. That nobleman, high-minded though he was and wholly devoted to the public service, yet refused to lead what he took to be a forlorn hope. "By insisting on our amendments," he argued, "we shall bring about a creation of peers which may overwhelm the present House and paralyse its action in the future without in any way retarding the passage of the Parliament Bill."

Mr. Balfour agreed with his colleague ; he would stand or fall, he said, with Lord Lansdowne, and the bulk of the Party inclined to accept the decision of the two leaders. The strength of the natural Englishman, and of the typical Conservative, is his sense of discipline—a tenacity in hanging together. It is beaten into him in his public schools ; it remains with him through life. And besides this deference to his own chosen authority, there was, no doubt, official pressure on the one side, hope of preferment on the other.

The timid man instinctively dreads the carrying of things to a crisis. Those easy-going peers who were content to enjoy the social advantages of their position disliked the cheapening which would come with the enlargement of the House of Lords. T. P. O'Connor, observing things closely, wrote to John Redmond of this " factor in the situation." " The backwoodsmen," in his opinion, " want the glory

and the show to remain, and would sooner be without the power than without the show." One of these
noblemen, in an argument with Carson, put it that
if three hundred peers were created, the House of
Lords would lose its prestige on the Continent.
" Oh, be easy in your mind if it's that you're thinking of," Carson retorted scornfully. " I always find
that, if you give him a big enough tip, the foreign
waiter will call ye, ' Milord.' "

There were, however, others, some from reason,
some on instinct, who were resolved to reject not
only the Bill but the advice of their leaders. Lord
Halsbury, whom Carson took to be the greatest
judge before whom he had ever pleaded, an indomitable little old man—he was then seventy-
eight—put himself at the head of the new Opposition. The greatest merit of this great lawyer, in
Lord Carson's opinion, was the intellectual power
to resolve a large and complicated question into
a simple issue. And in this case the old Tory Lord
Chancellor, after his habit, reduced the dilemma
between resistance and submission to a characteristic simplicity. " It seems to me," he said, " that,
upon a question of principle, if I believed a thing
to be wrong, I ought to do my best to prevent it."

On the night of the 26th July, 1911, Carson happened to be passing along Pall Mall when the Lord
Chief Justice strolled out of the Carlton Club.

" Where are you going ? " Lord Alverstone asked
him.

" I am going," said Carson, " to a dinner they
are giving to my revered leader."

" And who may that be ? " he asked.

" Who but Lord Halsbury ? " Carson answered.

" You ought to be ashamed of yourself," Lord

Alverstone retorted pettishly, " behaving as you are doing over this Parliament Bill."

" I have no reason to be ashamed of myself," Carson replied hotly ; " but I have had occasion to be ashamed of you, my Lord Chief Justice." And with that oblique reference to certain notoriously weak judgments, Carson left him and made his way to the Hotel Cecil, where he found a great company of his friends assembled. Lord Selborne was in the chair, and the cheerfully indomitable old man who was their guest of honour set the table in a roar by thanking those who were not present for " a most profuse quantity of advice, which he rather thought he had heard a good many years ago—he would not say how many years ago—from his grand-mother." George Wyndham, the Duke of Northumberland, Lord Salisbury, Lord Milner, Austen Chamberlain and Sir Edward Carson spoke to the various toasts of loyalty, defiance and good fellowship, and it may have sounded a little strange in this high-spirited company that Carson struck a note, not serious only but tragical, as one who even then felt the suffering that the blow portended for his people. He was, he protested, " an Irishman who looks upon your country as his own, and who has ever felt as deep a loyalty to your Sovereign as you feel." Then he denounced the conspiracy—" to sever your country from mine . . . to hand over those who have ever been loyal to the tender mercies of a disloyal dictator." As to the advice they had received, the loyal Irish, who had most to lose, ought to be the best judges, and they were all for resistance. Here Carson read a telegram from the Duke of Abercorn : " I stand fast to Lord Halsbury."

The Duke was the Ulsterman who had first said —" We will not have Home Rule."

" I often wonder," Carson went on, " if people realise the depth of infamy in the advice that the Prime Minister has given to his Sovereign—' Sir, as your adviser and counsellor, I must tell you that it is my determination to destroy your Constitution, which has existed for 700 years. . . . I can only do it by using men who are willing to sell their honour for a coronet. I ask you, Sir, as a Constitutional Monarch . . . as the guardian of the honour of your country, to lend yourself to so monstrous a proposal.' "

When they considered it in that plain way, was there any doubt as to their duty to resist to the end ? " We are told," Carson proceeded with gathering scorn, " that though we run away to-day, we will fight hereafter. My Lords, I prefer to fight to-day and to-morrow and hereafter. Courage is what we want," and here he thanked Lord Halsbury, " from the bottom of my heart, and on behalf of thousands of loyal Irishmen," for showing that courage.

Lady Halsbury treasured a letter which she received the following day from Sir Edward Carson. He had seldom been so moved, he said, as when he had listened to her " splendid Earl," and he prayed that her husband might be long spared " to teach us devotion to principle."

Carson, indeed, was very much in earnest, having the imagination to see all that hung upon the issue. On the 10th August, 1911, a young nobleman happened to meet him at the door of the House, the fate of which was that day to be decided. " What's the betting ? " said the young lord. " Betting ! "

Carson replied, " is that all you think of when the Constitution is in the melting-pot ? "

There was, nevertheless, good matter for a sporting bet, and tense drama and true humour as well, in that last day of the great debate on the Parliament Bill. Stout fellows had organised the Opposition well. Lord Willoughby de Broke and Lord Lovat were the Whips—" As calm and collected as though waiting outside a covert for a fox to break " —they had forgotten nothing and nobody. Lord Willoughby de Broke had even taken the precaution of hiding the coat and hat of a Duke who was thought to be doubtful ; but to no purpose : " the noble owner bolted off without either and was never seen again."

Feeling ran highest when Lord Curzon intervened in the debate, since he had led the ditchers to resistance and was then leading the hedgers to surrender.

" Let us realise what is before us——" Lord Curzon was saying.

" It is because 400 Peers are going to run away to-night," the Marquess of Bristol interrupted.

When Lord Curzon had recovered from the irreverence of this sudden assault, " I would sooner," he retorted, " run away with the Duke of Wellington than stand with the noble Lord."

" I would rather fight with Nelson at Copenhagen than run away with the noble Earl," Lord Bristol replied.

These sallies and stratagems were in vain.

The official Opposition abstained ; all the Bishops save two and a dozen Conservative Peers voted with the Government ; the Parliament Bill was passed by the narrow majority of seventeen votes. And none more than Sir Edward Carson deplored

CRAIGAVON

the result, since none more clearly saw that the passing of the Bill was not the end, but the beginning of the fight, the real object of attack being the unity of the United Kingdom, and that to make such a surrender at the beginning was to weaken the morale of the defence and greatly to hearten the enemy. Thenceforth Mr. Asquith could reckon on a Conservative Party which, in the last resort, would surrender rather than fight, and that, in the case of Ulster—which did not mean to surrender— might be a fatal miscalculation.

CHAPTER IV

CARSON GOES TO ULSTER

The Protestant North—History of Ulster—Falls Road and Shankill Road—
James Craig—Meeting at Craigavon—" We must be prepared."

ON THE 16TH FEBRUARY, 1886, Lord Randolph Churchill wrote to his friend Lord Justice Fitzgibbon: " I decided some time ago that if the G.O.M. went for Home Rule the Orange card would be the one to play. Please God it may turn out the ace of trumps and not the two." Sir Edward Carson came to the same shrewd conclusion as he surveyed the game in 1911. The Court cards had been played and lost : there remained the ace ; there remained Ulster.

Neither in 1886 nor in 1893 had there been any need for the resistance of that Province ; the attacks on the Union had been defeated in Parliament and at the polls ; but in 1911 the capitulation of the House of Lords left Ireland bare to the enemy, and in Ireland there was this stronghold where the fight could be continued, the Protestant North. " God help Mr. Birrell and the Nationalists if they come near us "—those grim words of James Craig's had passed almost unheeded, save by the men to whom they were addressed, in the elections of December, 1910. The Liberals were astute politicians ; but they knew little of Ireland and its people ; and of Ulster they knew less than of the

South. " I know that honourable members oppo-
site think they are better acquainted with the
North of Ireland than I am," Carson said in the
course of the Debates on the Parliament Bill.[1]
" Their information is overwhelming. I once met a
Liberal Minister who asked me something about
Home Rule in Ireland, and I said, ' Do you think
there is any use our discussing it ? Do you know
anything about it ? ' And he said, ' Something.'
' Have you ever been there ? ' I asked. And he said,
' Not exactly, but I have been round it in a
yacht.' . . . "

On that occasion Carson had used grave words of
warning. " You are," he said, " going to pass
Home Rule . . . by a pure act of force. . . . Your act
of force will be resisted by force." But the Liberal
Government had not heeded him. They could not
indeed so much as imagine any resistance other
than political, and, moreover, Mr. Redmond was
at hand to tell them that " all such apprehensions
are without any real foundation."

The root of Mr. Redmond's error may have lain
in his simple but fallacious faith that Ireland was
a nation. " Ireland," he kept saying, " is a unit. . . .
A unit Ireland is and a unit Ireland must remain."
Yet delve as we may into the history of Ireland we
shall never find this unity. In particular, it is true
that the North of Ireland, even in Celtic times, was
never part of any general Irish Kingdom.

Ulster lies by herself, curiously detached and
complete, like some little German duchy within a
fold of the Rhine, or Swiss canton tucked away
among its Alps. Behind its double line of lake and
hill, its natural fosse and rampart—through which

[1] To be exact on 8th August, 1911.

there are only one or two practicable roads—and these easily cut—it has always lain apart from the rest of Ireland. Its Southern ranges running from East to West, its large central plain of level country sloping down to the wide waters of Lough Neagh, its great straths of Foyle and Bann opening to the Atlantic in the North, these and Belfast Lough, the main facts of its geography, suggest its affinities and its history. Ulster has always been more closely connected with the West of Scotland than with the South of Ireland.

The O'Neills and O'Donnells of Antrim and Tyrone, the MacNeills and MacDonalds of Isla and Cantyre, had harried and married one another since the beginning of time. They made common cause against the South, and to a settled government they were something barbarous and inimical. Their feuds of clan against clan and sept against sept, their " evil customs of coyne, livery, bonnaght and cosherings " ; their primitive life—there was hardly a stone house anywhere and they tied their ploughs to the tails of their ponies—their savagery which reduced the country to a waste, made it natural enough in King James, who abominated all clans, whether Scottish or Irish, to propose a drastic reformation when the O'Neill (Lord Tyrone) and the O'Donnell (Lord Tyrconnell) gave him what he took to be a heaven-sent opportunity by fleeing the country. To vest the land in the Crown and thereby improve the revenue ; to recompense "well-deserving servitors" ; to plant towns and villages ; to substitute tillage for grazing and " civilise " a wild country—such were the respectable motives of the Jacobean settlement.

As the Crown lawyers did in the West of Scotland,

so they did in the North of Ireland, they ignored the communal tenure of the clan system, and parcelled out the land in individual holdings. They took care that the settlers should be of English or Low-land Scottish stock, and they drove those clansmen who were not allowed to remain as labourers and tenants into the hills. " The Irish," says Chichester in a letter to Salisbury, " were ready to do anything to avoid removing from the place of their birth . . . hoping at one time or another to find an opportunity to cut their landlords' throats, for they hate the Scottish deadly and out of their malice towards them they begin to affect the English better than they have been accustomed."

The feud which began in actual dispossession was confirmed by race, religion and circumstance. The Lowland Scot, who had been accustomed in his own country to constant war with the Highland clans, maintained that war in Ireland, just as the Irish MacDonalds under Colkitto joined Montrose in his wars on the Scottish Whigs. To the difference of race was added the difference of faith and, when the Civil Wars began, of allegiance. All these motives, pulling together, divided the settlers and the native Irish more sharply in the North than in the South. They were a garrison in a hostile country: " the King would protect them until they could protect themselves," they conducted their farming from fortified strongholds, driving their cattle in at night, yet for all their vigilance, " the wolf and the wood-kerne, within culver-shot of the fort, have oftentimes their share." Lord Carew was of the opinion that if the King of Spain were to send over a small force, armed with papal indulgences and excommunications, " all the modern English and

Scotch would be instantly massacred in their houses—which is not difficult to execute in a moment by reason they are dispersed, and the natives' swords will be in their throats in every part of the realm, like the Sicilian Vespers, before the cloud of mischief shall disappear."

What was prophesied in 1611 was attempted in 1641–1642, when what was a rising of the dispossessed against the possessors developed into a " general mania " of massacre. Some thousands of the settlers were slaughtered in three days, of whom some 680 were drowned or otherwise killed at Scarva Bridge over the Bann. The survivors, protected by the more humane against the fury of the more savage, took refuge in the fortified towns of Derry, Coleraine, Drogheda and Carrickfergus and the castles of their friends. The Lagan Force, recruited among the farmers, artisans and labourers of Tyrone and East Donegal, for the best part of nine years held their corner of the North against all the assaults of their enemies.

The original purpose of the Settlement as a garrison seems altogether lost in the embroilments of the seventeenth century. Wentworth antagonised the Protestant North by proscribing the Covenant and prescribing the Black Oath ; the Ulstermen, with some hesitation, took the side of Parliament in the Civil Wars ; they took the side of William III at the time of the Revolution ; and the circumstances of the Siege of Derry, the Battle of Newtown Butler and the Battle of the Boyne suggest something more ferocious than any dynastic quarrel—a war in which not merely men of one faith struggled against another, but men who had been dispossessed sought to exterminate their dispossessors. Even " religion and

liberty " were, as Carew suggested, no more than a
" veil " for something deeper and more nearly
primeval. The Rapparees of that time, the Houghers
of 1711, the White-boys of 1761, the United Irishmen
of 1791, were in reality ferocious Jacqueries, using
such weapons as the mutilation of cattle, the
burning of farm buildings, the torture and massacre
of isolated families. Thus in 1791 Alexander Barclay,
a Protestant schoolmaster of Forkhill, near Dundalk, and his family were massacred in such circumstances as do not bear telling. In September
1795 forty-eight Catholics were killed in private
battle at a place known as the Diamond in a village
of Tyrone, and that same night the first Orange
Lodge was founded.

These racial and religious feuds are criss-crossed
curiously with politics. The Presbyterians of Ulster,
Nonconformists and Whigs from the time of Wentworth, were in full sympathy with the rebels of the
Thirteen Colonies and threw up their hats for
Liberty, Equality and Fraternity. Wolfe Tone was
a Protestant ; the United Irishmen held their first
meeting on a rock called Macart's Fort above
Belfast. " The associations of the North," Castlereagh wrote to Pitt (from Dublin in October, 1796)
" are certainly as formidable in extent as the purpose
they have in view. Like yours they have artfully
availed themselves of the various descriptions of
Reformers, and have bound together in one solemn
Covenant against the State. . . . Their oath enjoins
the strictest secrecy and the whole is promoted by a
system of intimidation and guarded against dis-
covery by the assassination which inevitably awaits
those who are suspected even of a design of proving
unfaithful." For a while it seemed as if the United

Irishmen had bound together Protestant and Catholic populace in a general league in support of Revolutionary France; in November, 1796, the United Irishmen had 57,000 adherents, and were thought to be strongest in the Counties of Antrim and Down ; but race and religion were stronger to separate than politics to bind ; the Orange Order, which soon mustered twenty thousand strong, fought the United Irishmen with their own weapons. In 1796 they are said to have driven five thousand Catholics from Armagh " to hell or Connaught," and by 1798 the rebellion had crystallised the two factions. " It is a perfect religious phrensy," Castlereagh wrote in June of that year, " The priests lead the rebels to battle : on their march they kneel down and pray and show the most desperate resolution in their attacks. . . . They put such Protestants as are reputed to be Orangemen to death, saving others on condition of their embracing the Catholic faith."

In the century which followed the Union these fires subsided into a glow within their ashes but never died ; there were fierce outbreaks of the feud in every generation ; natives and settlers, Catholics and Protestants lived side by side but did not intermarry ; sometimes one end or one side of a street would be Catholic and the other Protestant ; there were Catholic villages and Protestant villages ; even Catholic roads and Protestant roads ; Catholic bridges and Protestant bridges.

Thus, for example, in discussing a grievous riot in the village of Columcille, the Attorney General for Ireland, Mr. Redmond Barry, explained to the House of Commons that, " there is a rule, which, I am glad to say, is a rule which prevails generally throughout Ulster, by which it is the custom of the

various parties so far to respect the districts or villages of the other party as not to make a demonstration particularly by band-playing in them. . . . I believe the rule is of this character : marching past is not objected to ; but the playing of bands is regarded as a form of demonstration that should be avoided by one party in the district of another."[1]

In Belfast the Falls Road was Catholic and the Shankhill Road was Protestant, and between these two quarters there was an armed truce, generally observed but liable to be broken upon religious or political occasion. We might illustrate the case from the year 1886, when Mr. Gladstone's First Home Rule Bill fanned these latent animosities into a flame. It happened that a gang of 180 navvies, mostly Catholic, were at that time excavating the Alexandra Dock. On the 4th June two of the workers had an argument on a matter of religion, and the Catholic, enforcing his point with a spade on the head of the Protestant, the latter, feeling himself in a minority of one, appealed for aid to the Protestant riveters of Queen's Island Dockyard, who responded with such spirit that some of the navvies sought refuge on a raft some little distance from the shore. The raft capsized, one of the lads was drowned in the mud ; the Catholics celebrated his funeral by waylaying the Protestant workmen in the Queen's Docks on their way home ; fierce riots ensued ; a strong force of police were drafted into Belfast from the South ; on the 10th June these newcomers, who were rather raw, mistook the blackened workmen, swarming out of Coombe's foundry at the end of the day, for a mob and charged them. The foundrymen retaliated with such energy

[1] *House of Commons 1911 Parliamentary Debates*, vol. xxxii., c. 1757.

that the police were driven into Shankhill Barracks and there hotly besieged until they were relieved by the military. In the course of that desperate affray several people were shot, many injured, and the police barracks almost reduced to ruin. In such circumstances it may be thought miraculous that the ensuing 12th July passed off without disorder ; but on the night of the 13th, when the Orangemen had gone in procession to Scarva for their customary sham-fight, the Catholics seized the opportunity to attack their houses. Women and boys rallied to the defence and a general action ensued between Falls Road and Shankhill Road, with heavy results of blood and mortality. There was further fierce fighting on 30th July when a Protestant band made rash music on " debatable ground abutting on a Catholic district," and the war was renewed with unabated zest on the 2nd, and again on the 9th August, when a party of Catholics, after attending the funeral of one of the victims, were disappointed in their expectation of finding whisky in a tram-depot, which was desperately defended by a Protestant garrison of three, armed with a rifle, a revolver and a pitch-fork. By that time the police and military of all Ireland had been drafted into Belfast, and forces five thousand strong laboured with infinite tact but indifferent success to keep the warring factions from one another's throats, until at last towards the end of September the fever faded out, and Falls Road and Shankhill Road relapsed into their normal peace.

Such was the historical background of a province over which the Liberals optimistically proposed to place a Nationalist Government—feud which never died but lived in the breast of every inhabitant !

Who began it ? The Saxon dispossessed the Celt ; the farmer shouldered out the herdsman. Who shall find the clue to right and wrong in this time-tangled skein, or indict before a Court of Justice a process of evolution ? The words used by Dr. Duigenan in 1793 remained true of 1912—" The Protestants of Ireland are but a British garrison in an enemy's country, and if deserted by the parent state must surrender at discretion "—save that in Ulster they had no intention to surrender.

Here we come to a point at which the theory of popular government breaks down. In Scotland or in England the minority of one election may be the majority of the next, a circumstance which gives to the vanquished hope, to the victors moderation. In Ulster either side so well understood the unassailable temper of the other that there was no attempt at persuasion : where the balance between the two communities was fine, the revision sessions were the only political argument. Dead men were sworn to be alive, absentees were sworn to be resident : the revising barrister held the fate of the constituency in his hands.

The Protestants of Ulster, although by no means the whole population, were in the main a solid community, a majority in six counties out of nine, surrounded by a Celtic fringe. On the light lands of the hills and the sandy coasts the natives remained, and did besides much of the menial and unskilled labour of the towns ; but the Protestants were a solid and integrated community, owning the land and the industries, with their own nobility—their Duke and their Marquess—their own gentry, business-men, farmers and workmen, knowing one another familiarly and keenly alive to their common

interests and the menace of their common enemy.

Such was the community which was to provide Sir Edward Carson, like another Oliver Cromwell, with the Ironsides of this civic struggle. The House of Lords capitulated on the 10th August, 1911 ; on the 23rd September following Carson faced a people who, as he knew in his heart, and could plainly see, would never capitulate.

Captain James Craig, at that time representing his native constituency of East Down in the House of Commons, was in himself a large epitome of those people, solid and big of body and mind, staunch, brave and practical. His house, Craigavon, looked over Belfast Lough from the slopes above the southern shore ; in front a pleasant meadow, cup-shaped and wood-encircled, sloped down to an old ivy-covered pump-house in the centre ; in this natural amphitheatre, near the crest of the lawn, Captain Craig had built a platform, and there the Unionist community of Ulster, ranged itself to meet its leader. All the Orange Lodges of Belfast, detachments from the County Grand Lodges and the Unionist Clubs of Ulster marched out from the City of Belfast in columns of fours, so considerable a body of men that it took two hours to pass a given point, and besides these a vast number of people flocked in from town and country. Altogether, or so it is estimated, there were a hundred thousand people in the meadow.

It was not merely a meeting but a muster and a demonstration of a whole community inspired by a single thought. Lord Erne expressed it in the immortal words used by Gustavus Hamilton to his friends, " divers of the nobility and gentry in the North-East part of Ulster," in 1689 : " We stand

upon our guard, and do resolve by the blessing of God to meet our danger rather than to await it." " We will never, never," said Mr. Thomas Andrews, " bow the knee to the disloyal factions led by Mr. John Redmond. We will never submit to be governed by rebels who acknowledge no law but the laws of the Land League and illegal societies."

Sir Edward Carson to this assemblage was not entirely a stranger. He had spoken at a public meeting in the Ulster Hall in December, 1910 ; on the 31st January following he had presided over a meeting of the Ulster Unionist Council. Yet as a man from the South, no Presbyterian, his brogue bewraying him, he had yet to make his way into the hearts of these people, and there he enthroned himself in the opening words of his speech, simple, direct, as his manner was, but weighted with the deep tones of his beautiful voice.

" I know," he said, " the responsibility you are putting upon me to-day." In their presence, " grave as it was," he " cheerfully " accepted it. And then with gathering emphasis, every word reverberating in the hearts of his hearers, slowly and solemnly he proceeded :

" I now enter into a compact with you, and every one of you, and with the help of God you and I joined together——"

Here indeed was a marriage of true minds——

" I giving you the best I can, and you giving me all your strength behind me——"

They felt themselves bound together in these words, and dedicated to what he proposed to them :

" We will yet defeat the most nefarious conspiracy that has ever been hatched against a free people."

Their hearts leaped as they realised that here was a leader they could trust to the uttermost, and he was telling them that the faith they already had in him he also had in them : " You realise the gravity of the situation that is before us . . . you are here to express your determination to see this fight out to a finish." They would fight this fight together.

Then, as they were thenceforth one, let them go on to consider the case. What they had to do was " to maintain the British connection and their rights as citizens of the United Kingdom." They had reason on their side ; under the Union, Ireland was " advancing in prosperity in an unparalleled measure." They had been cheated of their right to appeal to an electorate which " on two previous occasions refused to be a party to it"; as for the " paper safeguards " he could tell them as a lawyer that they were a mockery and a sham. The design was to place them under a Nationalist Government —" a tyranny to which we never can and never will submit." Their demand was simple : they asked for no privileges or special rights ; only " the same rights from the same Government as every other part of the United Kingdom.

" We ask for nothing more ; we will take nothing less. It is our inalienable right as citizens of the British Empire, and Heaven help the men who try to take it from us."

But what were they to do about it ? That was the question which those upturned faces were asking, and Carson was not the man to shrink from the reply, what he called the " logical conclusion."

" We must be prepared, in the event of a Home Rule Bill passing, with such measures as will carry

on for ourselves the government of those districts of which we have control.

" We must be prepared—and time is precious in these things—the morning Home Rule passes, ourselves to become responsible for the government of the Protestant Province of Ulster.

" We ask your leave, at the meeting of the Ulster Unionist Council, to be held on Monday, there to discuss the matter, and to set to work, to take care that at no time and at no intervening interval shall we lack a Government in Ulster, which shall be governed either by the Imperial Parliament or by ourselves."

There was the plan, in simple and concise terms : if the British Government would no longer govern them, they would govern themselves " in those districts of which they had control." " Our motto is," said Carson, " we rely upon ourselves " : if they could not, as they desired, remain part of the United Kingdom, they would take their own destinies into their own hands. The Liberal press laughed at the idea ; but the Loyalists of Ulster returned to their homes comforted and reassured. They had a leader and they had a plan.

CHAPTER V

MR. CHURCHILL AND BELFAST

Provisional Government—Legality—Churchill intervenes—The Ulster Hall—The meeting banned—Conference at Whitehall—The Celtic football ground.

" To meet our danger rather than to await it," such was the resolute nature of these Ulstermen, and it was sound policy besides. " Diligence and vigilance," Lord Randolph Churchill had told them twenty-six years before, " should be your watchword, so that the blow, if it is coming, may not come upon you as a thief in the night, and may not find you unready and taken by surprise." Such also was Carson's idea. The Government, as he knew, were proceeding slowly with their Irish policy : the Bill was only in the way of being prepared ; he proposed in the meantime a demonstration which would both frighten them and impress the country, and that must be done in Ulster. The Irish Nationalists, he calculated, would not have Home Rule without the North ; if he could prove that the North would not have Home Rule he would bring the whole thing to a stand. The Protestant community of Ulster, to his mind, was the key of the situation.

These people, certainly, would not have Home Rule ; so much he knew ; but to prove it was not so easy. The Liberals laughed at the idea ; Mr. Birrell found a convenient theme for his persiflage in an Ulster Army led by " an elderly barrister " ; Mr.

Redmond professed to disbelieve the Ulstermen, and the Liberals were guided by Mr. Redmond. Mr. Spender in his *Life of Lord Oxford and Asquith*, says (of the year 1912), " the Nationalists whom Asquith consulted were convinced that if the Government showed no signs of weakening in its policy, these troubles would subside and the inevitable be accepted," and, indeed, as late as November 24th, 1913, Redmond wrote to Asquith that " All our friends in Ulster have never ceased to inform me that all such apprehensions are without any real foundation." Between Ulster and the ear of Parliament, Government press and Irish oratory raised a barrage of ridicule and contempt. The Ulster people would have been grimly content to wait and show their true mind in the event ; but Sir Edward Carson desired above all things to *prevent* that catastrophe ; he desired above all that Ulster should save all Ireland from the impending blow. It was to those ends that all his plans were laid.

On the 25th September, 1911, two days after the Craigavon meeting, their new leader met four hundred delegates representing every interest in the community, concentrated as they were in the Ulster Unionist Council, the County Grand Orange Lodges and the Unionist Clubs. These four hundred agreed upon the policy without dissentient voice— calling " upon our leaders to take any steps they may consider necessary to resist the establishment of Home Rule in Ireland, solemnly pledging ourselves that under no conditions shall we acknowledge any such government." Those whom the delegates represented, it was added, would give their leaders " their unwavering support in any danger they may be called upon to face."

Fa

From that point they went on to arrange, as their first " imperative duty," " the provisional government of Ulster." The Commission appointed for that purpose—Captain James Craig, Colonel Sharman Crawford, Mr. Thomas Sinclair, Colonel R. H. Wallace and Mr. Edward Sclater—was " to take immediate steps, in consultation with Sir Edward Carson, to frame and submit a constitution for a Provisional Government of Ulster, having due regard to the interests of the Loyalists in other parts of Ireland : the powers and duration of such Provisional Government to come into operation on the day of the passage of any Home Rule Bill, to remain in force until Ulster shall again resume unimpaired her citizenship in the United Kingdom."

Here, then, was the frame of their civil resistance —" a Provisional Government to come into operation on the day of the passage of any Home Rule Bill " ; but civil government implies the power to maintain it, and that power was already taking shape in the instincts and the organisations of the Ulster people. Mr. Ronald McNeill (now Lord Cushendun), in *Ulster's Stand for Union,* describes how the volunteer force sprang from the Craigavon meeting. In the procession, he relates, " there was a contingent of Orangemen from County Tyrone who attracted general attention by their smart appearance and the orderly precision of their marching." They had of their own accord been learning military drill, and the example so set being taken up by others, not only Orangemen but Unionist Clubs also were soon drilling in many parts of the country.

It happened that one of the members of the Provisional Executive, Colonel Wallace, was both a

soldier and a solicitor, he had left his practice in Belfast to serve in the South African War, and had commanded the 5th Royal Irish Rifles, and he was quick to see both the possibilities and the implications of this military system.

Being a lawyer, his first idea was to put the movement on a legal basis. According to law any two Justices of the Peace had power to authorise drill and " other military exercises within the area of their jurisdiction, and application was duly made by Colonel Wallace and another Officer of the Belfast Grand Lodge of the Orange Institution :

" . . . for lawful authority . . . to hold meetings of the members of the said Lodge and the Lodges under its jurisdiction for the purpose of training and drilling themselves and of being trained and drilled to the use of arms and for the purpose of practising military exercises, movements and evolutions."

There was an undeniable candour and at the same time a certain irony in their statement of the purpose for which this authority was required :

" . . . they desire this authority as faithful subjects of His Majesty the King, . . . only to make them more efficient citizens for the purpose of maintaining the constitution of the United Kingdom as now established and protecting their rights and liberties thereunder."

This application, dated the 5th January, 1912, and duly granted by the Belfast Justices of the Peace, brings us face to face with the question of legality. As there was nothing illicit in the application so there was nothing unlawful in the authorisation to form this Volunteer Force. The Home Rule Bill was no law ; it had not been passed ; if it had been drafted it had not even been read a first time. Ulster was under the common law of England ; her justices were administering and her young men were acting within that law ; they proposed, indeed, to resist its abdication. They had even the right to arm, for the Liberal Government when returned to power in 1905 had chosen to relax the Coercion Act which forbade the importation of firearms into Ireland. They were acting within the law and within their rights. The Liberals, who themselves when in Opposition had patronised the breach of an actual Education Act, stormed and fumed against the " lawlessness " of Ulster ; but they had neither logic nor remedy. The Courts could take no account of a hypothetical breach of a hypothetical Act of Parliament.

The intention, however, was manifest. The Ulster Loyalists would defy the law if it should come into force, and Sir Edward Carson laboured to make that fact clear to Government and country. He was ready, as we shall see, to sacrifice himself in this cause ; he would, if he could, drag prosecution on his own head, hoping thereby to avert a more general defiance.

He had another motive : by promoting an ordered and disciplined movement he hoped to avoid the bloodshed of mere riot and anarchy. At Portrush, where he addressed a great meeting of Ulstermen shortly after the Craigavon demonstration, he made this purpose clear.

" Some people," he said, " say I am preaching disorder. No, in the course I am advising I am preaching order, because I believe that, unless we are in a position ourselves to take over the government of those places we are able to control, the

people of Ulster, if let loose without that organisation, might in a foolish moment find themselves in
a condition of antagonism and grips with their foes
which I believe even the present Government would
lament." The course they were following, he
added, " is the only course that I know of that is
possible under the circumstances of this Province
which is consistent with the maintenance of law
and order and the prevention of bloodshed." Carson knew well, none better, the dangerous stuff with
which he had to deal, the ferocious passions he had
to manage. And he succeeded. " Carson's influence," Tim Healy wrote two years later, " has
acted as a safety valve for the Orangemen, as they
would have got up sporadic riots if left to
themselves."

Thus Carson laid his plans to maintain the peace
by disciplining his forces. There would be no murder if he could help it, no cruelty and no terrorism.
" The Ulstermen," he said, " would never fight
from behind hedges, nor by the maiming of cattle,
nor by the boycotting of individuals." But what if
they came in conflict with the forces of the Crown ?
Carson did not anticipate any such collision. " God
forbid," he said, " that any loyal Irishman should
ever shoot or think of shooting the British soldier
or sailor." He did not believe it would go so far.
He knew, or thought he knew, the stuff of which
the Liberal politicians were made, and their
healthy fear of an outraged public opinion. " Any
Government," he said, " will ponder long before
it dares to shoot a loyal Ulster Protestant devoted
to his country and loyal to his King." " The situation," Tim Healy observed, " depends on whether
Asquith has the nerve to meet them unflinchingly."

Carson calculated that Asquith would flinch—and he was right.

All politics come down to a conflict of the human will. Carson was pulling, Redmond was pulling, Asquith was enduring : sooner or later one or other would crack. And chance, or the rashness of a politician, gave an opportunity for testing out the breaking-strain of these forces.

It was Mr. Churchill who made the occasion. Thanks to his great name as much as to his native ability, he had risen rapidly in a party to which neither by tradition nor conviction did he really belong. By nature audacious, by training military, he could not, like Mr. Asquith, endure and wait. His instinct was to quell, to dominate, to strike, like his great ancestor, at the heart of the enemy position, and in this case he had a double motive for activity : he smarted under the stroke of an old political friend and he burned to earn the gratitude of his new colleagues. There is evidence of these feelings in the speech made by the Home Secretary at Dundee on 3rd October, 1911. He spoke scornfully of " the squall which Sir Edward Carson was trying to raise in Ulster—or rather in that half of Ulster of which he has been elected Commander-in-Chief." " Are we never," he asked, " to be allowed to examine this great issue free from party rancour ? Sir Edward Carson says No. . . . He will attempt to set up in Ulster a provisional —that is to say a rebel—Government in defiance of laws which will have received the assent of Parliament and of the Crown. . . . These are his threats. . . . We must not attach too much importance to these frothings of Sir Edward Carson. . . . I daresay when the worst comes to the worst we shall find that civil war evaporates in uncivil words. . . ."

These jibes delighted the Liberal politicians, and set the fashion to the Liberal press. The Ulstermen were denounced illogically both as bigots and as bluffers ; their leader was described as a fanatic and a buffoon. The Irish politicians adorned the theme with their own more picturesque invective. " The majority of the people of Ulster," Jerry MacVeagh told a delighted congress of Liberals in Westminster, " wanted Home Rule and would not be deterred by the pantomime war which Sir Edward Carson was threatening. Sir Edward was not an Ulster member and not even an Ulsterman. He represented in Parliament the Episcopalian curates of Dublin University. Sir Edward would not discard his wig and gown for a spiked helmet and a khaki suit, and on the passing of Home Rule he would shoulder nothing more deadly than a brief-bag and march to no more dangerous a battle-field than the law courts."

Was all this true ? Would civil war evaporate in uncivil words ? Mr. Churchill rather rashly put the matter to a preliminary test by proposing to make a speech in support of Home Rule in the centre of Belfast. He would show by a practical demonstration that there was nothing in this Ulster bogey. The opportunity was provided by the Ulster Liberal Association which invited Mr. Churchill to speak in the Ulster Hall, in the company of Mr. John Redmond and Mr. Joseph Devlin.

The Liberal Party had at one time been strong among the Presbyterians of Ulster ; but had received a mortal blow when Mr. Gladstone introduced his first Home Rule Bill, and although some, out of fidelity to a tradition, still called themselves Liberal, the Liberal Home Ruler in Belfast could hardly be said to exist. As to its leader, the general opinion in Ulster was summarised by Carson, "Lord Pirrie," he said, "had sold them for a coronet, and Mr. T. W. Russell had sold them for a salary."

What infuriated his fellow townsmen was the zeal of the shipbuilder in creating an impression which they knew to be false, that outside the Roman Catholic District there was a body of Belfast Liberals in favour of Home Rule. "Feeling," said the *Northern Whig* (on the 9th January, 1912), "runs very high on both sides, and with a Falls Road mob invading a Protestant District while escorting a British Minister to the Ulster Hall to announce the impending doom of the Union, a spark might cause a general conflagration." As in the village of Columcille so in the city of Belfast, there was an unwritten law of political trespass.

The Ulster Hall had been taken by the Ulster Liberal Association for the 8th February, 1912 : on the 17th January preceding, the Standing Committee of the Ulster Unionist Council published a resolution which it had unanimously passed on the previous day—that " it observed with astonishment the deliberate challenge thrown down by Mr. Winston Churchill, Mr. John Redmond, Mr. Joseph Devlin and Lord Pirrie in announcing their intention to hold a Home Rule meeting in the centre of the loyal city of Belfast, and resolves to take steps to prevent its being held."

In this resolution, so " curst and brief," there was something which commanded and received attention. The terms were enigmatic ; but it was assumed everywhere that the statement involved illegality, and everywhere, in " a hundred different sharps and flats," the Liberal politicians and the Liberal press discussed and denounced it. That force should be used and free speech denied in our great and free democracy would never do : at all costs the meeting must be held ; otherwise there was an end to our constitutional liberties. Not the Liberals only were shocked by the announcement. " We cannot pretend," said *The Times*, " to rejoice in the decision of the Standing Committee of the Ulster Unionist Council. . . . As a matter of political ethics their action is hard to justify, and even from the point of view of mere political tactics its wisdom is open to question." Under the doubts of their friends and the abuse of their foes the Ulstermen remained disconcertingly silent. James Craig did, indeed, growl that the Liberals would now see whether it was all " bluff " and " Ulsteria " in Belfast ; but as for what they intended to do, " I cannot reveal what steps are being taken," sufficient to say that " the meeting shall not take place under any circumstances."

Excitement and speculation increased. On the 19th January it was reported that " the First Lord of the Admiralty " (as Mr. Churchill had by that time become) " has every intention of fulfilling his engagement." On the other hand, a " universal conviction " was reported " that if the meeting is held there will be violent and deplorable disorders in Belfast." The Irish Nationalist press insisted that the meeting must take place and " that all the forces of the Crown be put at Mr. Churchill's disposal " ; but the still small voice of the *Cork Free Press* hoped " for some such mediation as settled the railway and cotton strikes to avert bloodshed." Sir Edward Carson, speaking at Liverpool on the 22nd

January, said that he was on his way to Belfast, "where he ought to be and intended to be. . . . He endorsed the resolution passed by the Loyalists of Ireland with reference to Mr. Churchill's proposed visit—not with a light heart, God knew. He was the last man in the world to wish for a conflict with the forces of the Crown ; but if a member of the Government, either with or without its sanction, wished to create a situation that it was impossible for men in the condition of those men in the North of Ireland to bear, then the responsibility for the consequences was not upon those men, but upon the men who challenged them." As for free speech, Carson mentioned the notorious fact that " at Mr. T. M. Healy's last election campaign he did not hold a single meeting because he was not allowed to." And again, on the 23rd at Manchester, Carson referred to the " most provocative speaker in the whole party going under the most provocative circumstances to a place where the words of his own father are still ringing in the ear."

In the meanwhile prayers had been addressed to the Lord Mayor and Corporation to prevent a riot by closing the hall ; but the Lord Mayor stated to an interviewer on the 22nd January, that " the Corporation desired to keep their contract." Moreover the Ulster Liberal Association boasted that it had filled the three thousand seats by the issue of tickets and was firm in its resolve to hold the meeting. " Three regiments of infantry," it stated, " were to be drafted into Belfast from Dublin to strengthen the local garrison."

By the 24th January Sir Edward Carson was in Belfast, where he met the Ulster Unionist Council ; " the sole question before the meeting," it was reported, "related to the Unionist policy to be pursued in relation to the Churchill-Redmond meeting." No communication was issued to the press ; but rumour had it that the Council " enthusiastically endorsed the steps " recommended by the Standing Committee. On the same day it was nervously reported from Dublin that the Southern Unionists were in an " uncomfortable situation." They " had not been consulted ; but they would do nothing to dissociate themselves from the men of the North," and they expressed the conviction that " all the police and all the soldiers in Ireland will be unable to ensure peace."

If, however, there was nervousness in Dublin there was panic in London. True, the First Lord was still reported to " adhere to his intention " ; but the Liberal Party were beginning to fidget unhappily. They had said that there would be no trouble if a Home Rule Bill were passed and here was trouble over a mere preliminary meeting. The demands of Lord Pirrie and his friends for troops and police only increased their apprehensions. If the Belfast crowd resisted the soldiers there would be bloodshed ; if they submitted the use of force would still suggest that Home Rule could only be forced upon Ulster at the point of the bayonet. To enter upon a new campaign of coercion—against the Protestants—was the last thing they desired ; their fears conjured up terrible visions of riot, with Roman Catholics and Presbyterians locked in deadly strife, and their own supporters, the Nonconformists of England and the Presbyterians of Scotland, uneasily stirring, like a wood under a rising gale, with the revival of ancient bigotries.

The Master of Elibank, who had been enjoying a

vacation abroad with his bosom friends, Sir Rufus
Isaacs and Mr. Lloyd George, had returned to
town, and " had taken the matter in hand." Watch-
ful journalists reported, on 25th January, 1912, that
" Lord Pirrie and the First Lord of the Admiralty
reached the Chief Whip's Office about 3.30," as
also Mr. Graham and another representative of the
Belfast Liberal Association. The Attorney-General
also joined the Conference, no doubt to throw a
legal light on a situation of dubious legality. To say
that you intend to "take steps to prevent a meeting"
—there was nothing illegal there, since the steps
might be legal steps. By this time it was known that
the Ulster Unionists had hired the hall for the 7th
February, the night before the proposed meeting,
and Sir Rufus Isaacs was no doubt constrained
to point out that if a body of Ulstermen entered
the Hall on the 7th and remained there over the
8th, it would be extremely difficult either by force
or by legal process to eject them in time for the
meeting.

The Conference lasted until five o'clock ; but it
was after six before Mr. Churchill left the Whip's
Office. No doubt it was a hard task to dissuade him
from an enterprise to which his reputation, and his
dignity, were so heavily committed.

Mr. Churchill went from the Whip's Office to the
Admiralty, where he found inspiration to write a
letter to the Marquess of Londonderry. " If," he
wrote, " as I now gather from the newspapers, the
main objections of yourself and your friends are
directed against our holding our meeting in the
Ulster Hall, then, although such claims are neither
just nor reasonable, I will ask the Ulster Liberal
Association to accede to your wish. There will thus

be no necessity for your friends to endure the hard-
ships of a vigil, or sustain the anxieties of a siege."
If the First Lord had hoped to touch either the
compunction or the apprehension of the Marquess
he was doomed to disappointment. Londonderry's
reply had " vinegar and pepper in't." Mr. Churchill
was welcome to hold his meeting where he liked,
as long as he did not violate those " historical traditions and memories connected with the Ulster
Hall and your late father's visit in 1886 " ; as for the
right of free speech, Mr. Churchill's reference to
that elementary principle appeared " almost cynical, having regard to the action of your Government in repressing it in the House of Commons."

In this curious trial of strength the Ulstermen had
prevailed : they had carried their point : the
Liberal Government had, so to say, lowered their
eyes in a conflict of will, and thenceforth the Loyalists were to do as they liked in Ulster. They had,
moreover, won their point without breaking any
law or even threatening to break any law. They had,
in effect, forbidden a Minister of the Crown to do
a thing and the Minister had obeyed them. Sir
Edward Carson was not blind to the humour of the
situation. Speaking at the Holborn Restaurant, on
the 2nd February, he said he was glad to be able
to attend the dinner " through the somewhat
belated and reluctant consent of Mr. Winston
Churchill." Had events taken another turn, as
seemed possible a few days before, he might have
felt it his duty to be still in Belfast. . . . He hoped
Mr. Churchill's visit to that city would prove
peaceful, and his earnest wish was that, now Mr.
Churchill had seen it was best to pursue Nationalist
aspirations in Nationalist quarters, he would meet

with that respectful admiration from his Nationalist friends of which no one would in the least wish to deprive him.

Carson had won his first victory in this campaign, and he knew it, although he could not know the full effects. The Government sought to conceal a moral defeat by a physical display. On the 6th February, 1912, five battalions of foot, a squadron of cavalry and a detachment of Royal Engineers detrained at Belfast and marched to Barracks, " watched by curious and not unfriendly crowds." Yet that same day, after long, troubled and anxious debate in the Cabinet, Mr. Asquith wrote to the King that although the Bill as introduced was to apply to all Ireland, the Irish Leaders were to be warned that :

" The Government held themselves free to make changes, if it became clear that special treatment must be provided for the Ulster Counties, and that in this case the Government will be ready to recognise the necessity, either by amendment or by not pressing it (the Bill) on under the provision of the Parliament Act."[1]

While making a show of force the Government were already preparing to surrender.

As the Belfast Liberals would not consent to hold their meeting in the Nationalist St. Mary's Hall, a marquee was erected in the Celtic football ground. Seven battalions of infantry and a squadron of cavalry reinforced the police at various points ; but there was no need for such precautions. " The fact

[1] *Life of Lord Oxford and Asquith*, by J. A. Spender and Cyril Asquith, vol. ii., p. 15.

that the Unionist Leaders have put Belfast on its best behaviour," the Special Correspondent of *The Times* reported, "is the strongest guarantee of order, and I learn that Lord Londonderry, Sir Edward Carson and other prominent men in Ulster will be here exerting their influence against any interference with Mr. Churchill, his meeting or his supporters, so we may take it that the peace is unlikely to be disturbed."

It was not disturbed. Mr. Churchill drove to his meeting through Royal Avenue from the Grand Central Hotel, along streets placarded every few yards with the Unionist command to keep the peace. The crowd was under a discipline no less stern because it was unseen, yet it looked as if it might tear him to pieces. Mr. Churchill's car, at one time, was " poised on the near side wheels " by the force of the crowd. As the car slowly made its way through " the men thrust their heads in and uttered fearful menaces and imprecations." " It seemed to me," said the same observer, " that Mr. Churchill was running a graver risk than ever he had expected. But he never flinched . . . and no harm befell him."

He held his meeting, and got safely away ; but he had learnt far more than he taught, and years afterwards, with characteristic magnanimity he sent his son to Belfast to make up, as he said, for the biggest mistake he had ever made in the course of his life. That he escaped with his life that day seemed to those who saw the crowd which surged about him no less than a miracle : he was in fact protected by a sardonic yet benignant spirit. Late that night Carson appeared on the balcony of the Ulster Club in Castle Street, and over a scene of wild excitement congratulated the citizens of Belfast on their magnificent self-restraint during the day and advised them all quietly to go home. He himself stopped to write a letter to the Secretary of the Ulster Unionist Council, congratulating " all our friends " on that " very satisfactory and peaceful termination." " In the difficult times that are ahead," he wrote, " it is essential that any action which may be necessary from time to time shall be fully organised and disciplined, and that under no circumstances shall peace and order be thoughtlessly and wantonly disturbed. We have a splendid cause to fight for, and our friends may feel certain that we will shrink from no organised action which may at any time be necessary."

CHAPTER VI

THE CONSERVATIVE LEADERSHIP

Rebel and traitor—The Southern Loyalists—Carson at Dublin—Mr. Balfour resigns—Mr. Bonar Law—On Carson's arm—Taking the salute.

IN THOSE MONTHS between the Craigavon meeting and the introduction of the Third Home Rule Bill, Sir Edward Carson visited many cities and spoke from many platforms. The leader of his side, the centre of the struggle, like Ajax by the ships, he drew upon himself all the darts of the enemy : he received and returned their assaults with a certain glooming gusto all his own. Scornful, sardonic flashes of wit and touches of humour—there was never any doubt that Carson was an Irishman.

The Liberals, adept in every art of the politician, tried to sow distrust between the Leader and his followers. Sir John Benn, one of a party of the Eighty Club, which toured Ireland in September, 1911, declared (in Belfast) that " Sir Edward Carson and his friends were quite prepared to sell the Ulster Unionists, lock, stock and barrel, to save the House of Lords "—a reference to those intrigues during the Conference which we noticed in a previous chapter. Carson " resented the accusation, not merely because it was hitting below the belt but because it was a lie " and begged his accuser " not to offer him the additional insult of an apology." Thus admonished, Sir John made some attempt to prove his case in letters to the press ;

Gc

but he was out in his facts. There had indeed been an attempt to sell the Unionists ; but " Carson and his friends " had set their faces against it.

This line of attack failing, the Liberals tried another : they denounced Carson as a rebel, an arch-rebel, an instigator of rebellion. But as it was Carson's design both to frighten the Government and awaken the British people, these accusations exactly suited him ; the more he was denounced the more defiant he became. He was at one with his Belfast friends, he said at Liverpool, in proposing to prevent Mr. Churchill from speaking at Belfast. " If that," he added, throwing out his hands, " is inciting to riot, here I am." And again, speaking at Croydon, he said—" We will stop at nothing if an attempt is to be made to hand the Loyalists of Ireland over to those whom we believe to be the enemies of our country—and who certainly are the enemies of yours."

Carson, indeed, was a rebel, as honest Kent was rebel when he stood against the madness of King Lear :

> *Revoke thy doom ;*
> *Or, whilst I can vent clamour from my throat,*
> *I'll tell thee thou dost evil.*

Thus, for example, at Eastbourne, on 25th November, 1911, he described the fell designs of those who worked to destroy the United Kingdom, while fawning on the English people. " Let them have no faith in the smooth assurances of the Irish Nationalists : Mr. Redmond was performing on his patent bagpipes which played two tunes at one time—a strange mixture of ' Rule Britannia ' and ' The Wearin' o' the Green.' "

And with gathering scorn, he went on :

" I used to think I was a loyal Irishman. Now Mr. Lloyd George and Mr. Redmond inform me that I am a rebel.

" The times are out of joint. Things are strangely topsy-turvy.

" I am a rebel, a Sussex-Irish rebel, and all my Ulster friends are all rebels.

" The men who cheered the defeat of our troops in South Africa . . . and are now the colleagues of the Government in the House of Commons ; Mr. Dillon and his allies who went about Ireland asking and beseeching the people not to enlist in the army during the war in South Africa—they are all loyal subjects of the King, and I am a rebel. . . . When Mr. Lynch, the Nationalist M.P. for Galway, was firing at our troops in South Africa, I did not know where my son was. I had not heard of him for four months ; but he was fighting for his country. And I am a rebel.

" I have never shot against this country : I might have had a better time in Ireland if I had. I never said, as Mr. Redmond said, that Ford, the dynamiter, was the best friend that Ireland ever had ; but I am called a rebel.

" In the circumstances I am glad to be called a rebel.

" We have given of our best to build up the Empire. We recall the names of Wellington, of Roberts, of White of Ladysmith ; and we think of Coghill of Isandula, around whose body, where it lay dead, the flag of the British race, the old Union Jack, was found. All these were men of Loyalist Ireland, and mainly of Ulster.

" If you were to be told that you were to be

driven out of your present citizenship and your present unity, what would you do ? "

Here a voice answered, " Fight ! "

" That is what we are being told. We are given notice to quit.

" The men who made Belfast, which was a town of 12,000 when the Act of Union was passed, and has now something like 400,000 people, do you think they will accept notice to quit ? "

Here there were cries of " No, No ! "

" Would you advise them to ? "

" No," the meeting shouted.

" Then," Carson concluded, " you are all rebels."

Carson, indeed, was too sure of himself to be daunted by these accusations ; but the Liberals touched him more nearly in another and more subtle line of attack—the attempt to divide the Unionists of Southern Ireland from the Unionists of the North. His heart was with the people among whom he had been born and bred ; but he realised the difference between these two and the danger of division. In the North the Unionists were compact and powerful—at least half of the population, and in control of its territories, its industries and its economic power ; in the South they were a scattered minority, hostages where they were wealthy, defenceless where they were poor, protected only by the power of the British occupation, a smoking sacrifice, were that arm withdrawn, to the vindictive savagery of an ancient feud. Conceal it from themselves as they might, there was for these Southern Unionists a dilemma which grew the more dreadful as it approached, either to go into exile or submit to a triumphant enemy. For a minority so situated organised resistance was a course so desperate that it might be called hopeless.

There was thus a temptation, which as yet they put behind them, to make terms while terms could be made. Their position was put to them plainly and brutally by John Dillon, in October, 1911, when he demanded that certain landlords of the South should sell their land to their tenants.

" I tell these men," said Mr. Dillon, " that the sands in the hour-glass are running down fast. Home Rule is coming, and we will get it whether they like it or not. And when Home Rule is come and there is an Irish Parliament sitting in Dublin, I don't think they will get English Ministers to trouble themselves much about their woes in the future. They will make their bed with the people of Ireland, and, be it short or long, they will have to lie on that bed. It is better for them to make friends with their own people while there is yet time."

" To make friends "—those Protestants of the South had good reason to fear the rasping significance of that invitation. When an Irish Nationalist in the House of Commons appealed to Colonel Saunderson to join his Party, " we would give you," he promised, " the highest position in the land." " I don't doubt it," Saunderson replied, " —at the end of a rope ! "

Sir Edward Carson shared their knowledge and their apprehensions ; but he said clearly, nevertheless, that the one hope for the South lay in the resistance of the North. It seemed to him as plain as a pikestaff that to finance Home Rule would be utterly impossible without the taxable resources of Belfast. It would besides break the mainspring of Nationalism—Ireland a nation. To stop Home

Rule in Ulster, therefore, would prevent it for all Ireland. And as his habit was in advocacy, so it was in politics, he concentrated his attack on the vital point. That being won the minor issues would fall with the major.

It was this policy which Carson commended to the Unionists of the South at the great meeting held in Dublin on the 10th October, 1911. The Southern Unionists, although a scattered minority, were yet, at that time, a great multitude : they flocked into the capital from all parts of Leinster, Munster and Connaught—an intelligent, well-bred and high-spirited people. There were the old gentry, many of whom had sold their lands and lived happily if insecurely on their domains within a ring of friendly-seeming peasantry ; their talk mostly of horses, hounds, woodcock, snipe, and salmon, of sons and brothers in the Army, of the Services and the Frontiers of the Empire. There were also professional men—doctors and attorneys of the country-towns ; clergy of the Church of Ireland ; business men, who handled the prosperous and growing trade of Dublin, Cork and Waterford ; merchants, millers, brewers, distillers ; great graziers and cattle-dealers, breeders of hunters and race-horses ; farmers of broad acres ; shopkeepers, old soldiers, skilled artisans—altogether a fine set of people, gallant, keen, humorous, lacking the fanaticism of the North, but with a fine tradition of loyalty to the Union and the Crown.

They made a great show in the Rotunda, five thousand of them, the Irish peers filling a large part of the gallery. Lord Ardilaun presided, and Sir Henry Blake moved the principal resolution—a reasoned statement of their case—protesting against the creation of a separate Parliament, " whether independent or subordinate," protesting also against the creation of " an Executive depending for its existence on the pleasure of such a Parliament," foreseeing therefrom " the most dangerous social confusion . . . a disastrous conflict of interests and classes and a serious risk of civil war."

Looking back upon the events which followed, there is a melancholy interest in noting the fulfilment in all its terms of that grave statement by the Irish Loyalists, which foreboded their own doom :

" Because such a measure would endanger the commercial relations between Ireland and Great Britain and would cause in Ireland widespread financial distrust, followed by complete paralysis of enterprise.

" Because such a measure would imperil personal liberty, freedom of opinion and the spirit of tolerance in Ireland.

" Because such a measure, instead of effecting a settlement, would inevitably pave the way for further efforts towards a complete separation of Ireland from Great Britain.

" Because such a measure would hand over Ireland to the government of a Party which, notwithstanding professions the political purpose of which is obvious, has proved itself, during its long course of action, unworthy of the exercise of power, by its repeated defiance of the law, and disregard of the elementary principles of honesty and justice . . . "

It is fair also to say, where so much is forgotten which should be remembered, that those good subjects of the South took a wider point of view than their own interests—" being justly proud of the place we Irishmen have long held among those to whom the Empire owes its prosperity and fame, having been always faithful to our allegiance to our Sovereign and upholders of the Constitution, we protest against any change that will deprive us of our birthright by which we stand on equal ground with our fellow-countrymen of Great Britain as subjects of our King and as citizens of the British Empire."

It was to such an audience, of his own people, that Carson chose to justify the line he was taking in the North. Ulster, he told them, had made up her mind : " she would not have Home Rule on any conditions whatsoever." But let them not misunderstand what Ulster intended : she asked for no separate Parliament ; " she has never, in all the long controversy, taken that selfish course. Ulster asks to remain in the Imperial Parliament, and that she means if possible to do."

Here loud cheers interrupted the speaker, for to the Southern Loyalists the Union was something more even than to the North. In the North they could hope to protect themselves, but to their brothers of the South the Union meant life itself.

" And you need fear no action of Ulster," Carson proceeded, " which would be in the nature of a desertion of the Southern Provinces." Here he came to the core of his policy, what was for him its purpose and its justification :

" If Ulster succeeds," he said, " Home Rule is dead. Home Rule is impossible for Ireland without Belfast and the surrounding parts as a portion of the scheme."

If this indeed were true—and they all in Ireland

THE MEETING AT BALMORAL (BELFAST)
when Bonar Law made his famous speech

at that time believed it to be true—there was no need to argue further. It was sufficient. The whole speech, therefore, was an elaboration of this central point. Ulster, he explained, would set up her own Government in the event of Home Rule becoming law, but not till then, and it was part of her policy to consider how best to help her brother Unionists and Loyalists of the South. That the Ulstermen had elected him, a man of Dublin, as Leader, was some guarantee that this was to Ulster of the gravest importance. He suggested, therefore, that they should appoint a representative Commission to co-operate with Ulster in their defence. And again he drove the point home : " In this fight Ulster is the key of the situation. With Ulster strong there need be no fear."

The Southern Unionists were greatly reassured by this speech ; but although they so far took his advice as to appoint a Commission, they never accepted Sir Edward Carson as their leader. The difference in situation made a difference in temper and in policy ; the North put their trust in rifles, the South in resolutions, in influence, in reasonable argument. They could not bring themselves to believe that the House of Lords had become only the shadow and the simulacrum of power ; that the electorate could no longer intervene ; that, in fact, as Mr. Rudyard Kipling described it long afterwards, they were sold, like cattle, on the hoof. And so North and South, believing in different policies, gradually drifted apart.

A more immediate anxiety was the Unionist Party and its leadership. Carson had taken his share in those divisions which led to the resignation of Mr. Balfour ; but when it came he none the less

regretted it. They had differed upon several questions—on the Irish Land Bill, on the Chamberlain
policy, on the Parliament Bill, differences which
sprang partly from a dissimilarity of temper and of
character. The mind of Carson was positive and
intense, impatient of uncertainties, concentrated on
one end ; the Union was his Faith and he a zealot.
Balfour's temper was more cool, his mind more
fluid ; he hovered over a subject like a hawk which
does not pounce ; he delighted to play with the
opposition to the cause which he embraced ; and
was willing to admit that there was reason on the
other side. Moreover, there was a difference in the
ruling motives of these two men. What concerned
Balfour was to keep that Party together which he
had inherited, almost as a family trust, from his
uncle, Lord Salisbury ; what concerned Carson were
the lives and the religion of his friends in Ireland.

They differed from yet trusted each other, nor was
there any shadow of intrigue or of personal interest
to embitter the division. What the one wrote to the
other when he heard of his resignation we may
gather from the reply. " We have been," Balfour
wrote, " in many a critical engagement together,
inside and outside the House of Commons, and
I need not tell you how much I have always valued
your friendship, and how greatly I have admired
your courage."

This letter was written on the 15th November,
1911 ; Balfour had resigned on the 8th, and between
these two dates the question of succession had been
settled. Mr. Walter Long and Mr. Austen Chamberlain were both, as Mr. Long puts it, " pressed by
their friends " to accept the office. They had both
found fault with their leader ; Mr. Balfour, indeed,

had refused to rebuke Mr. Austen Chamberlain, for fear, as he expressed it, that his choice of Ministers, if he ever came to take office, might be narrowed to Mr. Walter Long and Mr. Henry Chaplin.

Their position was thus faintly invidious, and was made more so by the circumstance that their friends were less modest than themselves in the advancement of their claims. The rivalry, in sum, threatened to divide Unionists and Conservatives. There were some who thought that both gentlemen, strong as were their party claims, might be found to lack those rare qualities which make the natural leader of men, and thought they saw these qualities in Carson ; but when they sounded him they found him unresponsive. He had no love for politics ; such ambitions as he cherished were in the law. And there were other considerations : Balfour was his friend, and had been his benefactor. Moreover, in the main case, he desired to be free of all entanglements save Ireland alone.

There was another candidate, more modest than Austen Chamberlain and Walter Long, yet more successful, Andrew Bonar Law. He was, indeed, as Mr. Asquith described him, " meekly ambitious " ; but his diffidence was almost a disease, and he had neither talent nor inclination for intrigue. Yet the qualities which he lacked were supplied by a friend. Mr. F. A. Mackenzie, in his biography of Lord Beaverbrook, tells us that " Max Aitken, during the summer, made up his mind that when a new leader was elected, Bonar Law was to be the man, and set quietly to work." Part of this work was to win over the " discontented younger elements of the party " ; another part to win over the press. To this end, he arranged a meeting between his friend and Lord

Northcliffe, and so it came about that in the midst
of the crisis it was suggested in the newspapers,
as it were casually, that there might be a case for
Mr. Bonar Law as a " compromise candidate."

According to the Political Correspondent of *The
Times*, when the name of Bonar Law was put forward, Carson was again approached, and finding
no encouragement there, a deputation went to the
Whips and urged the nomination upon the Central
Office. " Carson," however, " on being again
approached, said definitely that in no circumstances
would he accept the honour proposed."

Three days later, that is to say on Monday, 13th
November, 1911, Bonar Law and Max Aitken drove
together to the meeting at the Carlton Club. " Don't
run yourself down," Aitken was urging his friend,
" don't try to keep in the background. Remember
you are a great man now." And Bonar Law replied,
with that despondency which seldom left him, " If
I am a great man then a good many of the great
men of history are frauds."

Before going to the meeting Bonar Law had gone
to Carson, and offered to stand down in his favour ;
and Carson, again refusing, had urged Bonar Law
to go forward. And so it came about that when Mr.
Long moved and Mr. Chamberlain seconded the
proposal, Sir Edward Carson left the room and
returned with Mr. Bonar Law, like a bride on the
arm of her father.

The arrangement, indeed, suited Carson very
well. The father of Bonar Law, a Presbyterian
Minister of New Brunswick, was born at Bally
Willan near Portrush—in birth and upbringing an
Ulsterman. Bonar himself inherited the serious faith
and earnest temper of his kinsmen ; a youth spent

among the Presbyterians of Glasgow confirmed these natal impressions ; Bonar Law was in all respects, even to the Covenanting vehemence of his language, at one with the Ulster people.

That these two men were of one mind was shortly made plain. The Home Rule Bill was to be introduced by Mr. Asquith on the 11th April, 1912. On the eve of that event Sir Edward Carson and Mr. Bonar Law went together to Belfast, and there and in public declared their unity of purpose. " Mr. Bonar Law and I," said Carson, " have shaken hands over this business, and we are going to see it through." And Bonar Law gave the Ulstermen " this message on behalf of the Unionist Party : though the brunt of the battle will be yours, there will not be wanting help from across the Channel."

These exchanges were preliminary to a more formidable demonstration. In the Show Ground at Balmoral, a suburb of Belfast, on the 9th April, before a crowd of people estimated at a hundred thousand, Mr. Bonar Law, Sir Edward Carson, Lord Londonderry and Mr. Walter Long took the salute of the Ulster Volunteers. We are now unhappily accustomed to force in civil affairs, but to the seventy or eighty Members of Parliament who looked on at that great Demonstration it must have been a startling phenomenon, a formidable threat to that system of government by consent which had been taken for granted in these islands for a hundred years and more. The manhood of Loyal Ulster, an Army, as we might fairly describe it, of between eighty and ninety thousand men, " in military order and showing in their carriage the effects of drill and discipline," divided into two columns, marched on either side of the little pavilion in which these four men stood. At once martial and democratic, " patrician and plebeian, clergy and laiety, master and man," the Loyalists marched past, Lord Hamilton at the head of the Prentice Boys of Derry ; and not the men of Ulster alone ; contingents of the four provinces of Ireland, " representing even distant Kerry, rebellious Cork, and Clare," were in those two columns.

A solemnity characteristic of Ulster made the demonstration the more impressive. The Primate of all Ireland and the Moderator of the Presbyterian Church opened the day with prayer ; the strains of the 90th Psalm were taken up by that huge assemblage :

> *Who knows the power of thy wrath ?*
> *According to thy fear*
> *So is thy wrath. Lord, teach thou us*
> *Our end in mind to bear.*

Of the fate of some at least of those contingents, the words might be thought prophetic :

> *As with an overflowing flood*
> *Thou carry'st them away ;*
> *They like a sleep are, like the grass*
> *That grows at morn are they.*

Although in their unity and their living strength they seemed invincible.

Shortly before, at a demonstration in Dublin, addressed by John Redmond, the flying of a Union Jack, not at but within sight of the meeting, had been denounced as " an intolerable insult." Here, on the other hand, the centre of the demonstration

was a flagstaff 90 feet high, on which the largest
Union flag ever woven, 48 feet by 25, was broken
and flew out as the resolution against Home Rule
was put to the meeting.

An upbringing in the South-West of Scotland gave
Bonar Law the key to the Cameronian spirit of the
demonstration. " You are men who know what you
are fighting for and love what you know," he said,
using the words of Cromwell to his Ironsides. And,
in telling reference to the history of the Province
he proceeded : " You are a besieged city. The
timid have left you ; your Lundys have betrayed
you ; but you have closed your gates. The Government have erected by their Parliament Act a boom
against you to shut you off from the help of the
British people. You will burst that boom. That help
will come, and when the crisis is over men will say
to you in words not unlike those used by Pitt—
you have saved yourselves by your exertions and
you will save the Empire by your example."

Inspiring as such words were, there was more in
the presence of Mr. Bonar Law than in his speech,
for, standing there and taking the salute, he was
making not only the Ulster cause but the Ulster
policy his own. There was a symbolism in this
presence at the saluting point of a military review,
of which, were it for good or ill, none could miss the
significance. And to make it the more obvious—
" the Ulster Leader and the Leader of the whole
Unionist Party," Carson and Bonar Law, " each
grasped the other's hand, as though formally
ratifying a compact made thus publicly on the eve
of battle."[1]

This seventeenth-century spirit enveloped the

[1] *Ulster's Stand for Union*, by Ronald McNeill, p. 86.

event in an ideal halo : Mr. Walter Long, with a
more prosaic and English bluntness suggested a
more modern and prosaic view of the alliance :
" If they are going to put Lord Londonderry and
Sir Edward Carson into the dock," he said, " they
will have to find one large enough to hold the whole
Unionist Party."

Thus on the eve of the Home Rule Bill not only
the Unionists of Ulster, but His Majesty's Opposition were ranged together in defiance of a proposed
law : since the Bill was not yet on the Statute Book
it was neither rebellion nor treason ; but it contained
the menace of both. It was plain that these men
meant what they said, and what they said implied
civil war.

CHAPTER VII

THE THIRD HOME RULE BILL

The Third Home Rule Bill—Carson on Union—The People's will and the public good—Exclusion—Carson states a case—" To wreck the bill "—Walter Guinness—Redmond prevails.

THE PRIME MINISTER presented the Third Home Rule Bill to the House of Commons on the 11th April, 1912, his exposition of the measure being at all points complete, except that it made no account either of the history or the nature of the country for which the Bill was designed. There was indeed, near the beginning of the speech, a dramatic passage to suggest a fatal antinomy. Mr. Asquith was expatiating on the verdict of the Irish Elections. " If," he said, " you refuse to recognise it, you are refusing to recognise the deliberate constitutional demands of the vast majority of the nation." . . .

" What nation ? " asked Sir Clement Kinloch Cooke.

" What nation ? " the Prime Minister replied, " the Irish nation."

The fierce cheers with which the Irish Nationalists hailed that fatal admission suggest the unhappy sequel. If the Irish were indeed a nation, then the Bill was sadly inadequate, since it allowed them only " local management of local interests." They were still to be ruled by an English King and protected by a British Army ; they were permitted to tax themselves, but not to collect their own taxes.

Hc

Their fiscal liberties were limited to 10 per cent on
or off existing duties ; they were, indeed, to be
financed by an allowance to meet a deficit—like a
young gentleman sent to the Colonies for the good
of his family. They were to be allowed to make laws
for the peace, order and good government of
Ireland ; but the Royal Irish Constabulary was to
remain—at least for six years—a reserved Service.
In matters religious they were refused discretion in
their own schools ; in matters of law there was an
appeal to the Privy Council. Mr. Asquith called the
Irish a nation, yet maintained, or so he boasted,
" in this Bill, unimpaired and beyond the reach of
challenge or question, the supremacy, absolute and
sovereign, of the Imperial Parliament."

Mr. Redmond might profess to be satisfied with
such a compromise ; but Sir Edward Carson, when
he replied to Mr. Asquith, quoted a more veracious
confession of what the Irish Nationalists intended.
" I say deliberately," Mr. John Dillon had said,
" that I should never have dedicated my life, as I
have done, to this great struggle, if I had not seen
at the end of it, the crown and consummation of
our work in a free and independent nation." " We
are always being told," Carson added sardonically,
" to trust the Irish Nationalist Members. I myself
believe that it is only in trust, if you can trust them,
that any guarantee exists at all. But upon what
ground are we asked to trust them ? Upon the
ground that we ought not to believe a single word
they have ever said ! "

We are not allowed to forget in this speech, as at
any time, that Carson is an Irishman. It was as an
Irishman that he loved the Union. Like Montesquieu a century before, he believed that Union was

of more advantage to the smaller country than to the greater. It was no longer a prophecy ; it was a fact. " The one boast of every Irishman now," he said, " whatever his political creed may be, is the advancing prosperity of his country and the progress that her citizens have made.

" What," he proceeded, " is the object of the United Kingdom ? As I understand it, it is that all parts shall be worked together as one whole, and with the object that the poorer may be helped by the richer, and the richer may be the stronger by the co-operation of the poorer."

Mr. Asquith had made an appeal to the parsimony of Parliament : he had pointed out that there was an annual deficit against Ireland in the balance of the accounts. " If," the Prime Minister had said, " you continue the present system, you will have to add to the deficit year by year. There is no other way in which you can finance Unionism as a working policy." The Union, in effect, was to be ended because the poorer country was getting too much out of the richer. Carson warmly denounced a separation which would allow " either Ireland or any other part of the United Kingdom, whether large or small, to go back in the race of progress and civilisation, and not to be kept up to the same standard as you yourselves or as near thereto as possible."

Carson has often been described as an extreme partisan, dominated by personal or factional hatreds ; but if we fairly consider such speeches as this of the 11th April, 1912, we see that the motive which gave it life, and throbs through it with a passion of sincerity, is solicitude for the poor people of Ireland, about to be delivered over to such misfortunes as no mere partisan but only the humane statesman could feel and foresee. And he based his conviction not on prejudice, but on a true philosophy of statesmanship. " I have," he said, " asked myself what are the benefits that the Prime Minister indicates for Ireland—and I have not heard one. Does he think that the separation of the poorer and the richer country will benefit the poorer country ? "

Here the biographer may be allowed to point a contrast between these two speeches. Asquith based his case on the " demand " of the Irish people— " repeated and ratified time after time during the best part of the life of a generation " ; Carson considered not the popular demand but the public good. If, however, elections were to be taken into account, the British people had as much right to maintain as the Irish to dissolve the Union. Nay, better, for Carson denied that the Irish were a separate nation : he believed, and with pride, himself and his people to be a true part of the United Kingdom.

Carson touched also on something which Asquith probably did not understand, and therefore could hardly consider—the historical division within Ireland herself which made Home Rule impossible without injustice—and danger—to the Minority.

He was ready to admit that he represented a Minority only—" but it is a Minority which has always been true to the United Kingdom. Some people," he went on, " say that this is really a religious question." It was none the less important on that ground ; " but, sir, it is a religious question added to various other questions "—and here Carson put the whole historical case in one profound and penetrating sentence : " In my opinion, it (religion) is the dividing line, because Protestantism has in history been looked upon as the British Occupation in Ireland."

Then Carson touched upon the cause which he had so recently made his own—" I would like to know when a statesman takes up a question with that line there, what argument is there that you can raise for giving Home Rule to Ireland that you do not equally raise for giving Home Rule to that Protestant minority in the North-east Province ? "

The question, as we now know, had already been debated in the Cabinet ; but Mr. Redmond stood out stiffly against any such compromise, and when he touched on the idea, it was in order to divide the Northern from the Southern Unionists. In this debate Carson had said that if it was right to give Home Rule to the rest of Ireland then it was right also to give it to Ulster. Was that his proposal ? Was that his demand ?

" Will you agree to it ? " Carson asked warily.

" I would like the proposal to be made first," Redmond no less warily retorted.

The one, we may be sure, hated such a settlement as much as the other, since neither could make it without sacrifice of principles and of friends. Neither would ever agree to it voluntarily : it was to be for both a last resort ; a surrender, when there was no longer hope, to save part of the whole for which both fought.

Certain of the English Ministers, however, as they had little understanding of these Irish predicaments, continued to press for such a settlement. Mr. Churchill referred to it in the debate on the Second Reading. " It was impossible," he said, no doubt with recent experience vividly in mind, " for a

Liberal Government to treat cavalierly or contemptuously . . . the sincere sentiments of a numerous and well defined community like the Protestants of the North of Ireland. We may think them
wrong ; we may think them unreasonable, but there
they are ! "

And there indeed they were : such men as James
Craig glowering across at him—grim, big and solid
—not merely the delegates of a community but the
leaders of a force.

" No Liberal will deny," Mr. Churchill went on
soothingly, " that it is the right of every citizen, nay
a duty, provided the circumstances are sufficient,
to resist oppression."

Then retreating from this dangerous ground, he
pointed out the dangers of unconstitutional resistance.
Ulster, moreover, could not stand in the way of the
rest of Ireland. " The utmost they can claim is for
themselves. . . . Do the counties of Down and
Antrim and Londonderry, for instance, ask to be
excepted from the scope of this Bill ? Do they ask
for a Parliament of their own or do they wish to
remain here ? Is that their demand ? We ought to
know ! "[1]

These questions found no immediate reply : Sir
Edward Grey, a few days later, touched on the
matter more vaguely : " if Ulster defeats the solution we propose, or makes it impossible . . . some
other solution will have to be found which will free
this House and put the control of Irish affairs in
Irish hands."

And a few more days later one wilier than either
tried his hand. Sir Rufus Isaacs cross-examined Sir
Edward Carson across the floor of the House on the

---

[1] 30th April, 1912, see *Parl. Deb.*, vol. xxxvii., c. 1720.

intentions of Ulster ; but he got very little comfort from the exercise.

It was not until the 11th June, 1912, when the Bill was in Committee, that this crucial question of the exclusion of Ulster really came to the surface. On that day a Liberal Member, Mr. Agar-Robartes, moved to exclude " the counties of Antrim, Armagh, Down and Londonderry " from the provisions of the Act. Then, indeed, the fat was in the fire.

The debate occupied three days. It was soon evident that Mr. Redmond had prevailed with the Prime Minister, for the Chief Secretary had " no hesitation whatever in saying that it is not the intention of the Government to accept this amendment," and Ministers set themselves to the congenial task of using the proposal to divide the Unionists of North and South. Knowing as we know now, and as the Irish Unionists knew then, that it was a matter of life and death for that loyal minority, it seems a cruel enough game, although in extenuation it may be allowed that as those English Liberals did not understand the Irish people, they could hardly know how cruel it was.

Thus the Prime Minister sarcastically asked " these chivalrous champions of the rights of the Protestant minority," the Ulster Members, if they were going to leave the scattered Protestant minority elsewhere " without any kind of redress or protection " and " take shelter in this oasis or Alsatia . . . in which they may snap their fingers at their Roman Catholic fellow-subjects." And Sir John Simon, who had just returned to the House from an inquiry into the sinking of the *Titanic* found what he took to be an apposite metaphor :

" I can quite understand," he said, " a certain

hesitation on the part of hon. gentlemen opposite to speak, for we have been told that Home Rule is a thing which may shipwreck the position of the loyalists in Ireland ; they feel a little hesitation in taking to their boats when they are leaving the most defenceless part of their body behind them."

" Why defenceless ? " Carson interjected, and there were both rebuke and logic in the question, for the Government had assured the House that the Minority in Ireland were protected by the safeguards in the Bill and, moreover, it was the duty not of Ulster but of the Government to defend loyal subjects of the Crown.

When, however, Carson rose to speak on the Amendment, it was not to make retort on the pleasantries of the Solicitor-General ; but to state the case of the Ulster Unionists. These people were not asking for anything—" they are only asking to stay where they are," to enjoy " the rights under which they were born, and under which they have lived and flourished." There had been " a great deal of scoffing on these matters " ; but did they really question their sincerity ? It was to Ulster " not a political matter," but " a matter affecting their lives, their liberties, their employment and everything that goes to make up what man holds dear in life." He believed that they were right in their attitude ; but if they were wrong—" that is what you have to conquer."

Belfast was a great city, which had prospered under the Union ; her citizens were free, they were loyal, they were satisfied. He pointed to her trade and to her industries, which enjoyed the markets not of Ireland alone but of the British Empire. Her people attributed their prosperity to their connection with Great Britain : " Do you not think that they are right ? Do you not think that these are the very kind of things that men will struggle to the very end to maintain rather than run the risk of what is at best a gamble on the future ? " And Carson proceeded, as his custom was, to reduce the position to its elemental simplicity :

" They say, ' We want to remain in this position.'

" They say, ' We have never yet been told what benefit we can get by being driven out of this position.'

" In the circumstances, is the statesman going to say, ' My business is to coerce you against your will . . . ? ' "

He went on to lay before Ministers the consequences of that policy. " I do not want to say one word by way of threat. . . . I am using no threat of any kind whatsoever. I shall assume for the purpose of my argument that you coerce Ulster. . . . I shall assume that the Navy and the Army are going to put Ulster down. What then ?

" Do you think that people with this burning passion in relation to the Government under which they are to live will be good citizens ?

" Do you really think that the Ulster Scot is the kind of man you can trample underfoot ? "

He agreed with the Chief Secretary, the good, amiable Mr. Birrell, that " Catholics and Protestants were not after all such bad friends as you might imagine " : he hoped they would be greater friends, as they would be were they let alone ; but there were " deep-rooted historical questions, traditions, ideas and race too, which you cannot get rid of but can aggravate by an Act of Parliament."

Then Carson faced the crux of the amendment

with a frankness which, if it did not improve its chances, leaves no doubt of his purpose. The Chief Secretary had said that without Ulster the Bill would be " truncated," and Carson agreed that it would make Home Rule " almost impossible." But what then ?—" The right honourable gentleman draws the conclusion that therefore you must force Home Rule upon Ulster. I draw the conclusion that you ought not to have Home Rule at all." Carson, indeed, supported the amendment with two objects in view—either, if it were accepted, to wreck the Bill, or, if it were rejected, to demonstrate that Ulster was not refusing a settlement for which, in the last resort, she was preparing to fight.

He worked, in fact, to save the South if he could but at least the North, always hoping that by saving the North he would save the South. And here he turned on the Prime Minister, " who gave us a very severe lecture on our daring to desert those who, according to us, were placed in peril in other parts of Ireland." " The people in Ireland," he retorted, " will not in the least misconstrue what we are doing on this occasion." Neither the Prime Minister nor any other Minister would succeed in driving a wedge between them. We feel in this passage of the speech the agony of the speaker's mind, the resentment against those political tacticians who were seeking to divide North from South, as hunters might divide the stags from the does of a herd devoted to destruction. " It will not," he said defiantly, " do us the least harm. They (the Southern Unionists) have perfect confidence that we—here he spoke for the North—are trying to do what is best for them, and very often on this kind of amendment, in very difficult circumstances, I admit."

It was the admission of a horrid dilemma :
" Is it desertion ? I do not agree. . . . Let me say
for myself, and in no egotistical way, that as a
Dublin man—the Solicitor-General was very
anxious to know my pedigree—I should be the very
last, with all my relatives living in the South and
West of Ireland, and in Dublin, and in various
places, who would for one moment consent to what
I believe would be in the slightest degree a desertion
of any other part of Ireland."

This understanding, this magnanimity, was expressed by one of the chief representatives of those
Southern Unionists in language which might have
brought a blush to the foreheads even of professional
politicians.

Mr. Walter Guinness, replying to Mr. Lloyd
George, who had taunted the Ulstermen with trying
to " save their own skins," described the true position of Ulster. They were opposed to the Bill ; they
were fighting for the Union ; they supported the
amendment only on the assumption that the
Government had the power, under the Parliament
Act, to pass the Bill into law. In such circumstances,
" for Ulster to refuse this salvation would not be to
help her friends, but would be merely taking up an
attitude of mock heroics. It is because we know the
earnestness of her opposition that we are anxious
to obtain this extrusion without civil strife and
rebellion."

Those who were left in the sinking ship bore no
grudge against those more fortunate who could find
a place in the boats. " It would," said Mr. Guinness,
" be merely a dog-in-the-manger policy for us who
live outside Ulster to grudge relief to our co-
religionists merely because we could not share it.

Such self-denial on their part would in no way help us, and it would only injure our compatriots in the North. We know perfectly well that Ulster fully shares our detestation of this Bill from a wider point of view than her own interests."

These magnanimous farewells could have no effect upon a Parliament whose existence depended upon the passage of the Bill. Mr. Redmond pronounced judgment. He would have no division of Ireland. " We put forward our claim for Home Rule," he said, " as a national demand. We claim that Ireland is a nation. . . . The idea of two nations in Ireland is revolting and hateful. The idea of our agreeing to the partition of our nation is unthinkable. . . ." He spoke with the humanity which no doubt he felt, for he also had the magnanimity of a ruling race. " Trust the people of Ireland," he said, " men will come together ; they will forget the past ; they will sit down at the same table, and endeavour to do all they can for the welfare and freedom of their common country."

Mr. Redmond chose to ignore " those deep-rooted historical questions " to which Sir Edward Carson had referred : nor could he foresee a future in which he was himself to feel, in the bitter moment of defeat, at the hands of those people, the full extent of his mistake. At the moment his word governed the situation. A British Parliament, engaged by his orders in dividing the British nation, accepted his view that part of it was one and indivisible. The second reading of the Bill had been carried by a majority of 101 ; the voting on this amendment to exclude the four counties suggests a certain falling away of Liberal support. It was nevertheless defeated by a majority of 61. The

Government had either repented or postponed
their own hesitations ; they had chosen to face the
resistance of Ulster ; but the Ulster Unionists, under
the wise guidance of their leader, had avoided the
snare which had been set for their feet. They could
go forward with their preparations to resist with
the better conscience because they had offered to
accept a settlement.

CHAPTER VIII

TROUBLE IN BELFAST

In the Albert Hall—Mr. Asquith in Dublin—The Blenheim pledge—Ancient Order of Hibernians—The shipbuilding yards—Joseph Devlin—The football match.

THE HARSH AND FLEERING WORDS of His Majesty's Ministers on matters which concerned the very lives of his most loyal subjects almost made Sir Edward Carson lose his temper. So at least we might gather from the language he used at that time. Thus on the morrow of one of those fierce discussions on the fate of Ulster—in the Albert Hall on the 14th June, 1912—he asked his colleagues, when they went back to Belfast, " to tell their friends there, in no uncertain voice, that the Government last night declared war against Ulster, and have announced that the only solution of this question is to drive them out of a community in which they are satisfied into a community which they loathe, hate and detest."

" We will accept," he went on, " the declaration of war. We are not altogether unprepared. I think it is time we should take a step forward in our campaign, and I will recommend that to be done." And at another meeting in London, on the 24th of the same month, he taunted the Government with their leniency to himself as the arch-rebel. They had been arresting Trades Union leaders for incitement to riot in the London Dock strike. Why did they leave him alone ? " One class of persons was sent to gaol for inciting to violence, and another class was forgiven when they had been guilty of exactly the same kind of incitement. . . . A craven Government . . . beneath contempt ! It had been said that he ought to be sent to gaol . . . he intended when he went over there to break every law that was possible. Let the Government take their own course ! He was not a bit afraid of them, for a more wretched, miserable, time-serving, opportunist lot never before sat in Parliament."

Yet there was policy behind this violence. Vague but compromising phrases of Sir Edward Grey and Mr. Churchill in the course of the debates had suggested to him—what we now know to be the truth —that the Government had almost made up their mind to make that exception for the North which he hoped would wreck the measure also in the South. But so far the pressure of John Redmond and the Radicals had overborne the compromising spirit of the Whigs. This was already plain in the discussion of the Agar-Robartes amendment, and it took dramatic form in the Theatre Royal, Dublin, on the 19th July, 1912, when, with their leaders around him, Mr. Asquith addressed his submission to an exultant meeting of Irish Nationalists. " I have come here to Dublin," he said, " to assure the people of Ireland—though, as Mr. Redmond has been good enough to say, I do not think any such assurance is necessary—of the resolute determination of the British Government, the British House of Commons and the British people to bring your great cause to a speedy and triumphant issue."

As for the case of Ulster, Mr. Asquith was not in the least embarrassed by the threat of a civil war in which he did not believe . . . " to say that a minority was entitled to . . . frustrate a great international settlement was a proposal which in my mind would never commend itself to the conscience or the judgment of the British people."

There was nothing, then, for Carson to do but to go on with his idea of freezing the Liberal blood. He must frighten them more ; if that failed he must raise the country against them. If he could not wreck the Bill, he must force a General Election : to such ends were those words of menace calculated.

Carson had gained an ally more zealous than discreet in the new Leader of the Conservative Party. It is difficult to imagine his predecessor identifying himself and the Opposition with the warlike preparations of Ulster. The more subtle mind of Mr. Balfour would have perceived that whereas the resistance of a small community, threatened in its rights and its religion, must embarrass the Government and win the sympathy of the country, the threat of an Opposition in arms was something, if not more difficult to justify at least more easy to misrepresent. The hope of placing a Constitutional Party in an unconstitutional position might even be irresistible to the Liberals, and Mr. Balfour would have been too wary to offer his opponents what was rather an incitement to proceed than a reason to desist.

The simpler and more ingenuous nature of Mr. Bonar Law foresaw none of these implications. The ancestral blood of Presbyterian Ulster kindled him to a fury altogether surprising in so mild-mannered a man. As at Balmoral, so at Blenheim. At the great Conservative demonstration of the 29th July, 1912, the courtyard of Vanbrugh's ornate palace rang

with words more warlike than it had heard since
the passing of the great Duke. After denouncing the
Government as " a revolutionary committee which
had seized by fraud upon despotic power," " I can
imagine," Mr. Bonar Law proceeded, " no length
of resistance to which Ulster will go which I shall
not be ready to support, and in which they will not
be supported by the overwhelming majority of the
British people."

Carson, speaking for the community whose rights
were to be attacked, used language better calculated
to frighten the Liberals and win the sympathy of
the country. " We will shortly," he said, " challenge
the Government to interfere with us if they dare,
and we will with equanimity await the result. We
will do this regardless of the consequences, of all
personal loss or of all inconvenience. They may tell
us if they like that that is treason. It is not for men
who have such stakes as we have at issue to trouble
about the cost. We are prepared to take the consequences." The cheers of the three thousand Englishmen who stood for the Conservative Party at that
great meeting showed how warmly these good
people felt for the loyal minority in Ireland ; the
result of a by-election at Crewe, which was
announced at the meeting, suggested that the
more general tide of opinion was flowing the same
way.

If there was one thing more than another which
roused the fury of the Irish Nationalists, it was the
presence of the Duke of Norfolk at this Blenheim
Demonstration. They felt it to be—as indeed it was
—significant and even symbolical. Thus we find
Joseph Devlin, in the House of Commons, shortly
thereafter, reserving his most scathing sarcasms for
Ic

" the great Catholic Duke . . . coming all the way to Blenheim . . . to give his benediction " to Carson and his policy of violence. The legend grew until even so careful an annalist as Mr. Denis Gwynn is raised high above the facts on the wings of a Celtic imagination :

" Not the least surprising feature of the occasion was the prominence of the Duke of Norfolk, who solemnly presented Sir Edward Carson with a golden sword, in appreciation of his strenuous resistance to the threatened tyrannies of ' Rome Rule ' in Ulster."[1]

The Duke of Norfolk presented no golden sword to Sir Edward Carson ; but his presence at Blenheim does suggest that many English Catholics understood and sympathised with Sir Edward Carson. Nor would it be surprising if they recognised in the Act of Union the best hope of religious and social peace in Ireland ; discerned the dark forces of anarchy which covertly inspired and directed the Irish Nationalist movement, and were loyal besides to the British Crown, which had given to those of their Faith equal rights and complete liberty, not in Ireland only but in every part of the King's Dominions.

Those English Catholics, moreover, understood Ireland better than the English Liberals, and that religious feud which they most feared soon began to show an ugly head. On the one side a fierce exultation, on the other a fiery resentment, were stirring Ulster out of an always unstable peace. The Nationalists had indeed been exhorted by their

[1] *The Life of John Redmond*, p. 211.

leaders to keep quiet, as things were " going their way." " In what remains of the struggle," Jerry MacVeagh commanded them, " let them neither give nor take offence ; but sit tight, keep quiet and rejoice that everything was going well with them." If they could not altogether follow such excellent advice, they yet confined themselves in the main to the subtle incitements in which they were expert—

> *Do you bite your thumb at us, sir ?*
> *I do bite my thumb, sir.*
> *Do you bite your thumb at us, sir ?*
> *No, sir, I do not bite my thumb at you, sir,*
>   *but I bite my thumb, sir.*

—to scrawling on the walls, " Home Rule is Coming," and sarcastically advising their Orange neighbours to make the most of the last chance but one to celebrate their " Twelfth " of July.

But their exultation could not altogether be restrained. On the 29th June, 1912, while the House of Commons was debating the political division of Ulster, a sudden spark luridly lit up the real division. It happened that a procession of Protestant Sunday-school children, returning from a " treat," were marching through the village of Castle-Dawson late in the evening with their banners, when a party of the Ancient Order of Hibernians emerged from their meeting-house and fell upon the children, tearing their flags from their hands, throwing some of them down and putting the rest into a sad state of panic. The ugly riot which followed was quelled by the police and some twenty or thirty of the Hibernians were brought to trial in the magistrate's court ; but the outrages continued ; Protestant children were attacked at Innisrush and Protestant women at Whitehouse. Ulster seemed to be taking fire in 1912 as in 1886.

Sir Edward Carson, who well understood what ancient feuds were stirring again in the hearts of the people, worked anxiously to prevent provocations. On the eve of the great Orange celebrations of the Twelfth of July, in a letter to the press of Northern Ireland, he "deprecated those spasmodic and sporadic rows . . . which could lead to no result of any kind except disaster to the various parties concerned." His friends in Ulster urgently reinforced these warnings, and the critical anniversary of the Battle of the Boyne passed off without any general breach of the peace.

There was, however, one inflammable zone upon which the flames for a moment took hold—the ship-building yards. In that flourishing industry more than twenty thousand men, most of them Protestant but a considerable number Catholic, worked side by side, and turned out after their work into one road, solitary except when it was crammed with a seething mass of humanity. There, and in nooks and corners of the yards, were both the stuff and the opportunity of trouble. How it actually began will always be disputed. Charles and James Craig, who knew Belfast well, put it down to such incitements as we have seen at Castle-Dawson. Mr. Birrell took that view of the case to be " a complete delusion." What is certain is that Catholic workmen were assaulted both in the yards and in the crowded approaches. Some were kicked and beaten ; others assailed by showers of iron nuts and rivets— " Belfast confetti " ; during the month of July 1912, there were twenty-five assaults inside and fifty-five outside the yards, "five of the most dangerous character, threatening the lives of the sufferers."

The Catholics employed by Workman & Clark were driven out of their employment, as they complained, by the threats of their Protestant fellow-workmen, and refused to return until their safety was assured. At Harland & Wolff's, several of the men were chased by a gang of youths, one into the dock, where he escaped by swimming across to the other side, and another into a workshop, where the foreman to whom he appealed for help was knocked down and kicked in trying to protect him. Things at one time looked so serious that Messrs. Harland & Wolff, " in view of the brutal assaults on individual workmen and the intimidation of others," decided to close their yards, and the loss of employment and the influence of the older men brought the hotheads to reason.

Sir Edward Carson had foreseen such troubles in the yards and had long been at work to prevent them. He had indeed spent a whole night at Craigavon talking things out with some of the foremen and Trades Union leaders, the upshot being a Unionist Workingmen's Association, which is still strong in Belfast—" the only true democracy in Ireland," as Carson proudly called it. It was those leaders among the Shipwrights and Riveters of the yards, good friends and faithful followers of Carson, who sweated through that sultry July to bring the hotheads to reason—and in the end they succeeded.

In the meantime Joseph Devlin might be trusted to make the best and the worst of those " shocking and unparalleled atrocities." Opening a debate on the subject, on the 31st July, 1912, he asked Carson: " Why, if the law was to be broken did the right

hon. gentleman not go over and throw the rivets ? "
To which Carson replied that he was glad to see the
Member for West Belfast " on the side of what we
would call law and order, considering the number of
years he has been engaged in championing the
party of intimidation, boycotting, and, to use his
own phrase, barbarism in other parts of Ireland."
As for the attacks upon himself—" I care nothing
about them. They will not influence me one hair's
breadth in anything I either say or do."

While " deprecating these occurrences," Carson
asked the House to consider their true causes.
There had been no " serious collision " in Northern
Ireland since 1886 ; but the policy of Home Rule
had " aroused feelings of deep passion," had moreover brought back historic memories, " which
unfortunately are never forgotten in those places,
and which render men very liable on provocation to
deal in a manner very much to be regretted with
those who are opposed to them." He ended with
the expression of a hope that there would be an end
of these riots, which, " even to put it on the very
lowest grounds, do not and cannot further anything
in the nature of a political cause."

The fires though damped down were not stamped
out, and Falls Road meditated a revenge for their
defeat on Queen's Island. Carson arrived in Belfast
on Saturday, the 14th September, 1912, and drove
out to Cushendun to stay with his friend Ronald
McNeill for the week-end. That very afternoon,
although he saw nothing of it, the trouble came.

It began in the Celtic Football Ground where
Mr. Churchill had held his meeting the previous
February. The Celtics, who were Catholic, were
playing on their own field against another Belfast

Club, called Linfield, of a Protestant complexion. The supporters of either side were thus of either faction, and there were altogether ten thousand people watching the game. A dispute began at half-time in the unreserved space, " and in a moment there was a seething mass of struggling men." As the fight developed it was seen that there were two mobs, some hundreds strong, one side carrying a Union Jack and the other the Celtic colours, and that they were fighting desperately with fists, feet, sticks, knives and revolvers. The police who interfered were contemptuously thrown aside, furious rushes of men, under whose feet many were knocked down and trampled, carried the swaying fortunes of the fight from one side to the other of the stricken field. Within a few minutes the casualties on both sides were staggering to the rear with bleeding heads and faces. The police, reinforced and supported by the more orderly part of the crowd, charged with batons, and at last the factions drew away from each other and left the field by opposite gates ; but the fight went on as the Protestants were gradually driven out of the Roman Catholic Quarter into their own Shankhill Road.

Such angry exchanges of words and blows must have convinced Carson of what he had long foreseen, the necessity of a diversion. If there were not to be an explosion, cruel, bloody, premature, disastrous both to peace and to the cause, he must have what Tim Healy called " a safety-valve for the Orangemen." He had referred, on the 14th June, 1912, to " a step forward in the campaign." By the end of the session that step had been thought out : by September the time had come to take it. If we consider the Ulster Covenant, as the historian

should consider such things, within its circumstances, we see how well calculated it was to raise
the minds of these people above the anarchy of
civil riot. As for the Ulster Volunteer Force, its
rules and its discipline were calculated to keep the
peace.

CHAPTER IX

SIGNING THE COVENANT

SOME TIME during the session of 1912, James Craig, as we are told by Ronald McNeill, was sitting in the Constitutional Club, with pencil and paper, working out that "step forward" to which Sir Edward Carson had referred. It was to take the form of a pledge to be signed by the people of Ulster, and as words never came easily to James Craig he was grateful for the suggestion of a friend that the Solemn League and Covenant might serve him as a model. They looked it up in the excellent library of the Club, and found by a strange coincidence that the original form of words had been drawn up by another Craig—that John Craig who so unwillingly proclaimed the banns of marriage between Queen Mary and Bothwell. The taking of oaths to stand by one another was, indeed, common form in the distractions of the sixteenth and seventeenth centuries ; but the Solemn League and Covenant was something loftier—a dedication of life and sword to a faith, and touched, moreover, those "historic memories" of which Carson had spoken. For in the Civil Wars the Solemn League and Covenant had been carried over to Ulster by four Ayrshire Covenanters, and accepted, not without misgivings, by General Monro and the Ulster

Army and by the Lagan Force. It was a sad, heavy, sanctified confession of faith, steeped in those institutes of Calvin which John Craig, or so it is said, had studied in the Library of the Inquisition ; but although the words had long faded out of the historical memory, the name of the Covenant still lived to remind these Ulstermen of stern and steadfast ancestors who had fought for life and faith three centuries before.

Thus it came naturally to the minds of those rather grim and serious men who looked to Craigavon as their Council Chamber. James Craig had a main hand in it, Thomas Sinclair drafted it, Alexander McDowell amended it in one important particular, and it was recommended to the people of Ulster by Sir Edward Carson in a series of meetings among the most remarkable in the annals of politics.

If it had been the fate of James Craig to be a soldier, he would have been a great Chief-of-the-Staff, an organiser of victory. He knew the country and the people ; he was master besides of detail ; his house was his headquarters, radiating at once his directions and his hospitality. He had designed the series of meetings as one vast demonstration, beginning in the West and sweeping up to its climax in the signing of the Covenant. In this demonstration Carson was the principal speaker. There was no thought of sparing him, nor had he any thought of sparing himself, but eleven great meetings within ten days were too much even for his resilient powers. There were others—Lord Charles Beresford, Lord Salisbury, Lord Willoughby de Broke, Lord Hugh Cecil, Mr. F. E. Smith, the last named brilliant, impetuous, a Rupert of the platform, yet, somehow not altogether favoured in Ulster, which may have been puzzled by his oratorical fireworks, or may have felt instinctively that he had no bottom of seriousness.

Sir Edward Carson arrived in Belfast on the 14th September, 1912 ; on the 18th he was at Enniskillen, frontier town of half-Catholic Fermanagh, western gate of the province, looking out over many-islanded Lough Erne upon an alien South and West.

A fortnight before the meeting, word had gone round that they should have a mounted escort for Carson, and in that short time, in that " great land for men and horses," they had raised almost a regiment of " comely young men," as a correspondent described them, among the gentry and yeomen of Fermanagh—238 strong, furnishing their own mounts and equipment—falling into line spontaneously, as frontiersmen in a wild country might come together for their defence. " There is a comradeship here," said the correspondent of *The Times*, " such as prevails in no other portion, I do not say of Ireland, but of the British Isles. It is comradeship of a race which has forgotten nothing of its history. . . ."

Two full troops of Yeomanry met Carson and his friends at the railway station and escorted them amid cheering crowds to the Town Hall, where fervent addresses were presented. But the great meeting was on Portora Hill where a platform had been built to hold a thousand people and a road cut for the occasion. Lord Erne welcomed the visitors in a speech which rang with the brave words of Gustavus Hamilton, oft repeated in this book and never forgotten in Ulster : " We stand upon our guard and do resolve, by the blessing of God, rather to meet our danger than to expect it."

Carson as he looked down upon that brave assembly, recalled the bitter words written a few days before by William Watson :

Spurned her, repulsed her—
Great-hearted Ulster,
Flung her aside.

They were not likely to forget their history in Fermanagh ; but Carson recalled to them the great day of Newtown Butler, when the Enniskillens and Derry together defeated James II and thereby " secured our civil and religious liberty." And he asked them over again the question asked of their ancestors by Colonel Wolseley : " You are in great difficulties. I put to you the question because it is your responsibility—'Will you advance or retreat ? ' " As in that case, so in this, the answer was, " Advance ! "

The Enniskillen meeting was on Wednesday, the 18th September ; on the 19th, Carson was back at Craigavon, arranging with the Standing Committee for the issue of the Covenant. We get a glimpse of him strolling out of the house, at four in the afternoon, bareheaded, smoking a cigarette, to give the crowd of journalists who waited outside the terms of the document. That same evening he was at Lisburn, a town of the linen-manufacture, some eight miles south of Belfast—escorted through the streets with fifes and drums playing the " Boyne Water " and " Protestant Boys " by an immense procession of men bearing dummy rifles and lighted torches, to a market-place packed with ten thousand people—the working-girls sitting under him, the men beyond them, line upon line in the light of the torches, until lost in the shadow beyond. "I pledge myself before you," he said, "that I will go to the end as long as God gives me strength." "The working men at Lisburn," the *Times* correspondent noted, "were more responsive than the agriculturists had been at Enniskillen. They seemed to be animated by a more desperate resolve, and as they carried the resolution with a roar of cheers, the multitude looked as dark and forbidding as the sea with a storm brooding over it."

In 1892 at a farmers' meeting in Enniskillen the Duke of Abercorn used words which had become proverbial in Ulster—"Men of the North, once more I say we will not have Home Rule." "We will not have Home Rule," was the resolution passed at all these meetings. "We will not have it" had become a watchword, a defiance, a battle-cry.

Next day as Sir Edward Carson set out for Londonderry from Belfast railway station, the porter who carried his bag whispered hoarsely to him as he thrust it under the seat, "You will have to change at Clones, Sir Edward, and will you tell the station-master, 'We won't have it.'"

This fierce conflict of the popular will—"We won't have it" against "Home Rule is coming"—threatened to disturb the peace of the maiden city, always a matter of delicate balances. A body-guard of a hundred well-disciplined men of the Unionist Clubs met their leader outside Londonderry railway station; his carriage was dragged across Foyle Bridge by a crowd of partisans, an enthusiastic Orangeman shouting on the box. As at Enniskillen so in Londonderry, the Muse of History seemed to brood with knitted brows over the vast meeting in the Guildhall. In that city of the Hamiltons it was natural that the Duke of Abercorn should preside, and natural also that he should refer to another meeting, as if it had been an event of yesterday, when the supporters of King William met to consider whether they should admit the emissaries of King James II and came to the decision : " Fight and resist and we shall win."

Natural also that Carson should say to such an assembly that they were " re-writing history . . . the old history of two hundred years or more ago . . . confronted with the old dangers and the old enemy they were going to have the old victory."

" They were going to make mutual pledges one with the other, and any man who, having made that pledge, went back on it or failed at the critical moment was a betrayer of his brother. . . . They were entering into that sacred obligation with the same spirit, the same determination, the same calmness and the same reasoning as influenced their forefathers when they resisted James II and all he attempted to do in relation to civil and religious freedom."

The past and the present were one in the city of Derry : the old enemy waited without. Carson was escorted from the Guildhall to his quarters at the Northern Counties Club by four hundred torch-bearers, and as the procession passed the Diamond, a mob of the opposite faction bore down upon them with sticks and stones. A shot was fired, an Irishman was borne to the infirmary imaginatively protesting that he was wounded ; the rumour that he had been killed roused the Nationalist quarter to fury ; four of the bandsmen of the No Surrender Band were laid out as they were returning from the Club ; the police charged, to be tripped up by a rope stretched across the street, two of the constables were wounded, and the fight continued merrily until two in the morning.

Lisburn looks to the south, Enniskillen faces the west, Londonderry is contested by the enemy within its gates ; but Coleraine lies at the centre of the " Black North," a town more Scotch than Irish, flourishing, industrious, Presbyterian. Carson was there the day after the Londonderry meeting, and the townsmen and their friends from the country round about mustered in the Diamond and marched out to meet him, in characteristic order and solidity, a great procession, five thousand strong, with Orange banners flying and drums beating, by the bridge across the Bann into the Manor House grounds. There Carson made the fourth speech of this series—like the others, strong, simple, vigorous, picturesque. " His command over the feelings of his Ulster audiences," says one who looked on, " is unquestionable, and never a phrase passes his lips which does not tell."

" What," he asked them, " was the Covenant they were going to sign? It was a contract between them as Ulstermen, and Ulstermen were not in the habit of breaking their contracts." He counselled them against precipitate action. " Organised men ought to do nothing in a panic : they ought to be calm and deliberate . . . there was such perfect mutual confidence between them that he knew that where he led there they would certainly follow.

" I will ask you a simple question," he went on, " Are you behind us ? "

They shouted that they were.

" Are you determined to go forward ? " he asked them.

They shouted, " Yes."

" Well, then," he concluded, " you give us the mandate and we accept it, and under Heaven I believe we must win."

With such assurances from the four quarters of the Province Carson returned to Belfast. On Monday, September 23rd, the Ulster Unionist Council met in the Old Town Hall formally to ratify the Covenant. It was characteristic of Lord Londonderry that, although he had been Lord-Lieutenant of Ireland, with so much to risk and to lose, he moved the resolution to enter into that solemn pledge to refuse, if need be, to recognise the authority of Parliament.

This resolution, too long to be recorded here, was a reasoned statement of the case for resistance. " By no law," it maintained, " can the right to govern those whom we represent be bartered away without their consent." Although the Government might drive them forth, " they may not deliver us bound into the hands of our enemies."

There were things which were incompetent in any authority, one of them being to appoint over them " men disloyal to the Empire, and to whom our faith and traditions are hateful."

And so they bound themselves : " Knowing the greatness of the issues depending on our faithfulness, we promise each to the others that, to the uttermost of the strength and means given us, and not regarding any selfish or private interest, our substance or our lives, we will make good the said Covenant."

SIGNING THE COVENANT

From left to right: R. J. McMordie, M.P., the Lord Mayor of Belfast, Lord C. Beresford, the late Marquis of Londonderry, Sir Edward Carson, Sir James Craig, Lord Glenavy (then James Campbell, K.C.), and Dr. William Gibson, J.P., who was largely responsible for the Belfast arrangements

This business over, Lord Londonderry entertained the delegates and their guests to a great luncheon in the Exhibition Hall in the Botanic Gardens, the only place big enough in all Belfast for such a company. There their host reminded them that he was of the same blood as Castlereagh, the man who had carried the Union, that the preservation of the Union was therefore an instinct inherent in him, and, moreover, Ulster, which had been the poorest province in Ireland before the Union, had become the richest, had everything to lose in losing it and much to keep in maintaining it. Then Carson, who was toasted as their Leader, brought their minds back to the Covenant—" the gravest matter," he described it, " that in all the grave offices I have filled I have had to consider ; but the more I consider it the more I believe it is right. I at all events am prepared to go to the end." Upon these words we are told, the whole company rose to its feet, and with one voice shouted : " We will back you." Leaders and followers were one.

The eleventh, the last and the greatest of these meetings was held in the Ulster Hall, Belfast, on the night of Friday the 27th. Those who had taken part in the campaign were on the platform ; but the demonstration was for Carson. " It was," one who was present reports, " an extraordinary welcome, and Sir Edward Carson remained standing until the great shout died away, seemingly much moved by the expression of loyalty and devotion."

Here again, as always in Ulster, history and cere- monial gave point and dignity to the occasion. Lord Charles Beresford had persuaded a friend at Hamp- ton Court to lend for the occasion a faded yellow banner which had been borne by a member of her

Kα

family before King William at the victory of the Boyne ; Colonel Wallace, Grand Master of the Orangemen of Belfast, put this piece of frail time-worn silk into the hands of their leader, and Sir Edward held it out before him for a dramatic moment—" a token " as he described it, of victory for civil and religious freedom. Then James Craig presented his friend and leader with a casket containing a key, another symbol to suggest that Ulster was the key to the political situation, and a golden pen with which to sign the Covenant.

Carson spoke, " for the most part in grave and measured tones," as he told the citizens of Belfast what was involved in their act of signature on the morrow. But there were inspired moments in which the orator seemed to transcend himself, his hand raised, as with a lifted sword, his tall figure seeming taller, his strong stern face kindling with an ardour that found instant reflection in the mirror of his audience, at the same instant and with the same emotion, as it were transfigured. He spoke with passion of the charge that they were " bluffers." " I am too old," he protested, " to be a bluffer." And then giving a turn to words of Parnell which were familiar to his hearers, " I would not have taken off my coat," he said, " if I had not been convinced that I could lead a people who will never even allow the first link that binds them to England to be severed." He reminded them of pre-union times when the Kingdom was liable to be run not in the interests of the United Kingdom but of one of the countries constituting it and of the progress made by the city of Belfast within the Union : in 1911 she had contributed through Customs and

Inland Revenue £4,915,000 to the Imperial Exchequer. " Was it any wonder that Mr. Redmond said he would not like Home Rule if they kept Ulster out of it ? " He reminded them of a suppressed paragraph in a resolution of the Ancient Order of Hibernians at their Convention in America in which it was stated that nothing else than absolute independence would be taken as a final settlement by the Irish race at home and abroad, and he described the struggle as the challenge of Constitution-wreckers to the upholders of the Constitution, the challenge of ascendancy to equality, " of the preachers of separation to the congregation of unity," of retrogression to progress. And then, after quoting the words of a great American—" Blandishments will not fascinate us, nor will threats intimidate us, for under God are we determined that wheresoever, whensoever and howsoever we shall be called upon to make our exit we shall die as free men "—he ended : " My last words before you sign the Covenant are, Be ready."

We should be misleading the reader if we left him with the impression that these speeches were mere incitements to a stubborn and passionate community. Carson indeed was an Irishman, and, therefore, a fighting man by his very nature. The English principle of government by consent has never yet, it may be admitted, taken more than a weak hold upon Irish soil. It was characteristic and natural in Carson, when he was presented (at Portadown) with a blackthorn stick, to brandish the shillelagh above his head and promise the givers that although he hoped he might never have to use it, " if I do I shall use it to the best of my ability." Yet we are able to trace a statesmanlike, even a

pacific, intention in these speeches. " The strong
man armed keepeth his house in peace." At Coleraine he let the people into the secret hope which
inspired these warlike preparations : " They will
never," he said, " coerce a people for being loyal."
And in Belfast, where there was most reason to
apprehend civil strife, he made the strongest appeal
for peace :

" He pledged himself from the bottom of his heart
that when they gave him their confidence by the
help of God they would never be betrayed. On the
other hand the leaders had a right to demand from
their followers that no kind of action should be
taken by them . . . without having the sanction of
their leaders. He knew they had often to submit to
taunts and jeers, but let those who used them stew
in the juice of their own falsehoods. . . . The stronger
they were the more moderate they could afford
to be."

These exhortations over, there remained the signing of the Covenant. Saturday, the 28th September,
1912, was the day appointed for that event ; to be
celebrated, after the manner of Ulster, with prayer
and praise and sermon. James Craig, co-operating
with the Protestant churches, the Orange Order,
the Unionist Clubs, had organised a universal and
simultaneous demonstration. Our concern, however, is only with Belfast, and with Carson's share
in the ceremony. After service in the Ulster Hall
Sir Edward Carson went on foot to Donegall
Square. " Two companies," we are told, " one
representing the Orange Order, the other the
Unionist Clubs, had formed fours, and Sir Edward,
bareheaded, took his place before the banner (that
same flag of the Boyne which had been presented to

him the night before). Behind the second company marched Lord Londonderry, Lord Charles Beresford, Mr. F. E. Smith and the other lieutenants." So they proceeded very slowly through thick crowds in Bedford Street and the Square till at last they reached the Hall. There a table had been placed just below the grand staircase, and there Carson signed the Covenant.

Here it may be thought appropriate to give the words of that famous pledge which that same day was signed by a great multitude not in Belfast alone but in every part of Ulster.

" Being convinced in our consciences that Home Rule would be disastrous to the material well-being of Ulster as well as the whole of Ireland, subversive of our civil and religious freedom, destructive of our citizenship, and perilous to the unity of the Empire, all, whose names are underwritten, men of Ulster, loyal subjects of His Gracious Majesty King George V, humbly relying on the God whom our fathers in days of stress and trial confidently trusted, do hereby pledge ourselves in Solemn Covenant throughout this our time of threatened calamity to stand by one another in defending for ourselves and our children our cherished position of equal citizenship in the United Kingdom, and in using all means which may be found necessary to defeat the present conspiracy to set up a Home Rule Parliament in Ireland. And in the event of such a Parliament being forced upon us we further solemnly and mutually pledge ourselves to refuse to recognise its authority. In sure confidence that God will defend the right we hereto subscribe our names.

And further, we individually declare that we have not already signed this Covenant. God save the King."

When Carson stepped aside from the table Lord Londonderry took up the pen, then the Moderator of the General Assembly, the Bishop of Down, the Dean of Belfast, James Craig, whose mind had conceived and organised that great demonstration, and his fellow members of the Unionist Parliamentary Party in Ulster. Desks had been arranged running in corridors from the centre of this table, and the public came to sign in batches of four or five hundred at a time, following one another in continuous procession. All was done quietly and in order, as became so solemn an occasion. The Duke of Abercorn, then in failing health, signed the Covenant under an oak-tree outside the little church at Baronscourt, Newtownstewart ; at Portadown two thousand people signed the Covenant in half an hour ; at Armagh Sir John Lonsdale and the Dean of Armagh led the signatories ; at Enniskillen the first to sign was Lord Erne and the second the Bishop of Clogher ; the Bishop of Derry and Lord Hamilton were among the first to sign at Londonderry, and Lord Templetown, founder of the Unionist Clubs of Ireland, signed the Covenant at Castle-Upton on the old drum of the Temple-Patrick Infantry. At Ballymena the first signatories were that Grand Old Man of Ulster, John Young, and his son William Robert Young, Hon. Secretary of the Ulster Unionist Council. It was signed in Dublin by two thousand men who gave proof of their birth in Ulster ; it was signed by Ulstermen in London, in Liverpool, in Glasgow and elsewhere throughout

Great Britain. In Edinburgh it was signed by a thousand Ulstermen on the flat gravestone in Greyfriars' Churchyard, where, according to tradition, the Solemn League and Covenant had been signed in 1638. Thus the Ulstermen everywhere bound themselves to stand by one another in their resistance to Home Rule.[1]

Carson made his way with difficulty to the Reform Club through all Belfast converging with one intent upon the Ulster Hall, every Orange Lodge and every Unionist Club in martial order with its own insignia under its own banners. At the Reform Club he was entertained to luncheon ; he dined at the Ulster Club at half past seven ; he left by the Steamship *Patriotic* for Liverpool at 9.15 p.m., and all Belfast seemed to be gathered round the water-edge to bid him farewell. A searchlight played upon him as he leant over the rail of the upper deck. He wished them " good-bye," told them to " keep the flag flying," said that he longed for the time when he could come back—" whether the occasion be for peace—I prefer it—or to fight, and if it be to fight I shall not shrink." And then he added in a parting shot characteristically Irish and Carsonian : " One thing I feel perfectly confident of is that to-day we have taken a step which has put our enemies into such a state of difficulty that they are wondering what on earth they are going to do."

[1] Altogether 218,206 men signed the Covenant in Ulster, and 19,162 Ulstermen signed it elsewhere ; 228,991 women signed the Declaration in Ulster and 5,055 Ulsterwomen signed it elsewhere. The grand total of signatures of men and woman was 471,414.—See *Lord Carson of Duncairn* (by Sir Thomas Moles), pp. 29–30. Also Ronald McNeill, *Ulster's Stand for Union*, pp. 123–4.

CHAPTER X

IN COMMITTEE

Liverpool—Glasgow—Cracking sinews—Challenge to prosecute—The guillotine—Safeguards—Another prophecy—Federalism—The case for exclusion—Bereavement.

SIR EDWARD CARSON left Belfast in a glory of farewells. From the Ulster Club to Donegall Quay he had made his way through " solid masses of people tens of thousands in number," cheering him as he went. His good friends the working men of Queen's Island, organised as a Unionist Club, had formed a guard of honour round the shed of the Belfast Steamship Company, and as Carson crossed the gangway the white flashes and sharp reports of their revolver shots were his parting salute.

He went to his cabin with the last salutations bursting over the ship in rockets of coloured sparks, reflected in the waters of the lough from bonfires on the immediate hills of County Down or shining like stars from the more distant hills of Antrim, and he slept so soundly through a tempestuous night that when he awoke he thought himself still in Ulster, for there, on the Mersey, lined along the main and upper landing-stage and on Prince's Quay was the same crowd, singing the same familiar strains—" O God our help in ages past."

Liverpool, sister of Belfast, rough, big-hearted, Protestant, Unionist, gave Carson a great welcome.

Alderman Salvidge was on the landing-stage : " I shake hands with you across the sea," said Carson as he met that stout veteran. " I bring a message from the democracy of Belfast to the democracy of Liverpool. All that they ask is to be allowed to stay with you, and I do not think you will permit them to be driven out." Mr. F. E. Smith, then on his own ground, promised that the two cities would stand together—no matter what the hazard might be.

This was on Sunday morning, the 29th September, 1912 ; on the Monday following there was a greater demonstration. The working classes of Liverpool and the surrounding districts joined in a procession of Unionists and Orangemen, something bigger than even Belfast could show—100,000 men with banners and torches—marched to Shiel Park to cheer Carson again, and to pledge themselves " to unite with Ulster in resisting Home Rule." Then to the Conservative Club where Carson stood for two hours on a platform in front of the building, in a blaze of electric light, while they went past, four deep. " If and when it comes to a fight between Ulster and the Irish Nationalists," said F. E. Smith, " we will undertake to give you three ships that will take over . . . 10,000 young men of Liverpool."

On the 1st October Carson was in Glasgow. Sir T. Comyn Platt, a friend of Carson's, describes that great meeting of six thousand people in the Saint Andrews Hall and the extraordinary power of Carson's oratory : " His voice, always sympathetic, was richer and deeper—owing no doubt to the fatigue of the recent campaign." He raised those sober Glasgow people to their feet in uncontrollable enthusiasm at one passage, at another " hundreds were moved to tears."[1]

On the night of 4th October the Sussex village of Rottingdean was illuminated to welcome Carson home. By that time, it is plain, the Liberals were urging one another on to grasp this nettle of Ulster. Mr. J. A. Pease and Mr. Gulland had said that Carson ought to be prosecuted for " heinous crimes and misdemeanours." " They know where I am," Carson replied. "I am always ready! The only reason they give why I am not prosecuted is that if I am there might be riots—the most extraordinary reason for not carrying out the law that ever I heard."

From Rottingdean, the day after, Carson wrote a letter to Dawson Bates,[2] thanking him as Secretary of the Ulster Unionist Council, " and all our friends who helped to make the demonstrations preceding Ulster Day and Ulster Day itself such a huge and magnificent success." They had taken "a step forward in defence of their rights " ; he praised them for their good order, their self-control, and decorum, and warned them against " isolated or unauthorised action." " We are now bound in solemn covenant each to the other : let us each prove a worthy covenanter."

In all these meetings and demonstrations Carson had an eye on the political effect : " That the Government," he wrote, " professes to take no heed of our action let no man trouble himself about." In that tremendous tug-o'-war he was waging against John Redmond, his ear could detect the cracking

[1] T. Comyn Platt, " The Ulster Leader," in the *National Review* for October, 1913.

[2] Afterwards Sir Richard Dawson Bates, Minister for Home Affairs in the Government of Northern Ireland, and always the most staunch, able and devoted of Ulstermen.

of sinews. Mr. Redmond with closer opportunities had more ample evidence. The Irish Nationalist Leader had been invited to speak on Home Rule in Mr. Churchill's constituency ; but on the 31st August was informed that to spare him unnecessary fatigue, Mr. Churchill would be glad to arrange for a meeting in Sheffield instead of Dundee. " I have been pondering," the First Lord wrote to Mr. Redmond, in the course of a tactful but too transparent letter, " a great deal over this matter, and my general view is just what I told you earlier in the year—namely that something should be done to afford the characteristically Protestant and Orange counties the option of a moratorium of several years before acceding to the Irish Parliament. I think the time approaches when such an offer should be made. . . . Much is to be apprehended from the rancour of a party in the ascendant and the fanaticism of these stubborn and determined Orangemen."[1]

Mr. Redmond, although he was told that these opinions were " personal," had good reason to suspect that the doubts of the First Lord reflected the hesitations of the Government.

Other members of the Cabinet, however, hastened to disguise these signs of wavering. Sir Rufus Isaacs, then Attorney-General, asserted that the Government would not be moved a " hair's breadth from its course," and Mr. Asquith himself, referring to " what is popularly called, and which, for the purpose of the argument, I will call, the Ulster problem," while admitting that it was " serious and indeed formidable," refused to " dwell for more than one moment on the organised demonstrations," which had " revealed nothing not

[1] Denis Gwynn, *The Life of John Redmond*, p. 214.

perfectly well known before." " I need not tell the people of this country that the Government and Parliament of the United Kingdom are not going to bow to such a threat."

As for " the reckless rodomontade at Blenheim " which with " this Ulster campaign furnishes a complete grammar of anarchy . . . a more deadly blow—I say it with the utmost deliberation and with the fullest conviction—a more deadly blow has never been dealt in our time by any body of responsible politicians at the very foundations on which democratic government rests."

Mr. Asquith, as we know, had long before arranged for a line of retreat if this threat, to which he was not going to bow, should materialise. The passage, however, suggests new difficulties. His Radical following saw in the " capital blunder " of Mr. Bonar Law their opportunity to put the Conservative Party in an unconstitutional position. They were already raising the cry of Democracy in Danger, already denouncing any idea of compromise on such an issue. If it was becoming more danger-ous for Mr. Asquith to go forward, it was becoming more difficult to go back. " You know perfectly well," said Carson when the session opened, " that your party cannot hang together unless you give a bone to each dog."

On 10th October, 1912, the Prime Minister moved to apply a time-table to the remaining stages of the Home Rule Bill. As Mr. Churchill put it, " those who talk of revolution ought to be pre-pared for the guillotine." In the debate which followed the chief concern of the Liberals was to exploit the " capital blunder " of Mr. Bonar Law. Thus—

Mr. Lloyd George : The right honourable gentleman said he would give his moral support—I think he said his " moral support," and not his physical support.

Mr. Bonar Law : I did not make any distinction.

Mr. Lloyd George : No distinction. Very well, I will put this to him. He said he is prepared to give his support to the Protestants of Ireland, whatever action they take. That is a very remarkable doctrine to come from the Leader of a party which claims to be the Constitutional Party, the party of law and order.

Mr. Bonar Law : May I put that quite plainly ? I said that if this Government attempted, without first appealing to the country, to impose this rule upon Ulster by force I would support them at any length in resistance to such an attempt.

Mr. Lloyd George : Supposing there were an election and supposing that at that election the country approved of Home Rule, does the right honourable gentleman then say it would be the duty of Ulster to obey ?

Mr. Bonar Law : If the right honourable gentleman makes that offer quite specific and definite I will at once answer it.

Mr. Lloyd George did not make the " firm offer " and Mr. Bonar Law did not at that time reply. " I will tell the House why he will not answer," said Mr. Lloyd George. " He dare not. There sits his master." And he pointed to Sir Edward Carson.

" And there sits your master," a Conservative retorted, pointing at John Redmond.

Here Carson intervened, formidable, sardonic, glowering darkly at the Treasury Bench. " I have been," he said, " in such close contact with the more serious side that I have not the least ambition to follow the right honourable gentleman into the foolery we have listened to."

His glance was like Chatham's : those on whom it was directed grew uneasy : " I do not envy the man who goes to laugh Belfast out of it," he said.

Then he turned to the threats against himself. " I was waiting," he said, " to hear some of them say something—they do it in the papers—about my lawlessness, and the necessity of prosecuting me "—here his eye seemed to search for the Law Officers of the Crown ; then, with infinite scorn, " and all the other ridiculous rot."

He paused, and resumed : " Even if you wanted to do it, you would not have the courage to do it."

Not one of the lawyers ranged on the Treasury Bench took up the challenge, and Carson proceeded.

" I noticed the other evening that one of the Whips "—here he seemed to search in vain for Mr. Gulland—" who is not here at the present time, said that I would have been prosecuted ; but "—he paused again to give full effect to the thrust—" but that they were afraid there would be riots."

He waited awhile as if expecting some observation, some denial, and then added in slow solemn and measured tones : " I can only say this—I hate referring to a personal matter, and I only say it to leave it once and for ever—let no man suppose that I am claiming immunity from anything to which the humblest man in the country is subject."

There had been Government prosecutions of strikers for rioting in the London docks : the whole House understood and appreciated the weight of the rebuke.

Then Carson challenged the Treasury Bench to

say if they had, even yet, made up their minds to coerce Ulster. And he put the case of that community :

" They made an audacious claim," he said, " to stay under the Imperial Parliament. Terrible blackguards ! It really astonishes me more than anything in the world how anybody ever cares to stay under the Imperial Parliament. It is a kind of crime. . . . Ulster is making no claim at all. All Ulster asks—I know it is a very extravagant thing— is to stay as she is."

" And to resist the claims of the rest of Ireland," Mr. Lloyd George interjected.

" She asks to stay as she is," Carson replied. " That is the only claim she has made that I know of."

" That is fatal to the Bill," said an honourable member.

" I cannot help it," Carson retorted, " I think the honourable gentleman is probably right : the whole object is to get hold of Belfast and the Northern Counties so that you may tax them. After all, it is not a very extravagant thing for the people who are there, the people who have made Belfast, to say, ' We are not altogether agreeable to that : we prefer to stay as we are. We are doing very well.' You say to them, ' No we must turn you out because it is fatal to the Bill.' I do not understand that argument."

Between the 10th October, 1912, the date of this debate, and the 16th January, 1913, when the Bill was read a third time in the House of Commons, the guillotine was so applied that out of the fifty-one clauses of the Bill only twenty were even partly and only six fully discussed. Not a single amendment proposed by the Opposition was accepted by the Government. These discussions, futile as they were in their results, have an interest to this biography.

Carson's whole heart was in the fight ; everything he loved was at stake, the fate of his country ; the fortunes, the very lives of his friends. " Feeling strongly and bitterly, and hating, loathing and detesting the whole of the Bill, I am not going even under these circumstances," he said, " to lose either my head or my temper. . . . It is far too serious for my own people. . . . We will fight it to the end, even if you have tied our hands behind our backs." And he was as good as his word. Over the wide range of a complicated subject, he showed everywhere an astonishing dialectical resource, an impressive intellectual power. He had law to meet Asquith's, wit to meet Birrell's, he was as alert as Lloyd George ; the two Jews in the Cabinet, Sir Rufus Isaacs and Mr. Herbert Samuel, had sedulously mastered the financial and commercial aspects of the question ; he had practical knowledge to confound them both ; and he knew well what they ignored—the real interests of Ireland ; had besides a far truer insight into the nature of her problems and the feelings of her people than John Redmond and the whole pack of the Nationalist Party.

Broadly we may say of these speeches of Carson's in Committee, that they deal with Constitutional Law, the safety of the United Kingdom and the welfare of Ireland. As to the first he was chiefly concerned with the validity of the " guarantees " or " safeguards " in the Bill. They were all, as he pointed out, vitiated by the grant of responsible powers to a popular Government.

" Suppose they say to the Lord Lieutenant, ' If

you veto this '—say it is a case of taking away property without compensation—' we resign.' . . . Nobody else will take office. What is to happen then ?

" And then the Solicitor went on to say, ' Even if you are not satisfied with the Veto, you have the supremacy of the Imperial Parliament.' How is that to be exercised ?

" Suppose you were to try to exercise it to-morrow under this Bill, how would you carry it out ? You would go to the Courts in Ireland, which are under the executive you are going to override, and where are your powers to carry it out in Ireland ? "

Moreover, wrongs were not done chiefly by unjust laws, but in the course of administration : " Nobody supposes that any Government would pass an Act of Parliament to permit of the cruelties of boycotting. . . . This is not done by law. People do not do these things by law . . . it is carried out either by conniving at it or by not enforcing the law against it. . . ."

And Carson summed up this whole subject of safeguards in one comprehensive sentence : " The truth of the matter is, the moment you have set up your subordinate Parliament, or your co-ordinate Parliament, or what I think it will be, your dominating Parliament, there is only one way in which it can operate, and that is by absolute trust."[1]

Absolute trust : the only safeguard where power is given. But could they or did they trust the Irish Nationalist Party ? They did not trust them with the Customs, nor did they trust them with the money lent to Ireland for the purchase of land : these were reserved services ; " but where it is an

[1] *Parl. Deb. Com. 1912*, vol. xlii., c. 2221 *et seq.*, vol. xliii., c. 295 *et seq.*
Lᴄ

ordinary, simple, elementary matter of the deprivation of life, liberty and property, you say, ' All these we hand over to Ireland.' "

In the light of experience and of history, had they any right to trust these people ?

" . . . Anyone who knows Ireland, or who knows the history of Ireland for the last twenty years, the methods of intimidation, the methods of persecution, the methods of the leagues, which, unfortunately, permeate the whole South and West of Ireland, knows the oppression and the cruelty which are the ordinary weapons of the Nationalists in Ireland and knows perfectly well that the only protection against these methods is the proper protection of the Executive power." Were it withdrawn, " there are many men now living in Ireland who could not continue to live there for another day."[1]

To reserve your customs, to protect your loans, but to surrender your own loyal people—we can see through the coldness of the printed word how the shame of such a transaction revolted the soul of the speaker. Mr. Birrell had confessed that, " having regard to the enormous stake which English credit has in the success of the operation . . . it would be impossible for the scheme to retain its hold on the public, if we were to . . . hand over Land Purchase to the Irish Government," and this thrifty reservation inspired Carson, like Cassandra, to prophecy :

" . . . Everyone knows perfectly well that when you have a separate Executive in Ireland the stability of your security will rest no longer upon the Imperial Executive, but upon the local Executive. . . . All the £108,000,000 which you have advanced

[1] Ibid., vol. xliv., c. 2326.

on British credit would be absolutely imperilled."[1]

If Carson could not foresee the exact manner in which De Valera appropriated the annuities, his foreboding mind could yet discern the essentials of that transaction.

We have already shown how Carson detected in the Bill a Liberal design to be rid of the administration of a poor country, the costs of which were being vastly increased by Mr. Lloyd George's programme of " Social Services." Here we come to a passage which illuminates the true tenderness of a heart often misrepresented as hard and ruthless.

" The whole object of Governments," said Carson, " the whole idea of government, and the whole reason why people amalgamate together and consent to a Government, is that the rich may help the poor, and that working as one harmonious whole, you may carry on to the best advantage of every individual in the country."

Carson pitied the common people of Ireland : he foresaw the impoverishment which must follow the separation of the richer from the poorer partner. "But the moment," he proceeded, "that you go to Ireland, what is your whole case ? You say, ' Ireland is a poor country : we are running it at a loss ; we must cut the loss.' . . . When you tell me that you are going to cut the loss, what you mean is that you are going to let the standard of living in Ireland lapse back to a different grade from that which it has attained to-day . . . you cannot benefit by a dissolution of partnership where the poorer partner is driven upon his own resources and dissociated for ever from the advantages of being connected with the richer partner.[2]

[1] Ibid., vol. xlii., cc. 1271–1281.   [2] Ibid., vol. xlii., c. 1565.

" What was it all for ? To satisfy a Nationalist sentiment : for that they were to have ' retrogression, rags and an empty stomach.' "

He did not despise sentiment ; but what of those people who did not share it, and were yet to suffer the consequences ?

This consideration of Nationalism, as Carson foresaw and foretold, made it certain that the settlement proposed was no settlement.

" What you have at the bottom . . . is the contrast between real local self-government and a step in the claim for national independence. . . . There is no use shirking it. It is nationality that is at the bottom of the whole claim of the Nationalist Members below the gangway, and that is why in reality you never can make, and never will make, this Home Rule scheme any part of a general federated scheme for the United Kingdom."[1]

Mr. Churchill, whose restless and resourceful mind was trying to find a way out for Ulster (and the Government) had been entertaining the electors of Dundee with a federal project, to recognise the local claims to self-government not only of Wales and of Scotland, but of Yorkshire, Lancashire, the Midlands and London. The implication was sufficiently plain, as Mr. Churchill intended it to be : if England could be divided, Ireland could also be divided. Ulster could be treated differently from the South. But the Irish Nationalists would have nothing to do with the idea, and Carson pointed out the reason why. The lion of Nationalism and the lamb of Federalism would never lie down together. The Nationalists intended to use the Irish Parliament not to federate with England but to

[1] Ibid., vol. xlii., c. 1091.

force a further separation : for that reason, " the system of the half-way house is absolutely and practically impossible." The logical result of the Home Rule Bill was separation.

Such arguments, true as events have proved them, had no effect on the Government, and once more Carson took up his blackthorn shillelagh. In the Christmas vacation of 1912 the nineteen Unionist Members for Ireland wrote a joint letter to the Prime Minister giving notice that they proposed to move, in the report stage, an amendment excluding the Province of Ulster from the operation of the Bill. Their opposition to the whole measure was unaltered ; the resistance to which Ulster was committed they still thought right ; but : "We cannot be blind to the grave mischiefs which are involved even in righteous resistance," and it was their plain duty " to do whatever we can to avert the violence we foresee." They therefore asked the Prime Minister to accept the amendment as " the only way to preserve the threatened peace of the realm," and assured him that if he rejected it, he would incur " a most heavy responsibility."

The Liberal press, strange to say, found encouragement in this letter. They had been watching Ulster with growing discomfort of mind. The Radical *Star* had even made open confession that it was " impossible to impose Home Rule upon Ulster by force," and proposed " so to shape the Home Rule Bill that Ulster may at some stage or other . . . come into the Irish nation of her own free will." But the letter was taken as a sign that Ulster, or her Leader, was wavering ; and had brought the amendment forward because " the game was up." It was even said that Carson had gone to Belfast to persuade that refractory people to make their submission by way of the amendment.

This illusion, were it shared by the Government, could hardly have survived the speech of the 1st January, 1913, in which Carson proposed to except the Province of Ulster from the scope of the Bill.

It was a speech, as the Prime Minister afterwards described it, " very powerful and moving." " Everybody knows," Carson said in a tone that withered such doubts at the root "—or, if they do not, I think they are very ignorant of the situation—that Ulster is a serious fact and a stern reality, which will not be got rid of either by turning myself and others into ridicule, or by pretending that the facts are different from what they are." In his characteristically plain way he proceeded to lay that bleak certainty before the Government.

" People come to me and say—I think in perfect good faith—' After all how can you fight in Ulster ? We have got the Army and the Navy.'

" Of course I am not fool enough in these things to dispute that point.

" They also say, ' What are you going to fight, and whom are you going to fight ? '

" Can any man measure beforehand—if you once try to drive people out of a Constitution they are satisfied with into another—where the forces of disorder, if once let loose, will find their objective, or what will be the end of it ?

" . . . It is enough for me to say that my opinion is that they will not accept and that they will resist.

" Where their resistance will come in will be where they find it best for giving vent to their views and their determination to keep their solemn pledges in the Covenant that they have entered into."

Then Carson turned once more to those scattered minorities of the South and West who were always in his heart and in his mind. When their case had come up before, on the Agar-Robartes Amendment, the proposal to exclude the four Counties had been to him no more than a means to divide Liberals from Nationalists : his intention was still to wreck the measure : " We are," he said, " opposed to the whole Bill, root and branch . . . compromise is . . . absolutely impossible." But it was plain, never-theless, if we may judge from this speech, that the course of events was forcing upon his mind this loathsome alternative of division. He had to con-sider it, and in this notable speech we find him considering it from the point of view of those scattered minorities in the South and West of Ire-land.

" My firm conviction is," he said, " and I believe it is now shared by the majority of these people, that, even by the exclusion of Ulster, these people would be in a far better position than they would be if Ulster were retained in the Bill." And he went on to argue the case from that point of view. In a Home Rule Parliament, " a few representatives from Ulster would really have no power," but if Ulster were excluded, " they would have the same representation here, in this House, as they have now, and would take care, as far as they were able, at all events that some watch should be held over the way they (the Southern Unionists) were treated under the administration of the New Government of Ireland."

Moreover, " they would have in Ireland itself an

Imperial power and an Imperial force which could not be disregarded by the rest of Ireland."

Carson, then, was by that time considering the exclusion of Ulster, if the worst came to the worst, as an ark and a refuge in Ireland. But he knew— he must have known—that the amendment which he proposed would be defeated. John Redmond— it was his calculation—would refuse it. That calculation envolved an estimate of statesmanship of the Irish Nationalist Party, for if that Party had been led (and controlled) by a Bismarck or a Cavour, it might have accepted the Bill without Ulster, on the calculation that in due course that Province must come to them. There were, it is true, 200,000 more Protestants (or Unionists) in that Province than there were Catholics (or Nationalists) ; the Unionists, moreover, had the power of business and of industry ; but politically the population of Ulster was so arranged as to give the Unionists, over the whole Province, a bare majority of one Member in the House of Commons. The Nationalists might well calculate that, as sometimes happened, a majority of one might be turned into a minority of one and that the harvest of time would bring Ulster into their rickyard. But (as Carson no doubt knew) if the Irish Nationalists could calculate, they could not wait. The heady stum of Nationalism and of victory intoxicated their minds. " Ireland for us is one entity," said John Redmond. He would have none of the proposal. And Mr. Asquith, who—as we now know—had himself provided this line of retreat, was as emphatic in rejecting it. Carson, as he saw the defeat of this offer of a way out, must have been glad that at least he had made it.

One other passage of this debate must here be

mentioned, since it has its influence on the course of our story. Mr. Bonar Law had supported Ulster in its determination to use force if force were necessary. He had been challenged to define his attitude if the Bill were submitted to the country and approved at a General Election, and in this debate he supplied the omission in his speech at Blenheim :

". . . So far as I am concerned, if it is submitted to the people of this country as a clear issue, so long as I speak for the Unionist Party, I shall do nothing to encourage them in resisting the law."

For Ulster, as Mr. Bonar Law admitted, he could not speak : ". . . If you put it before the country as a clear issue, then it is a problem for Ulster and not for me." Yet he could not resist quoting the opinion of two Liberal statesmen, the Duke of Devonshire and the Duke of Argyll, " That if the people of this country did give a majority, in their opinion Ulster would still be justified in resisting.

" And for this reason : a community had a right to say to another community, ' We do not wish you as part of us ' . . . but they had no right to say, ' You must not only leave us, but you must submit to another Government.' "

Over such refinements on the ancient rules of right and might the historian may be permitted to pass without gloss or comment. The main thing to note is that the Government at that time rejected both exclusion and election as a way out of the difficulty.

Sir Edward Carson was not among those who voted against the Third Reading of the Government of Ireland Bill a fortnight after.

His wife all through that winter lay critically ill at their seaside house in Rottingdean. There, after lingering on through many painful weeks she died, on the 6th April, 1913, and the death left Carson desolate. "Carson," a friend reports, "married very early, and on an income that to many a youth to-day would be but pocket-money. . . . And so, with a wife to whom he was devoted, and who used to share his toil and encourage him by her presence, he would work at his briefs—that were few and far between—night after night until the early hours. His first was a great event. It was quite a small case but he won it, and as a result a day with his wife in the country followed, when all sorts of similar expeditions were planned—expeditions they were to enjoy together when his work should increase."[1] As he stood with his family and James Craig and his other friends of Ulster round the grave in Rottingdean Churchyard, such old memories must have crowded in upon him ; it must have seemed to Carson that his life was ended. " I am glad to be here to-night," he said to his old friends, the working-men of Belfast, on the 16th May thereafter. " Heaven knows, my one affection left me is my love of Ireland."[2]

[1] " The Ulster Leader," by T. Comyn Platt, in the *National Review*, October, 1913.

[2] At the Willowfield Hall, in the Woodstock Road, Belfast.

CHAPTER XI

THE MARCONI CASE

Rumour—Godfrey Isaacs—American Marconis—" This Company "—
Le Matin—The Three Musketeers—" A good investment "—Leo
Maxse—Cecil Chesterton.

A GOVERNMENT which does not rest upon its
own majority must go into the market of the House
of Commons for support, and make deals with men
and parties of different views and interests, for which
reason it must inevitably fall into disrepute.

So it was with the Asquith administration, which
contrived to get along, as Mr. Balfour described it,
like " one of those old comedies of intrigue, in
which the chief schemer goes to each one of the
subordinate characters in turn, and gives to each a
different version of his object, induces them by
separate methods to carry out his policy, and at the
end, leaves them all duped." Mr. Balfour was
speaking of the case of Ireland, but similar methods
were followed over the whole field of politics : the
Irish Nationalists were bought with Home Rule,
the Nonconformists with Welsh Disestablishment ;
the Socialists with Payment of Members. The poor
were caught with abuse of the rich and the rich were
told that the poor were being reconciled to their lot.
Mr. Lloyd George, the most enterprising in this
system of purchase, did, however, miscalculate in
his Health Insurance, which Mr. Asquith gloomily
described as " a liability rather than an asset," and

there was something else which added so much to
this disrepute as nearly to bring down the Government—that cloud of rumour, scandal and fact,
the Marconi case, in which Sir Edward Carson
played a professional part.

To understand the political side of that once
notorious affair, we should remember that it did
not begin as a political issue. The Conservatives,
more than the Liberals, saw the importance of
wireless telegraphy to the economy and the de-
fences of the Empire, as had been recommended
by the Imperial Conference and the Committee of
Imperial Defence. The German Government were
at that time developing the Telefunken system, and
it seemed common prudence for the British Government to encourage Signor Marconi.

The terms of the agreement, indeed, did not
please certain critics upon both sides of the House :
Sir Henry Norman thought it a bad bargain for the
State ; Major Archer Shee disliked a monopoly ;
but they both dissociated themselves, expressly and
emphatically, from any charge that the contract
was tainted with corruption, a suspicion which the
former described as " preposterous " and " without
a shadow of foundation " : " I have not seen," he
said, " any such charge put forward by any Member
of the Opposition." Nor will this seem strange to
those who know English politics at that time : both
Parties, and especially both Front Benches, although
fierce enemies on political issues, had a common
regard for certain traditions in British Government :
even to hint insinuations on the personal honour of
Ministers, showed, as one of these critics said, " a
lamentable falling off from the high standard of
public controversy in this country." Certain more

detached critics outside the House, like Mr. Hilaire Belloc, the two Chestertons and Mr. Leo Maxse, put these scruples down to the " Trade Unionism " of politics ; but they seem upon the whole, looking back upon them, an excellent convention in our Parliamentary life.

It was outside politics that the rumours started : they began in the City, were taken up by certain journals independent of party, probably had their origin, as we shall presently see, in the indiscretions of the Ministers concerned, and were given point and currency by certain circumstances of the agreement. It had been negotiated by the Managing Director of the Marconi Company, Mr. Godfrey Isaacs, whose reputation did not stand very high at that time in the City of London, but who was a familiar member of the National Liberal Club, and was brother besides of that influential politician, Sir Rufus Isaacs, then Attorney-General. Mr. Herbert Samuel, the Postmaster-General, had negotiated the agreement on behalf of the Government. Rumour, no doubt, was given wings by the unworthy suspicion that among Jews and Liberals kissing sometimes goes by favour.

The preliminary tender—not yet a contract— for the erection of certain wireless stations was accepted by the Post Office on the 7th March, 1912, and what gave the more point to this gossip was that the shares of the Marconi Company, which had previously stood at about 14s. or 15s., rose by a delirious progression to £9 15s. The Company had been allowed (in a letter to their shareholders) to announce (without official contradiction) the acceptance of " our terms," which was not strictly accurate, nor was it made clear that the tender was

subject to the veto of Parliament. The critics con-
tended that information which had been partially
given to the shareholders should not have been
withheld from the House of Commons ; but Mr.
Samuel replied, reasonably enough, that he could
not control the Company, that the tender was
merely provisional, and that the contract had still
to be negotiated. It had to pass the scrutiny of
various Government Departments, including the
Treasury, it was subject to alteration, and, as a
fact, was not completed until the 7th July, when it
was laid on the table of the House.

In the meantime the bubble of the shares grew in
size and iridescence ; the wreck of the *Titanic* adding
to the optimism of the market. At the height of the
boom Mr. Godfrey Isaacs, with Signor Marconi,
went across to America to create a company there,
and it was thought indiscreet, to say the least, that
Sir Rufus Isaacs, being Attorney-General, should
have sent a telegram, to be read at a public banquet
in New York, congratulating these two on the
success of their " marvellous enterprise." The
American company was not indeed a party to the
agreement which was then in negotiation ; but it
was controlled by the English company, and was in
fact one of a group commonly described as Marconis
in the City. Signor Marconi and Mr. Godfrey Isaacs
were on the boards of both companies, and the one
could not but share in the prestige and prosperity
of the other.

The American company thought it opportune to
issue shares to the amount of £1,400,000, and as
there were fears that they would not be taken up in
New York a large part of them were brought over to
London. Mr. Godfrey Isaacs, who had " made

himself responsible " for £500,000 of these shares at
£1$\frac{1}{16}$ per share, returned to London on the 8th or
9th April, 1912, and on the 18th of that month
American Marconi shares were offered to the
British public at the opening price of £3 5s. od.
What happened at that time gave rise to the rumour
that certain Members of the Government had been
gambling in Marconis. These rumours grew in
definition in the months which elapsed between the
hectic but short-lived boom and the completion of
the contract, and they chiefly concerned, although
no names were mentioned, Sir Rufus Isaacs, the
Master of Elibank, then Chief Whip, and Mr.
Lloyd George. " The rich man's hatred of a great
People's Minister," said the *Daily News*, " winged
the lies and double-distilled the poison." The
Postmaster-General had hoped to get the contract
passed amid the rush of business before the autumn
adjournment, but on the 7th August, 1912, he was
compelled to postpone the matter until October,
and on the 11th of that month the debate occurred
of which we have already given extracts.

The Opposition, as we have seen, were hardly less
indignant than the Government at those rumours,
the currency of which indicated " a lamentable
falling-off from the high standard of public controversy in this country." But Mr. George Lansbury, who had never been to a public school, was
less punctilious, and blurted out an indecent
reference to " a statement broadcast publicly " :
" that considerable sums of money have been made
by the sale of these shares, and that they have been
made by people who had information in connection
with this matter previous to other people—information which was not available to other people."

This statement, which, as we shall see, closely
accorded with the facts, brought Mr. Lloyd George
to his feet in a fury. " The reason why the Government," he exclaimed, " wanted a frank discussion
before going to Committee was because we wanted
to bring here those rumours that have been passed
from one foul lip to another behind the backs of the
House." In the heat of his desire for a frank discussion, Mr. Lloyd George neglected to make any
denial of the rumours which he denounced, an
omission only remarked by those over-suspicious
cynics who are the bane of our public life.

Sir Rufus Isaacs was, or appeared to be, more
definite. From beginning to end he had taken no
part in the negotiations " in reference to this
company," and " Never, from the beginning . . .
have I had one single transaction with the shares of
that company." The Postmaster-General was, or
seemed to be, still more explicit, not only on his own
behalf—as he had a right to be—but on behalf of all
his colleagues. " I say that these stories that Members of the Cabinet, knowing the contract was in
contemplation, and thinking that possibly the price
of shares might rise, themselves, directly or indirectly, bought any of those shares, or took any
interest in this Company, through another party—
these stories have not one syllable of truth in them."

" This company," " that company," who would
suppose such insignificant adjectival pronouns to be
so pregnant with vital limitations ? Mr. Lco Maxse,
one of those too cynical people, in the *National
Review*, attacked both the agreement and the circumstances in which the terms had been made
public, and referred to the persistent rumours then
current in the City. When brought before the

Parliamentary Committee which had been appointed to go into the case, he refused to be bullied or browbeaten into a withdrawal, and demanded to know " why the Ministers themselves had not appeared at the first sitting to state in the most categorical manner that neither directly nor indirectly had they any shares . . . in *any* Marconi Company."

" This," " that," " any " : the Ministers concerned, as we shall see, fully appreciated the distinction in these particles of speech. This terrible Maxse, they must have thought, was in their secret.

Then a strange thing happened. Mr. Maxse, as was his habit, had been careful to say nothing beyond what he knew and had excepted the Postmaster-General from the scope of his censures. Thus he had said, in his memorandum of evidence : " . . . The rumours about particular Ministers—not the Postmaster-General—are circumstantial and persistent." Yet, two days after Mr. Maxse faced the Committee, *Le Matin* published from its London correspondent a complete travesty of his evidence which was at the same time a gross libel on the Postmaster-General and the Attorney-General.

Just those charges which Mr. Maxse had not made and which Ministers thirsted to deny were concisely put in this amazing paragraph : it was published on the 13th February, 1913 ; it was withdrawn with apologies on the 18th February. There was no defence possible, nor was any attempted, when actions were brought against *Le Matin* by Mr. Herbert Samuel and Sir Rufus Isaacs before Mr. Justice Darling on the King's Bench on the 19th March following. For both plaintiffs Sir Edward Carson acted as Senior Counsel ; Mr. F. E.

Mc

Smith, Mr. Schwabe and Mr. Raymond Asquith were also briefed by the plaintiffs.

The case seemed perfectly simple and straightforward : the libel was untrue and undefended ; *Le Matin* apologised ; damages were waived ; there was to be " no difficulty " about costs ; the two plaintiffs entered the witness-box to deny the allegations on oath—which might have seemed a mere formality, were it not that the occasion was utilised to make confession of something which was not alleged in the libel, and therefore, it might have been supposed, like the flowers that bloom in the spring, had nothing to do with the case.

Sir Edward Carson asked the indulgence of the Court to explain " one transaction in one of the Companies," by the Attorney-General, " although it is a little outside the libel." On the 17th April, 1912, " six weeks after the tender had been made public," Sir Rufus Isaacs had bought 10,000 shares of the American Marconi Company—" an entirely different company "—he had sold a thousand of these shares to Mr. Lloyd George, and another thousand to the Master of Elibank—" two intimate friends of his own." . . . "At the time, neither of them knew of the shares, probably had never heard of them, and the Attorney-General, believing that they were a good investment, having nothing whatever to do with the shares of the British Company, offered them, and they bought a thousand each. I am afraid that it turned out a loss for him. . . ."

Never, in effect, since the somewhat similar affair of the apple in the Garden of Eden had there been so innocent a transaction attended by such prejudicial results.

Sir Rufus Isaacs confirmed and amplified in the witness-box the statement of his Counsel. There was, of course, no cross-examination of the Attorney-General, which may be thought fortunate, since otherwise it might have been brought out that the shares were not in the open market on the 17th April when he bought them at £2 (not indeed from brother Godfrey but from brother Harry, who had bought them from brother Godfrey) ; that they were only offered to the public in the Stock Exchange on the 19th April at the issuing price of £3 5s. ; that, in effect, the Attorney-General had been favoured with special information and a special price in advance of the general public, that he had passed on these advantages to two of his colleagues in the Government, and that the source of these favours was at that time in negotiation with that Government. For it might also have been elicited—it was indeed stated in evidence by the Postmaster-General —that the " contract," which the Attorney-General said had been announced six weeks before, was not completed until nearly three months after this transaction—and even then required the sanction of Parliament to make it valid. Moreover, these transactions were only made public after it had become clear that they were known to others who might disclose them.

The facts, indeed, were not even then fully disclosed. On the crucial question of whether Ministers were given an advantage by Mr. Godfrey Isaacs, it appeared before the Committee that the information which Sir Rufus had from his brother on 9th April and shared with his colleagues on the 17th April, when they bought the shares at about £2, was only given to the public by the issue of a circular on the 19th April. Ministers were in effect given an advantage—and this a little scandalised even the most enthusiastic Radicals—not only over the general public but over the Liberal Party. The Chief Whip had been " investing " money of the Party Fund, and it was thought a little invidious that, whereas the Master of Elibank and Mr. Lloyd George should have had 2,000 shares for £4,000, the Party of Progress, a day or so later, should have paid £8,000 for 2,500 shares.

Under the partial examination of the Committee, an intimate picture of life at 11 Downing Street on that thrilling 17th April came gradually to light. Mr. Lloyd George, the Attorney-General and the Master of Elibank were intimate friends, " meeting continually " (as Mr. Lloyd George explained) " at meals, and, I think, at golf, and other transactions of that kind. That is the real reason " (he went on) " why the Master of Elibank and I were brought in ; it was not as if he were picking a Minister here and there ; it is purely and simply because we happened to live under the same roof and we three were constantly together." It might almost be said of them that, like the Three Musketeers, they had one purse. " I knew," said the Attorney-General, " what was their financial position approximately, and I said to them as regards the money, because both of them said, ' what about paying for them ? ' ' They need not bother about that . . . as I would always give them plenty of notice before I required the money.' "

If the affair had continued in this spirit of intimate informality it might never have become known to a censorious world ; but on the 19th April, when the shares were rising, the nerve of our Three

Musketeers began to waver under the strain of that haunting dilemma, whether to snatch a profit or to hold on for a rise. They consulted their brokers, who told them that the market was "very much too high," and they started to sell.

Not only so : on the 22nd May Mr. Lloyd George, plucking up courage again, bought 3,000 more American Marconi shares at $£2\frac{5}{32}$, with money lent to him by his broker, who took up the shares on his behalf. In the light of these transactions Mr. Lloyd George's defence, that he bought the shares as "a good investment" and (alternatively) that he made a loss on the transaction, was by some thought unworthy of such a financial expert as the Chancellor of the Exchequer presumably was or ought to have been. But as it was explained by a fellow Liberal, Mr. John, the Member for East Denbighshire, "the Chancellor of the Exchequer is a child in these things, artless, ingenuous, impulsive and confiding."

Their friends on the Committee did their best for these maligned Ministers. We find Mr. Falconer asking Sir Rufus Isaacs if it were not true that "the highest dignitaries in the Church who had money to invest might properly have made an investment in the American Marconi Company." They laboured also to draw a distinction between the British Marconi Company and the American Marconi Company, and to show that the latter had no interest in the contract with the British Government. Nevertheless, on the 18th June, 1913, in the House of Commons, Conservative opinion was put by Mr. Cave, afterwards Lord Chancellor : "It seemed," said Mr. Healy, "as if he were at the Day of Judgment summing up as Counsel against a sinner but presenting everything that could be said in his favour." There was no charge of corruption against the Ministers ; they had, however, broken certain rules which should govern conduct. " They had," said Mr. Cave, " made a big profit. They had made it in consequence of the information given to them by Mr. Godfrey Isaacs, representing the British Company, a company which was contracting, or about to contract, with the Government. They owed that profit to him, and if so, there was a clear breach of the rule, to which I have referred, that no Minister can take any favour or advantage from a man who is contracting, or about to contract, with the Government.[1] . . . They had also broken the second rule ; they had become interested in a company the profits of which undoubtedly depended upon the conclusion and confirmation of the contract that was then being negotiated."

It is fair to add that the House of Commons, taking a milder view of the affair, refused to censure the Ministers concerned ; but contented itself with accepting the rather perfunctory expressions of regret offered by the Attorney-General and the Chancellor of the Exchequer.

According to Mr. Healy, " Sir Edward Grey insisted that both Lloyd George and Rufus Isaacs should apologise to the House," a circumstance which might account for the fact that even after his death Mr. Lloyd George pursued Grey with rather more than that malice which may fairly be expected from one colleague to another.

Mr. Asquith made a speech which his party thought both tactful and discreet, since it severely condemned the offence and completely absolved the

1 *Parl. Deb. Com. 1913,* vol. liv., c. 397.

offenders. And the more signally to vindicate the honour of the Administration, the Chancellor of the Exchequer continued to occupy his high office ; the Master of Elibank was raised to the Peerage ; and the Attorney-General was made Lord Chief Justice of England.

Sir Edward Carson did not speak in that debate : he had thought it his duty, apart from friendship and against his party interests, to take the brief of the Attorney-General. Leo Maxse deplored the circumstance that " our Front Bench lawyers should have allowed themselves to be enticed into such a trap," and their action he described as " professionally correct but a public disaster." Carson did not trouble to reply, his view being that he could make no political distinction between clients, and that every man was entitled to a fair trial.

There was besides the tradition of the House of Commons, not yet broken down by the new Democracy, which was expressed by Mr. Balfour in the debate. He would, he said, " with or without evidence," no more dream of entertaining doubts of the honesty of the Ministers concerned than " I would believe a similar charge against my own nearest relations."

Friendship, indeed, and the strong traditions of the Inns of Court may have played their part, and it is certain that Carson was entitled to the gratitude of Lord Reading, who wrote to him on the 22nd October, 1913, on becoming Chief Justice :

" MY DEAR NED,—You behaved to me with all that nobility which is characteristic of you—there I must leave it—it almost overwhelms me."

The other case in which Sir Edward Carson took
a hand in connection with this affair need not long
detain us. Mr. Cecil Chesterton, a journalist of no
political attachments, had plunged into the controversy with more ardour than discretion. In that
dangerous sort of journalism which concerns itself
with the exposure of public abuses courage is an
essential but an inadequate equipment. The writer
—it is a wise precaution—must know something of
the subject, or, failing that, ought at least to have
a bowing acquaintance with the laws of evidence
and of libel. Innocent apparently of both, Cecil
Chesterton, in the *Eye Witness* and afterwards in the
New Witness, wrote a great deal which no eye
witness or new witness or witness of any sort could
be found to substantiate. The charge was of criminal libel, the case was tried before Mr. Justice
Phillimore at the Central Criminal Court, and Sir
Edward Carson, who appeared for the prosecution,
that is to say for Mr. Godfrey Isaacs, had an easy
task. He had only to ask the defendant to prove and
to justify such libels as this for example :
" Isaacs's brother is Chairman of the Marconi
Company. It has therefore been secretly arranged
between Isaacs and Samuel that the British people
shall give the Marconi Company a very large sum
of money through the Agency of the said Samuel for
the benefit of the said Isaacs. . . . Another reason
why the swindle or rather theft—impudent and
bare-faced as it is—will go through is that we in
this country have no method of punishing those who
are guilty of this kind of thing."
" Those who are guilty of this kind of thing " in
journalism, find soon enough that there are methods
of punishing them. The rash offender was found

guilty and mulcted in a heavy fine and the heavier costs of the prosecution, as is apt to happen in law when youth, with its generous impulses, in its headlong enthusiasm, makes a bad case of a good cause.

CHAPTER XII

LORD LOREBURN INTERVENES

The British League—Lord Roberts—Touring the North—The Sackville case—The German Emperor—Miss Ruby Frewen—The Loreburn letter—Durham.

THE YEAR 1913 was ominous to England at home and abroad. Two clouds, the one of civil the other of foreign war were gathering in a blue sky, although as yet only the weatherwise paid much heed to either. In the spring of the year that gay and gallant Englishman, Lord Willoughby de Broke, organised his British League for the Support of Ulster and the Union : the Duke of Bedford stood behind him : a hundred Unionist Peers and a hundred and twenty Members of Parliament were among its original members. " It is clear," they said, " that the men of Ulster are not fighting only for their own liberties : Ulster will be the field on which the privileges of the whole nation will be lost or won." Tom Comyn-Platt, an old friend of Carson's, as secretary, appealed for members and for means, and Carson himself, in a letter published on the 28th March, 1913, thanked Lord Willoughby de Broke and his friends on behalf of the Irish Unionists. " I always felt certain," said Carson, " that our determination to resist Home Rule would have behind us all those who were not prepared to sacrifice their friends for the purpose of placating their enemies." The League thus founded grew and spread over the Kingdom and the Empire. Before long it had four hundred agents and ten thousand men prepared to fight for Ulster if required.

In the meantime Ulster was working on steadily and methodically, preparing the frame of civil government, courts and magistracy, and drilling Volunteers. Early in the year the Standing Committee gave orders that the various contingents be organised as the Ulster Volunteer Force, an Army of 100,000 men, and Lord Roberts himself was asked to choose a Commander. That great little old man, who had learnt in many campaigns to know the enemies of his country, was at the time warning England of the dangers which threatened her from Germany, and he saw no less clearly the perils which lurked behind Irish Home Rule. He was therefore all ardour in these affairs, and on the 4th June, 1913, wrote to his friend, Colonel Hickman, that he had found " a Senior Officer to help in the Ulster business, Lieut.-General Sir George Richardson, K.C.B. . . . a retired Indian Officer, active and in good health . . . not an Irishman, but settled in Ireland." Richardson was, in fact, very much like Roberts, one of those small, wiry, keen, old soldiers who had learnt to know men and war fighting the Afghans and the Pathans on the North-West Frontier. He found material to his mind in the Ulster Volunteers, with whom he was soon as completely at home as with the tribesmen of the Tirah or Zhob Valley.

While these preparations were going forward, the ponderous and slow machinery of the Parliament Act was steadily rolling along to its appointed end. The Bill had been read a second time on 9th May, 1912 ; as it had to be passed by the House of

Commons in each of three consecutive sessions, it could not become law before the 12th June, 1914, and the distance in time made most Englishmen oblivious of the danger. Mr. Balfour, on the Second Reading, in its second year—on the 9th June, 1913—recalled to the House the loss of the *Victoria*—when during manœuvres in the Mediterranean two battleships started upon a course in perfectly calm weather, and to the eyes of landsmen, in perfect safety—" Yet a point was reached when, to those who knew, it became perfectly certain that no skill upon earth could avoid a collision between those two great vessels, and that one or both must sink with all their crews, to the bottom." If they had not reached the point at which collision in Ulster was inevitable, they were moving in that direction.

Sir Edward Carson, in scornful reference to the " automatic process " of the Parliament Act, said that he and his Irish friends " refuse to help you to play out this pantomime." " Our duty," he went on, " is not here : our duty is to help our own people to organise and also to ask those people of Great Britain who would never be a party to your wretched, miserable and scandalous betrayal to organise for our assistance."

To make these words good, a few hours after the end of the debate, all eighteen Irish Unionist members were on their way North to make urgent and united appeal to the chief cities of Scotland. On the 12th June, they were in Glasgow, on the 13th at Edinburgh, appealing to great audiences, whose blood and faith made them sympathetic to Ulster. Then South again. On the 16th they were at Norwich, on the 19th at Bristol. Everywhere

Carson's words were moving, simple and direct. " We are citizens of the United Kingdom just as you are," he said at Crewe Railway Station, " we want to remain with you, and with your help and God's help we will." At Edinburgh a sigh of weariness escaped him. " For my own part," he said, " I would only wish at this crisis of my life that I could have left politics altogether. I have been twenty years in the House of Commons and certainly if I acted on the mere dictates of my own convenience I should never put foot there again. But there are crises in history in which, whatever may be his personal feelings or sufferings, a man owes a duty towards those who have relied upon him. . . ."

Carson, however, could not altogether neglect his profession, and we must turn aside for a moment from the stream of politics to give a brief account of a celebrated case in which he was engaged at that time. It concerned the will of Sir John Murray Scott, a bachelor who had bequeathed a great part of his vast fortune to Lady Sackville of Knole in Kent. A large family of brothers and sisters, his heirs-at-law and next of kin, had always supposed that his money would be divided among them : it was, indeed, part of their case that Lady Wallace, who had left this fortune to Sir John, had desired that it should be so divided. They had watched with profound disquiet the growth of a friendship between their eldest brother and Mrs. Sackville-West (afterwards Lady Sackville), and when Sir John died (in January 1912) and the will came to be read, their fears were realised. Sir John had given Lady Sackville large sums in his lifetime ; he left her £150,000 in cash free of duty and—what were of greater value—his " fine things," as he called them—his pictures, furniture and plate in his houses in London and Paris. The net value of the estate was £1,180,000; but the Scotts protested—although this was denied—that when all claims were paid it was " extremely probable that there would be no residue." " Who shared in the residue," said their Counsel, Mr. F. E. Smith, " was not really an important matter at all." The Sackvilles, he said, had taken the kernel and left only the husk.

The case for the family was that Lady Sackville —her husband colluding—had spent many years in establishing so complete an ascendancy over Sir John that " his mind had ceased to be his own, but had become Lady Sackville's." They represented her as a designing woman of " uncanny " cleverness and charm, who had wound herself into Sir John's life like a serpent, ruling his household, estranging him from his relatives, dominating his mind and will, and exploiting this undue influence in extracting from him most if not all of what he had meant should be theirs.

The trial of the action occupied Sir Samuel Evans and a special jury some eight days of the summer of 1913 and excited enormous interest. The case for the parties cited, as put by Sir Edward Carson, was that Lady Sackville and Sir John Scott were kindred spirits, united by their love of " fine things," and in particular by the great and historic house of Knole, and its glorious furnishings, of which the lady was the proud and embarrassed heiress. To save Knole with all its fine things intact, to disencumber it of a vexatious law-suit ; to recollect and re-endow it with the rare old silver which had been distributed and sold ; to secure them all for Lady Sackville and her daughter, and to place these charming people high above the vicissitudes of an impoverished estate—such legitimate and worthy objects became an absorbing interest with the testator.

Sir John Scott had been a great connoisseur—he had first met the lady when he was arranging the Wallace Collection ; he was a trustee of the British Museum and the National Gallery ; and the finest *objets d'art* which had ever swum into his ken were the great house of Knole and its high-bred owner. If this unencumbered bachelor cared to engage in so congenial a task, and devote part of his fortune to the work, what was there in law or equity to prevent him ?

The testator was a rational man, competent in business ; he was described in the course of the case, as a huge old gentleman of twenty-five stone, dividing his serious attention between a *pâté* and a picture, and pathetically grateful for the platonic attentions of a high-born lady. He had clearly testified to the high value he had set on the friendship, and his intention to make Lady Sackville " comfortable and independent . . . in return for her goodness and sympathy." No attempt had been made to prove the testator insane, nor was there any suggestion of immoral relations in the case. The will, which had been drawn up in October, 1900, had remained for upwards of eleven years unaltered in its main provisions. To prove that before the will was made " undue influence " was already established, and that all those years it had been used to prevent an alteration, was beyond the power of the relatives. Moreover, Sir John Scott, as Sir Edward

Carson showed, had treated his family well, giving them and leaving them handsome allowances in houses and money : he had done everything to justify, and nothing to forfeit, the right of a man to do what he would with his own.

The Scotts had some unpleasant things to say of Lady Sackville ; but the Judge held that undue influence was something much nearer to coercion than anything which had been proved, or even alleged, and the Jury after retiring for twelve minutes upheld the will.[1]

This great case was decided on the 8th July, 1913 ; Lord and Lady Sackville wrote Carson gratefully on the result. " I do thank you also from my heart," Lady Sackville wrote, " I am rather a wreck still." Her Counsel also was "rather a wreck." He had overtaxed his strength in the ardour of the action and was unable to be present at the Third Reading of the Home Rule Bill in the House of Commons. On the following day it was stated in the press that he was " confined to his house with an attack of neuritis "—a painful malady which dogged his steps through life ; by the 12th July he was nevertheless in Belfast ; on that great day of the Orange Order he addressed a heartening speech to 150,000 Orangemen assembled at Craigavon, who heard also a more courageous than judicious message from Mr. Bonar Law : " Whatever steps they might feel compelled to take, whether they were constitutional or whether they were unconstitutional, they had the whole of the Unionist Party under his leadership behind them." On the 16th, with his good friend, James Craig, he was enjoying the fresh

---

[1] Capron *versus* Scott and others, Probate Divorce and Admiralty Division, the 25th June to the 8th July, 1913.

sea breezes of Tyrella ; a few days later he was cruising in the Hebrides ; and then, still in pursuit of health, we hear of him at his habitual Homburg.

There at the table of an English friend, one day in the week ending 23rd August, 1913, Sir Edward Carson met the German Emperor. It was a luncheon-party mainly English—the Emperor, Lord Acton, Sir Edward Carson, Sir Adolphus Fitz-George, Sir Charles Crutchley, Sir Archibald Hunter and the Hon. Mrs. Chichester. The Emperor chatted pleasantly on many subjects, the talk running on gardens, which led naturally to the management of States ; the Emperor suggested that England did too little to consolidate her Empire. " We have our own ideas," Sir Edward replied, " and we give them self-government."

Then the Emperor remarked that he would have liked to go to Ireland ; but that his grandmother would not let him, adding with a smile in a half-aside—" Perhaps she thought I wanted to take the little place."

" I think, Sir," said Carson, " you are well out of it."

Upon this the Kaiser began upon Ulster, in which no doubt from his own point of view he was already interested ; but Carson had an ear con-veniently deaf, and replied to his question with an irrelevant but well-calculated remark about certain plans then in hand for an extension of the suburbs of Berlin.

The Emperor, easily turned by this shrewd flattery, exclaimed : " I did it. I can explain it all to you," and, to illustrate the improvement of his beloved capital, drew a plan of the place on the table-cloth.

Na

Such was the ground of a portentous rumour, which may be found even in serious books, of a desperate intrigue between the Ulster rebels and the arch-enemy of England.

Carson lived with his physician, Dr. H. L. Richartz in the Ferdinandstrasse, and there survives a letter from the Herr Doktor dated 31st August, 1913, which suggests both Carson's state of mind and his state of health at that time.

"You were asking me the other morning," Richartz wrote to his patient, "how soon it would be possible for you to return to work. I fully realise how important it is for you and your country that you should not be absent too long from your post ; but a physician is pledged to absolute truthfulness and I am bound to tell you that, if you leave Homburg now, I cannot be responsible for the consequences. In my opinion you are in urgent need of another two or three weeks' rest before you are fit for the exertions of public speaking."

If there was one circumstance which might make Carson differ from his doctor it was a chance meeting with a charming English lady, Miss Ruby Frewen. The two thus opportunely brought together fell in love at first sight : the marriage of twin minds made nought of the difference between Spring and Autumn : the one found her hero, the other such sweetness, joy and tranquillity of life as he had never known nor had dared to anticipate.

The wedding, however, was not yet. Carson, returning to London on the 9th September, 1913, was in time for such a development in politics as must have driven everything else—but the happiness of his good fortune—out of his head. Two days later Lord Loreburn's letter appeared in *The Times*.

If we are to understand the importance of this
letter we must remember that Lord Loreburn was
one of the stoutest of British Radicals. He was not
indeed at that time a Minister ; for reasons of health
he had left the Woolsack the year before ; but he
had a great name and great influence in his Party
and it was generally supposed that as ex-Lord
Chancellor he must still be in touch with his recent
colleagues. The plausibility of this attribution gave
point and currency to the rumour.

Not only so, the letter seemed to claim that some
at least in the Government agreed with the writer.
Thus Lord Loreburn quoted a speech made by the
Secretary of State for India in the House of Lords
two months before. " Certainly we do not believe
for a moment," Lord Crewe had said, " that this is
the only Home Rule Bill, I would even say the only
kind of Home Rule Bill, which Parliament might
be asked to consider." He had touched besides on
Lord Grey's scheme of Devolution and Federation,
with which certain members of the Government had
been toying ; he quoted Lord Lansdowne as being
ready to treat such a scheme " with the utmost
respect " ; he quoted Lord Curzon as saying of
" the Irish question "—" I agree that it must be
solved," and there was an implied rebuke of the
Prime Minister in Lord Loreburn's question :
" Is there, then, nothing that can be done except
to watch the play of irreconcilable forces in a spirit
of indolent resignation ? "
There followed a grave warning of the havoc
those forces might work in Ireland, and an exhortation to the Government to do something to avoid
such dreadful consequences.
Not only so : the Conservatives had an equal

interest in a settlement : the Home Rule Bill would be upon the statute-book in the following June ; threats had been used which must have caused the gravest misgivings in that Party, " for lawlessness is opposed to all their traditions, and no one stands to lose more than they in every way by its encouragement." There were good reasons, then, to believe that a settlement could be reached, if this formidable question could only be discussed in private between the responsible men, with " no preliminary conditions."

Both the tone and the temper of this letter made a powerful appeal to many men and to many interests. The Government, itself, as we have seen, had long been furtively but anxiously considering various expedients. It was indeed a grievance with Mr. Winston Churchill and Mr. Lloyd George that when they, two years before, had proposed in the Cabinet special terms for Ulster, Lord Loreburn had been their most vigorous opponent. Since then they had been given good reason to doubt Mr. Redmond's smooth assurances that there was " no Ulster question." They knew of the Ulster Volunteer Force although they could still congratulate themselves that the Force had few arms or none. Not only Ulster : the British League for the support of Ulster and the Union was drawing many thousands of adherents all over the country.

If these did not frighten them there were hints that the Army had dangerous sympathies with Ulster. They knew that Lord Roberts had recently found a Commander-in-Chief for the Ulster Volunteer Force—it seemed incredible yet it was true. The Army was not a political force and with non-political forces they were unaccustomed to deal ;

but there were demonstrations among their own people. The Ulster Presbyterians were busily working among the English, Welsh and Scottish Presbyterians, and although these in the main had so far been true to their Liberalism, there was no knowing, once the religious temper began to rise, how long the political moorings would hold.

As for Sir Edward Carson, he had defied them, and although certain members of the Government were always against it, they even contemplated a prosecution. But would they get a conviction— and would it end the trouble ? Altogether, a horrid situation, although (as they must have assured themselves) almost as horrid for the Opposition as for themselves.

As for the Opposition, to do them mere justice, they were still in the main faithful to the Union and wanted nothing better than to refer the issue to the Electorate. What were the " People " thinking about it ? The Unionists could point to two recent by-elections in Cambridgeshire and Cheshire, in both of which they had won notable victories. Yet, divided and distracted as they still were over fiscal tariffs, and formidable as were the Radicals in raising new cries and preparing new measures, they had to admit to themselves that the issue was by no means certain. Were they to risk all on the hazard or seize a chance to get this troublesome Irish question out of the way for good and all by some sort of settlement ? Lord Loreburn's letter suggested prospects which were certainly tempting.

These prospects, if they tempted some, did not tempt Carson, not only because of his passionate faith in Union as a policy, but because he knew well that no compromise between Union and Separation was in Ireland possible : between two such hostile forces as were there arrayed there could only be the issue of victory or defeat. In the previous May, when already there had been rumours about conferences, he had said (in Belfast) that, for himself, if ever a time came when the people of Ulster thought it better to compromise for any reason, he must stand aside—" I never could, under any circumstances be a party to compromise."

This letter of Loreburn's was, therefore, for Carson, both welcome and unwelcome : as far as it signified weakening on the other side, he liked it ; in so far as it might weaken his own he distrusted it. The letter, as we have seen, appeared on the 11th September, 1913 ; on the 13th Carson was given the opportunity of facing the issues which it raised.

At Wharton Park Lord Londonderry had organised a great meeting of the people of Durham : Carson was the principal speaker, and he hailed the letter as a sign that " serious and thinking men are beginning to realise the gravity of the situation." With it the Home Rule controversy entered upon a phase entirely new : " this question can no longer stand as it did." Lord Loreburn, however, did not grasp its rudiments, as he failed to see the width of the gulf which separated the speaker from Redmond. " With Ulster it is no question of petty details ; we shall never give up the principle for which we have fought—to be governed only by an Imperial Parliament and by an Executive responsible to it." With Redmond also it was no question of detail, but of a " separate nationality "—" two positions you cannot reconcile." It was, therefore, " not of the slightest use to meet in a conference which must be abortive. Nothing could shake the determination of

Ulster not to be expelled from the Union and placed under a Dublin Parliament. If that were attempted, " we are going to make Home Rule impossible."

Carson had a simpler remedy : let Mr. Asquith take the vote of the country. " The Government," he said in his sardonic way, " trust the People everywhere but at the polls." And he repeated, " No conference on the assumption of Home Rule."

But, " if it were a question of considering the better government of Ireland . . . if it were a question of the expansion of local government or of doing something which might unite the people in one common cause for the progress of Ireland, I would be the first to say : ' Above all things let us have a conference again.' I myself would make many sacrifices to come to an agreement."

To some these words suggested a weakening : Carson then, was ready to enter a conference. " You will observe too," T. P. O'Connor wrote to Dillon and to Devlin a few days later, " that they got Carson into line." Carson had indeed got into line ; but on such a line as John Redmond would never agree to stand.

CHAPTER XIII

ROYAL SOLICITUDE

The King takes a hand—At Balmoral—Bonar Law reports—The Royal Prerogative—Carson in Ulster—The Provisional Government—The Ulster Volunteers.

"LORD LOREBURN'S LETTER," says Mr. Denis Gwynn, " came as a bombshell to Mr. Redmond[1] among the Wicklow mountains." We may well believe it. " Asquith's overpowering love of compromise," Mr. Gwynn adds, " was his most constant anxiety," and he had besides been labouring all the summer to prevent Mr. Churchill from breaking away on Ulster. An even shrewder observer shared his fears. " The Government," Tim Healy wrote to his brother on 23rd September, 1913, only want an excuse to abandon Home Rule. There is no enthusiasm for it among any of them. The Redmondites will throw the blame on Lord Loreburn if they are sold by the Cabinet. I think they will be sold."[2] Openly to forbid the banns of peace would not make the Irish more popular with the English people. " The Nationalists received Loreburn's letter," the Dublin Correspondent of *The Times* reported, " with an anger all the more bitter because it has to be disguised." Mr. Dillon, indeed, denounced intervention as "futile and mischievous"; but John Redmond, for the moment, said nothing. He would wait a little.

[1] *The Life of John Redmond*, p. 228.
[2] *Letters and Leaders of my Day*, p. 529.

Mr. Asquith, as soon as he read the letter, wrote to Lord Loreburn, asking him to tell him precisely what he meant. Lord Loreburn replied, proposing a conference, not on the Home Rule Bill, but to see if there was " any, and what meaning in the language which Lansdowne used, and Redmond used, and even Carson used quite lately about co-operation for the good of Ireland." This letter, printed for the Cabinet as a secret memorandum, was sent to Redmond and did not allay his anxiety. And what disturbed him even more—reports reached him of meetings and conversations between Ministers and Members of the Opposition at Balmoral.

The King, by that time, was taking a hand, His Majesty's aim being impartially to bring together the contending parties. It had, indeed, become plain to His Majesty that he could not well keep out of it. His peace, his Army, his subjects were threatened, and there was besides a disposition, on the Conservative side, to " take sanctuary in the Royal name." We have to remember that to force a General Election was the policy of the Conservative Party. Their amendment to the Second Reading of the Home Rule Bill in the House of Lords put their intention in a sentence : " That this House declines to proceed with the consideration of the Bill until it has been submitted to the judgment of the country." As the Government refused to comply with this demand, as the House of Lords had lost the power to enforce it, there was only one remedy left—that the King should use his prerogative of dissolution.

Great lawyers on the Conservative side—Lord Halsbury, Mr. Cave, Sir William Anson, Professor Dicey—supported the case for a Royal intervention.

There were precedents. Truly the last was nearly a hundred years before, and precedents, like brandy, although they keep long in bottle, lose their strength with time. Moreover, it was not of the best, for when William IV called upon Lord Melbourne to resign, that Minister went to the country and was returned with a victorious majority for a term of years. Nevertheless, there was the undoubted right : Lord Lansdowne was of opinion that the King should use it ; Mr. Balfour's more balancing mind agreed that there was a fair case—the better if His Majesty were to put himself right with his people by writing to his Ministers beforehand, to make his intentions and his reasons clear. Mr. Bonar Law, when he found the opportunity, pressed this point of view, that the Royal function was not " purely automatic."

Lord Loreburn's letter, it may be recalled, was published on the 11th September, 1913. On the 13th Mr. Bonar Law and Lord Curzon visited Balmoral Castle, Mr. Churchill being at that time Minister in attendance on the King ; Mr. Balfour arrived a few days later—as his two Conservative colleagues departed. These comings and goings were not lost upon Sir Edward Carson and John Redmond—the one in County Wicklow, the other in County Down.

Mr. Bonar Law left Balmoral on the 17th September. On the day following he wrote Carson a characteristically despondent letter, which, however, is of such consequence that, despite its length, it must be given in full.

"Pembroke Lodge,
"Kensington.
"18th September, 1913.

"MY DEAR CARSON,—I think it is necessary that you should know all that I know about the position, and as arranged with you, I am sending this letter by messenger.

"I had a long talk with the King, and he asked me to put in writing a summary of the conversation. I did so, and enclose a copy for you which gives all the information so far as my talk with the King himself is concerned.

"Churchill was there, and we had a talk about the whole situation in the course of which he told me that he had a letter from Asquith suggesting that he should speak to me.

"My talk to Churchill was practically confined to this : I told him that it seemed to me that the position was a desperate one for both political parties. I said it was bad for us ; but it seemed to me much worse for them. I told him that if the thing was to go on on their lines they themselves had taught us no half measures were any use, and it was certain that we would stick at nothing when it came to the point. I told him it was idle to suppose that they could leave you alone and trust to your movement breaking down from its difficulties. I said to him that most certainly the moment the Home Rule Bill was passed you would not only set up your provisional government, but that you would allow no force of any kind in your area except the force appointed by you ; that you would appoint your own police, and allow no other body to interfere with your action. He then spoke in a half-hearted way, as if it would be possible to allow even this to go on without interference by force. He spoke, for instance, of stopping railway communication ; but I pointed out the absurdity of this, as it would interfere not only with Ulster but the whole of Ireland, the whole of England and Scotland, which traded with Belfast, and I think he realised that that was impossible. I told him also that here in England there would be no half measures ; and I said to him, suppose it comes to this : the whole of the Unionist party say that Ulster is right, that they are ready to support them, that if necessary all the Unionist members are turned out of the House of Commons—does he suppose that the Army would obey orders to exercise force in Ulster ? I said to him that in that case undoubtedly we should regard it as civil war, and should urge the officers of the Army not to regard them as a real Government but to ignore their orders. I said to him also that of course we realised as clearly as he did not only the serious-ness but the actual calamity of allowing things to come to such a point. I said also I saw no way out of the difficulty. I spoke to him of the two possible bases of a conference (suggested in my memorandum to the King) dwelt even more strongly on the impossibility of our agreeing to any form of home rule with Ulster left out unless there were a large measure of agreement in favour of it among Unionists in the South and West.

" Now that is the position, and I feel sure that Asquith will suggest a private meeting either with Lansdowne or with me. If it is with me I am most anxious that before it takes place I should have a talk with you. As you know I have long thought that if it were possible to leave Ulster as she is, and have some form of home rule for the rest of Ireland, that is on the whole the only way out, because a discussion of the larger question of general devolution, even if the Government were ready to consider it, would involve a discussion, for instance, of the House of Lords, and probably other questions, and would really be impossible, I think, unless there were something in the nature of a coalition.

" When do you came back ? for it is really not possible to have a proper understanding by letter ; and you know that I have not only so strong a personal friendship for you but so much belief in your judgment that I do not think in any case I would go on with any proposal to which you were strongly opposed. I think I would rather give up the whole thing than do that. I do not think you should show this to any of your Irish colleagues, but of course you are free to show it to F. E. and perhaps you could arrange for him to see me as soon as he comes back to England. I do feel, however, that it is vital that before there is any meeting with the other side I should personally see you. The whole question as to the exclusion of Ulster really turns upon this—whether or not it would be regarded as a betrayal by the solid body of Unionists in the South and West.

" Yours very sincerely,
" A. Bonar Law.

" P.S.—I very much liked your speech at Durham and the speeches yesterday. Nothing that has happened in my opinion should alter your position in the least, but you have always made it clear that it is the inclusion of Ulster against her will which justifies your resistance."

As we have seen, Sir Edward Carson was in Ulster when these conversations were in progress. There was much to be done in Belfast—ill as he was : thither he went from Wynyard Park on the 16th September to be met by his dear friend, James Craig, and taken to Craigavon, by that time another home to him. Thence to Mourne Park, the seat of Lord Kilmorey, and thence to open his " autumn campaign " with an inspection of the Volunteer Forces at Kilkeel and Newry.

It is evident from the speeches there delivered—if evidence were needed—that Carson had no faith in conversation ; but that his whole design still was to force or frighten the Liberals into a sense of the danger to which they were heading. At Newry he spoke of the Provisional Government then being organised. " Of course," he said, " it was illegal : so were the Volunteers ; but they dared not interfere." At Kilkeel he made direct reference to the Loreburn letter. " They were not," he said, " going into a conference which meant not even a compromise but absolute surrender. They knew no surrender. A nice conference ! Just look at the position of the parties that would enter it ! Why, there would not be a free agent among the lot ! "

This was on 18th September, after Carson had seen in the contingents of County Down good evidence of the resolution of his Protestant friends in Ulster. But bigger events were pending : the leaders and business heads of these staunch people had been busy with systematic preparations for the work in hand : on the 24th September, 1913, the scheme for a Provisional Government in Ulster in the event of Home Rule becoming law was laid before a great conference of five hundred delegates of the Ulster Unionist Council in the Ulster Hall.

In coming to this critical decision Lord Londonderry, true and staunch as always, stood beside his adopted leader. Carson had implored him not to undertake a thing which led straight into danger. " They can," he said to this dear friend, " do little to me : therefore I have little to fear. But you have great possessions, a great title, friendships at Court, a seat in the House of Lords. You have to consider also the future of your son, Charlie. The Government, when they grow vindictive, as they will, may strike at you—and him. For these good reasons keep out of it." But Londonderry, with tears streaming down his face, said that he must not even be asked to stand aside when his friends and when Ulster were going into danger.

Lord Londonderry, therefore, presided at this fateful meeting, where besides the Duke of Abercorn, James Craig, Lord Erne, and indeed all the notables of Ulster were assembled. The business to be done was nothing less than to establish the machinery of an administration, to govern if need be in defiance of the law, and Lord Londonderry, speaking of the event as the most important step in his political life of thirty-five years, begged them to realise " the awful responsibility of their position." He proposed to them Sir Edward Carson as Chairman of the Central Authority. What action they would take in repudiating and resisting the decrees of a Nationalist Parliament and Executive and in taking over the Province in trust for the British nation would be made public when their leaders deemed it expedient : " We shall place ourselves in that respect entirely in their hands. . . . We believe in our leaders and they believe in us. Powerful enemies will seek to overcome us in the open and to undermine us in secret ; but we have weighed the consequences and they are nothing compared with the loss of our rights and privileges under one King and one Parliament."

Here Lord Londonderry shrewdly summed up their purpose in one pregnant sentence :

" It is easy to baton an undisciplined mob into surrender ; but it is a harder task to coerce a disciplined and organised community."

Carson in his speech struck the same grave and warning note. He spoke of their loyalty, of the disastrous effect of this division, which, if the Government drove them to it, would "split our society from top to bottom." He spoke of the disastrous effect on the Empire and on the forces of the Crown. "I know from my correspondence," he said, " that men who ought to have before them nothing but one steady aim,—the government and defence of the Empire—are already dividing into hostile camps." And he quoted from a letter of Lord Wolseley to the Duke of Cambridge in a previous Home Rule crisis pointing out what would be the disaster to the Empire if men were sent to coerce those whose only crime was that they had been always loyal to their Sovereign and the Crown.

Then Carson turned to review the work of two years, rising out of their anxiety to avoid sporadic riots and mere chaos, and to present their loyal democracy with a logical courageous and determined

THE CHURCH MILITANT IN ULSTER

The Moderator (Presbyterian Church), Dr. D'Arcy, Primate of all Ireland, and other leading clergymen dedicating the colours

policy. As surrender was impossible—" I would like to see the man who would come out to this democracy of Belfast and say, ' I advise you to surrender ' "—their duty was to guide and direct into its proper channels the methods of resisting this Home Rule Bill if the Government persisted in forcing it upon them, and that was exactly what they were doing by setting up a Provisional Government.

Such was the business of this memorable meeting, which proceeded to delegate its powers to a Provisional Government consisting of seventy-seven members, with a Commission of Five, of whom Carson was Chairman, as its Executive. There were besides the various Departments—the Military Council, the Ulster Volunteer Committee, the Finance and Business Committee, the Legal Committee, the Education Committee, the Publications and Literary Committee, and the Customs, Excise and Post Office Committee. Everything was to be in readiness when the day should dawn.

At the end of the meeting Sir Edward Carson made a proposal to create an indemnity Guarantee Fund of a million sterling, in aid of the prospective disabled, and widows and orphans of the Ulster Volunteer Force. He himself headed the list with a guarantee of £10,000 ; his friends followed suit ; a quarter of a million sterling was guaranteed on the spot, and by 1st January, 1914, the Fund stood at £1,043,816.

Such was the civil side of this formidable demonstration, nor was the military side neglected. On Saturday, the 27th September, there was a muster of the Belfast contingent of the Ulster Volunteer Force—four regiments of fourteen battalions, 12,000

Oa

men in all. The review was held in the Balmoral grounds ; all Belfast was gathered to see it ; the band struck up " The British Grenadiers," and the Infantry, by that time well drilled, marched forward in a line of about three hundred yards to where Carson, Londonderry and their friends awaited them on a platform. Then General Richardson called for three cheers for the Union. The men waving their hats in the air gave the cheers with such spirit as brought the whole assembly to its feet in wild hurrahs. The great Union Jack was broken ; the band played " Rule Britannia," and then the whole vast multitude joined in " God Save the King."

CHAPTER XIV

NO SETTLEMENT

Negotiations—Mr. Asquith states the case—A hint of menace—Mr. Lloyd
George—Redmond's ruling—No compromise.

BONAR LAW, who leaned heavily on Carson's
arm, wrote from Margate on the 24th September,
1913, to express his delight " that so far as I can
judge you and I take exactly the same view about
the present position. The only thing I see from your
letter I didn't make clear is that W. C. had no doubt
that the Nationalists could be made to agree to the
exclusion of Ulster."

And in a postscript Bonar Law added :

" H. M. told me that both Grey and Harcourt
had told him that none of the Cabinet knew anything about Loreburn's letter, and I gather from
Churchill that they resented it very strongly. I
am sorry to hear that you are ill again ; but I am
not surprised. I have told Lansdowne that I have
communicated all I know to you."

And on the day following the Conservative Leader
wrote again to congratulate Carson on his " very
great speech . . . the best you have ever made, in
my opinion," and to admire " the moderation and
reasonableness with which you have conducted the
whole campaign." Carson was to come to see him
as soon as he returned to London. And the letter
ended with another postscript :

" By the way I did not say yesterday that I was pleased that you should show my letter to James Craig. The only reason why I suggested that you should keep it to yourself was that I am most anxious not to have any secrets, even in small matters, with Lansdowne, and he is naturally more reserved than I, and more inclined to keep things to ourselves."

To unravel the tangled skein of those close events we must now turn again to Balmoral. The Prime Minister did not himself go North until the 6th October ; but in September 1913 he wrote two memoranda, evidently intended for the eye of the King, which are of consequence to this story.[1]

In the second, Mr. Asquith discussed " the prospective situation in Ireland." If the Bill were passed there would " undoubtedly be a serious danger of organised disorder in the four North-Eastern Counties of Ulster." The men were drilled ; but, on the other hand, " the importation of rifles has, so far, been on a small scale." There was besides a " considerable and militant minority " in Ulster (Devlin's Nationalists) who were " ready to render active assistance to the forces of the Executive."

Mr. Asquith did not think that the Ulster Protestants could " stand up against regular troops " ; but he admitted " the certainty of tumult and riot and more than the possibility of bloodshed."

Then the Prime Minister turned to consider the alternative—if the Bill were rejected or indefinitely postponed. In that case, he argued, the prospect was " much more grave." If the Nationalists were disappointed—" if the ship, after so many stormy

[1] They are to be found in Mr. J. A. Spender's *Life of Lord Oxford and Asquith*, vol. ii., chaps. xxix. and xxx.

voyages were now to be wrecked in sight of port "
—it would be " difficult to overrate the shock or
its consequences." Ireland, in effect, would " become ungovernable—unless by . . . methods which
would offend the conscience of Great Britain and
arouse the deepest resentment in all the self-
governing Dominions of the Crown."

Having thus considered a position in which the
Government could go neither forward nor backward
without disaster, Mr. Asquith proceeded to discuss
the demand for a general election. To that course
he saw " objections of the most formidable
character."

Having stated these objections, Mr. Asquith proceeded to what is probably the key to his whole
policy at that time. Here, therefore, must be in-
scribed the passage in its naked literalness :

> " It is quite another matter to suggest that,
> after the Bill has passed, a General Election should
> take place before it has come into active opera-
> tion. Parliament will then have completed, or
> nearly completed, four out of its possible five
> years ; and if the country were either on general
> or particular grounds averse to the Government,
> the new Parliament would consider, before any-
> thing irreparable has been done, whether to
> repeal or to amend the Irish Government Act.
> If, moreover, it were known beforehand that this
> would happen, any outburst of disorder in Ulster
> would everywhere be regarded as premature and
> inexcusable."

We must pause to admire, in their full beauty, the
implications of this proposal. The Government

would be able to remain in office for four-fifths of
its quinquennial term ; the Irish Nationalists would
be brought not merely " within sight of port " but
into the harbour before being scuppered. Although
the lesser disappointment would make Ireland
" ungovernable," the greater could happen without " anything irreparable " being done. Mr.
Asquith, in effect, would get the very most and the
very last out of Mr. Redmond, and would keep
Ulster quiet besides, with expectations which must
disappoint either the one or the other.

With these possibilities in mind, Mr. Asquith, as
we can readily understand, had little use for the
Loreburn proposal. Neither Sir Edward Carson
nor Mr. Redmond, he pointed out, was likely, at
the moment, to accept an invitation (from any
quarter) to come into a room and sit round a table
for the purpose of talking in the air about the
government of Ireland, " or about Federalism and
Devolution."

There was " a deep and hitherto unbridgeable
chasm of principle between the supporters and the
opponents of Home Rule," although, if the principle
and the urgency of Irish Home Rule were admitted,
there was no point—finance, Ulster, Second Chamber, representation of minorities—upon which Mr.
Asquith was not " ready and anxious to enter into
conference."

There must, however, be a basis, and at present—
" it may be different nearer the time "—no such
basis could be found. In all these circumstances,
" an abortive conference would be likely to widen
differences and embitter feeling."

Thus Mr. Asquith stamped firmly on the Loreburn proposal, and (in his other memorandum) he

was—naturally—even more emphatic against the Conservative idea that the King might force an appeal to the country. He scornfully dismissed William IV as " one of the least wise of British monarchs." " We have now," he proceeded, " a well established tradition of 200 years, that in the last resort, the occupant of the Throne accepts and acts upon the advice of his Ministers. . . . If the King were to break that rule, he would, whether he wished it or not, be dragged into the arena of party politics, and at a dissolution, following such a dismissal of Ministers as has just been referred to, it is no exaggeration to say that the Crown would become the football of contending factions."

There was a hint of menace in the words, which we hear rather more clearly repeated in a remarkable conversation a few days later. On the 30th September, 1913, Mr. Lloyd George sent for Mr. T. P. O'Connor to sound him, on behalf of Mr. Asquith, on the views of the Irish leaders, and " T. P." reports the conversation to Messrs. Dillon and Devlin. " L. G.," he says, " reassured me with regard to the attitude of the King. He has been told quite plainly that a refusal to sign the Bill would be very perilous."[1]

Mr. Lloyd George gave " T. P." a not altogether accurate account of what had passed at Balmoral. " The Tories," he said, " were willing to go into a conference, but on the condition that the Liberals should consent to the right of Ulster to decide by plebiscite whether she should come under the Irish Parliament." And, incidentally, he set himself right with the Irish in characteristic fashion :

" He (L. G.) recalled that he had proposed at the

---

[1] Denis Gwynn, *The Life of John Redmond*, p. 230.

beginning of the struggle that Ulster should get this option, feeling confident then that it would be refused, and that he still thought this would have been wise tactics."

He accepted the fact that the plan was " out of date," he assured Mr. O'Connor that " all Ministers, with the possible exception of Winston, are quite determined to act with us " ; he said that Loreburn's letter had been written " without consultation with a single Minister " and had created " the bitterest indignation," and he assured the Irishmen that Haldane, then Secretary of State for War, " was most firm on the question of Ulster—even going the length of saying that he would begin to send troops there already."

The Prime Minister's Mercury went on to hint—it was no doubt his main object—that " Asquith had been expecting to hear from Redmond ; and certainly wants to know his views." Redmond should therefore be asked to communicate with Asquith " by wire if possible." Such a telegram would also be useful to " put a bridle " on Mr. Churchill.

Mr. Redmond had, as a matter of fact, already given his ruling. On Sunday, the 28th, two days before this interesting conversation took place, he had spoken at Cahirciveen in County Kerry, and had recalled an offer he had made to Carson in the previous June to discuss the question of Ulster with him—" on one condition, that Sir Edward Carson should frankly accept the principle of a local Parliament in Ireland with an Executive responsible to it." To this offer he still held, but he had nothing to add : as to going into a conference in which the whole question of Home Rule would be put back in the melting-pot—" that," he said, " we cannot and will not do."

In these circumstances, so unpromising of peace, Carson went on with his preparations for war. On the 1st October, 1913, we hear of him with General Richardson, James Craig and F. E. Smith—escorted to Killymeen Demesne by mounted men, inspecting the Cookstown battalion of a thousand men under Mr. MacGregor Greer ; then at Dungannon inspecting the West and South Tyrone battalions under the Duke of Abercorn, Lord Northland and Mr. William Coote. There Carson had a word to say in reply to the Irish Nationalists : " Redmond said, ' I will meet Carson in conference if he will accept the principle of Home Rule.' Well, I say, ' Thank you for nothing,' and I tell him I won't." The time for argument was over, Carson went on. There was no use talking about peace when there could be no peace.

On October 2nd the Party were at Strabane, and went to inspect the Donegal Regiment of the Ulster Volunteer Force. Lord Leitrim was the Commanding Officer and the regiment on parade was 1,500 strong—" the greatest turn-out in Raphoe or any part of Donegal since '98, when your ancestors beat the rebels," said Carson. " I hope to inspect you again," he added, " with a rifle on every man's shoulder." On the 4th Carson was at Baronscourt, Newtownstewart, the guest of the Duke of Abercorn, who had three hundred men of Tyrone for musketry training in the Park ; on Saturday, the 4th, he concluded his tour with a visit to Armagh as the guest of the Bishop. There again he expressed his suspicion of conferences. " Your course and my course," he said, " is perfectly clear. We have got authority to set up provisional government, and we are going straight ahead—day after day—perfecting all the arrangements which may be necessary."

On the 5th, Carson returned to London and went straight to Bonar Law at Pembroke Lodge.

The air and the press were full of rumours of conference and settlement. The King had intervened : Asquith was " weakening " ; Redmond was " weakening " ; Bonar Law was " weakening " ; Carson was " weakening." These two men knew better. Lord Loreburn's intervention had failed to budge any of the embittered opposites.

It was in these circumstances that the first attempt to act upon the Loreburn letter failed. The King was assiduous in his solicitude ; Asquith, certainly, was no less anxious ; so were they all ; but by that time there could be no satisfactory settlement. There could be, as Carson plainly saw, only victory or defeat.

CHAPTER XV

CONVERSATIONS AND DEFIANCES

Near Leatherhead—Lord Lansdowne—Irish noblemen—Asquith and
Bonar Law—Asquith and Redmond—Redmond and Lloyd George—
Carson on tour—Joseph Chamberlain.

WE SHALL PRESENTLY SEE the Prime Minister
wrestling, secretly and desperately, with John
Redmond and Sir Edward Carson, to extricate
himself from the dilemma in which, by his own
policy, he was involved. His advances were both
private and public, and we have to trace through
the autumn and winter of 1913 two curiously
parallel negotiations, one shouted from platform
to platform, the other conducted with every precaution of privacy, in a series of furtive and clandes-
tine assignations.

The first of these latter was made by Asquith
from Balmoral, " with the King's hearty approval,"
on the 8th October—a confidential invitation to
Mr. Bonar Law, as a result of which these two met
" with elaborate precautions for secrecy," six days
later, at Max Aitken's house near Leatherhead.
" The atmosphere," according to Mr. Spender (a
specialist in atmosphere), " was friendly." Mr.
Bonar Law seems to have been more than usually
despondent : " the two men were now agreed that
almost insuperable difficulties lay ahead of both
parties." " Neither," moreover, " was sure how far
he could carry his own party." Mr. Spender tells

us, on the authority of Asquith's pencilled notes of the conversations, that Bonar Law made a proposal :

" . . . the permanent exclusion of the four north-eastern counties, ' plus perhaps Tyrone and one other,' with an option of inclusion at some later date, if these counties so decided."

It could not have been a firm offer, as Mr. Bonar Law was " doubtful whether Lord Lansdowne, who thought that North and South should sink or swim together, and held strong views about deserting the Irish Loyalists, would consent to this." They never-theless discussed " the various permutations and combinations of the Ulster exclusion plan . . . exploring the ground," Mr. Spender calls it—with " very discouraging results."[1]

This secret and gloomy conversation was on the 14th October, 1913 : the day before Lord Lans-downe had written a letter to Sir Edward Carson which helps us to understand the hesitations on the Conservative side.

" If," Lord Lansdowne wrote (from Meikleour in Perthshire, evidently in reply to a letter from Carson), " if the overture which has been made by Asquith to Bonar Law leads to further discussion, we shall have an extremely difficult hand to play."

So much, certainly, Carson did not need to be told, and as for the case which his friend proceeded to put to him, it must already have occupied his waking—and his sleeping—hours :

" The Unionists of the South and West," Lans-downe went on, " are, it is very true, helpless and

[1] *Life of Lord Oxford and Asquith*, vol. ii., p. 35.

inarticulate ; but I do not know that one can blame them. They probably feel that it may be better to have no meetings at all than the poor little gatherings which they are able to collect. But they are quite powerful enough to provoke a serious outcry against us if we throw them over. They will argue that in the past we have resisted Home Rule, not merely owing to our affection for Ulster, but because we regarded it as dangerous to the United Kingdom as a whole and disastrous to the Unionist minority in other parts of Ireland, where that minority is in special need of protection. You have, of course, seen Barrymore's letter, which will, I should think, receive a good deal of backing. If matters go further, would it not be possible for you to meet him, and see whether a *modus* of any kind is attainable ? It will be difficult for him to answer your argument that your men cannot be expected to fight if they are offered a settlement satisfactory to themselves.

" But I have grave doubts whether such a settlement will, after all, prove to be within reach. The geographical puzzle to which you refer (your second point) is one of the rocks upon which it will probably split, and it seems to me that if you are charged with the betrayal of a section of your Covenanters, you will be in a place just as tight as that in which we shall find ourselves if we lay ourselves open to the imputation of having bartered away the liberties of our friends in the South and West.

" These are, however, only some of the obstacles in the way of a transaction. It is impossible to discover from Winston Churchill's speeches what is really meant by the ' exclusion ' of Ulster (be the same more or less). He insists on maintaining

' the national integrity of Ireland,' and so does
Redmond. What kind of integrity would it be that
left either the larger or the smaller Ulster outside
the arrangement !

" I am afraid I regard the suggestion for a conference with profound mistrust. Loreburn's letter
forced the Government to do something, and my
impression is that they mean to offer us terms which
they know we cannot accept, and then throw upon
us the odium of having obstructed a settlement.
Personally I should much have preferred to go on
pressing for a General Election with all the risks
involved.

" I shall, of course, come South if I can be of any
use."

The letter to which Lord Lansdowne referred had
appeared in *The Times* a few days before. Lord
Barrymore, an old man well trusted by the Irish
Loyalists, Chairman, besides, of the Executive
Committee of the Irish Unionist Alliance, put a case
for those people, which was " in danger of being
overlooked," because " the determination of Ulster
to resist by physical force overshadowed everything." They were none the less opposed to Home
Rule ; they had held great meetings in Dublin,
Cork and Limerick, and in almost every county
of the South and West ; they had subscribed, mostly
in small sums, £10,000 ; they deserved well of their
country ; they foresaw " with the greatest alarm "
the financial ruin, the social disorder, the disruption
of Empire involved in Home Rule, and their
demand was to lay the facts before the British
people in a General Election.

Carson knew it all ; he himself was a man of the
South ; he had been fighting their battle as well as

he knew how. Another old Irish friend, Lord
Rathmore, had written to him, a few months before,
" to say with what admiration I have been watching
your gallant and most able efforts, in and out of
Parliament, fighting against almost hopeless odds—
(and I fear weighted heavily all the time by
domestic anxieties and troubles !)—but I really
don't think you have ' missed a bar ' anywhere."
It was true : Carson had not missed a bar anywhere ; but was he playing the right air ? He was
a man of the South. He had taken up the North,
as his manner was in his law cases—to concentrate
on the strong point of his own, on the weak point
of his enemy's case, never thinking that the Liberal
Government would ever seriously attempt—or the
Irish Nationalists permit—the alternative of Irish
Home Rule without Ulster. His whole design was
to wreck the Bill.

Yet this mad alternative—mad because Home
Rule was manifestly bankrupt without Belfast—
was coming gradually more and more into practical
politics. It was being seriously considered. Carson,
at that time, had another indigestible letter from
another Irishman. On the 9th October, 1913,
Lord Arran wrote to him from County Louth,
arguing urgently and strongly that Ulster, or part
of Ulster, could not compromise by accepting
exclusion, " as they had sworn in the Covenant to
take all means necessary to defeat the present conspiracy to set up a Home Rule Parliament in
Ireland.

" Many of us outside Ulster," Lord Arran proceeded, " signed this Covenant relying on the word
Ireland, and my point is that if Ulster accepts, as a
compromise, a Home Rule Parliament with herself

excluded, she would be false to the Covenant she
swore. I entirely agree with you that we must use
all our physical and armed force to prevent Home
Rule, but not only for Ulster, but for the whole of
Ireland, as sworn by the Covenanters."

We must hold all this in suspense while we proceed with the tale of these negotiations. The next
move of the Prime Minister was public. At Ladybank, in his own kingdom of Fife, on the 25th
October, 1913, Mr. Asquith invited the Opposition
to " an interchange of views and suggestions, free,
frank and without prejudice." Yet, characteristically, this " free " and " frank " invitation was
governed by three considerations, neither frank nor
free : Nothing was to be done to interfere with the
setting up in Dublin of a subordinate Irish Legislature with Executive responsible to it; no " permanent or insuperable " obstacle was to be put in the
way of Irish unity ; and, in the matter of devolution
in other parts of the United Kingdom, " the claim
of Ireland is paramount in point of urgency and
must be dealt with first."

As for Ulster, " We are not," said Mr. Asquith,
" and shall not be intimidated by the threat of
force "—although, indeed, it was fairly obvious
that only the threat of force had induced him to
make these overtures. The Loyalists of the South,
who had been entirely constitutional in their
opposition, were not even mentioned.

Mr. Bonar Law made his reply to this invitation
from Newcastle on the 29th October, 1913. He
accepted the invitation, although governed by
conditions, " so obscure that I do not know and I
do not think anyone knows in the least what they
mean." Carson, who also spoke, did not conceal his

contempt for all this "kite-flying and political jockeying":

> "Mr. Asquith said, 'Let us have a frank interchange of views upon a basis which I will lay down.' It reminded him of two business men falling out, and one writing to the other to say : 'Our differences are so great that there is no use you calling upon mc or me calling upon you ; but if we happen to meet at the corner of the street, perhaps we can settle the matter.' "

It was at this meeting also that Mr Bonar Law said something which reminds us of Tim Healy's shrewd observation—" Carson's influence has acted as a safety-valve for the Orangemen." " Now Sir Edward and I are friends," said the Unionist leader. " In his presence I shall say no word in his praise. His influence is greatly, in my opinion absurdly, exaggerated by our opponents. They think, or pretend to think, this movement in Ulster to which they have given his name, is due to him, and without him would disappear. There never was a greater delusion. That movement rests upon forces far deeper and stronger than the personality of any man." In Carson's speeches, he pointed out, there had been no hostility to his brother Irishmen ; no claim of ascendancy, no word of religious bigotry—" no word that can offend the feelings of any Catholic. . . . Determination and restraint "—for these Bonar Law praised Carson and the people of Ulster.

But let us turn again to the negotiations. On the 13th November, 1913, Mr. Asquith, in a letter marked " Secret " implored Redmond not to
Pa

" close the door to the possibility of an agreed
settlement," assuring him at the same time of " the
firm and unshaken determination of my colleagues
and myself to attain with your help our common
object."

Redmond's comment on that letter is to be found
in the speech he made at Newcastle on the following
night (the 14th November), where he protested
against any surrender to a " gigantic game of bluff
and blackmail," and scoffed at the idea of excluding Ulster, " which for us would mean the nullifi-
cation of our hopes and aspirations for the future.
. . . I shut no door," he said, " to a settlement by
consent ; but we will not be intimidated or bullied
into a betrayal of our trust."

Mr. Asquith, in his letter, had asked Mr. Redmond for a consultation, which took place on the
following Monday (November 17th). These two
men who thus met in secret, were they adversaries,
or colleagues, or were they a little in the relationship
of master and servant—or of Dr. Faustus and
Mephistopheles ? The reader will judge for himself
from the two accounts of the interview—one,
brief, in Spender,[1] the other more detailed, in
Denis Gwynn.[2]

It appears from the second that Asquith began
by relating his conversations with Bonar Law. They
had discussed and " dismissed " the idea of a
General Election. Bonar Law had then professed
his desire for a settlement, had said that he could
count upon " the official Tory Party," had added
that, although he could not count upon the extreme
men, " Carson was quite as anxious for a settlement

---

[1] *Life of Lord Oxford and Asquith,* vol. ii., p. 36.
[2] *Life of John Redmond,* p. 234, *et seq.*

as he was." Bonar Law had " said that he thought
the matter could be settled on the basis of the
total and permanent exclusion of Ulster from
the Bill—' Ulster ' to mean an area to be settled
by agreement and discussion."

Mr. Asquith, although, as he explained to
Redmond, he " had given no countenance whatever to this idea," had " considered it his duty " to
report it to his colleagues ; and then the Prime
Minister proceeded to report to Mr. Redmond the
discussion of this matter in the Cabinet.

Here he disclosed the true origin and purpose of
a proposal of which we shall hear more later :

" The only suggestion," said Mr. Asquith,
" which seemed to justify serious discussion was
one made by Mr. Lloyd George, to the effect that
a certain area, to be agreed upon, should be excluded for five years from the operation of the Bill,
but should come in automatically under the Bill
at the end of that period."

Here, indeed, was the proposal afterwards to be
advanced in the sacred name of Peace and to be
described by Carson as " sentence of death with a
stay of execution for five years."

" It was," Asquith went on to tell Redmond, " the
opinion of the whole Cabinet, and of Mr. Lloyd
George himself, that such a suggestion would not
form the basis of a settlement by agreement, as Sir
Edward Carson and his friends could never agree
to a proposal which would really mean the giving
up of the whole principle for which they had been
contending.

" It was, however, argued by Mr. Lloyd George
that if such a proposal were ever put into the Bill,
or even that if such a proposal were made by the

Government and rejected by the Opposition, it would have the effect of preventing an immediate outburst in Ulster, as men could not possibly go to war to prevent something that was not going to happen for five years."

The proposal, then, was not seriously intended ; it was no more than a trick—characteristic of the inventor ; Mr. Asquith was evidently a little ashamed of it. Although he reported that it had supporters in the Cabinet—among the chief, Lord Morley (Honest John !) and Mr. Winston Churchill, he assured Mr. Redmond that neither he nor the Cabinet had come to any conclusion on the proposal ; also of " the unshaken determination of himself and his colleagues to carry into effect our common object." Then he gave Mr. Redmond some alarming information from the War Office ; and asked him to " send a memorandum at my convenience." And he ended with a piece of information—was it in malice ?—that " two years ago, or at least early in this matter, Mr. Lloyd George had formally proposed the exclusion of Ulster from the Home Rule Bill, but that the Cabinet had unanimously rejected the idea."

Now John Redmond knew very well that when Mr. Asquith spoke of " unshaken determination," he meant " shaken determination," and he accordingly pitched his memorandum hot and strong. There might, he said, be a riot or two ; " but nobody in Ulster, outside a certain number of fanatics and leaders, believes in any organised rebellion, active or passive." Further, the Tories were bluffing ; Sir Edward Carson had " powerful enemies . in his own ranks " ; his movement had been losing ground when Lord Loreburn came to his rescue ; he

flattered Mr. Asquith on his " firmness " and ended
by expressing his " strongest conviction " that " any
offer at this moment of concessions would bring
disaster to our cause " and give " new strength and
new hope to the Orange movement."

This memorandum was sent to Mr. Asquith on
the 24th November, 1913, and the very next day
brought Mr. Lloyd George from the Cabinet in a
panic. The Cabinet, indeed, or so the Chancellor of
the Exchequer reported, were unanimous in agreeing with Mr. Redmond that any suggestions or
proposals by the Government " at the present
juncture " would be " a fatal step in tactics " ;
nothing, therefore, " for the present." But " the
time would come when some offer would have to be
made—sooner than we thought."

We can hear in imagination the dramatic whisper
in which Mr. Lloyd George proceeded to tell Mr.
Redmond that " the Government had discovered
ninety-five thousand rounds of ammunition in
Belfast," that they had made up their minds to seize
it ; that " the next move of Sir Edward Carson
would be to hold a review of armed men " ; that the
Government intended to suppress it at any cost ;
that they would " issue any necessary proclamation
and use any force." But—and here Mr. Lloyd
George came to the real purpose of the interview
—the Cabinet felt that when the time came to
use these " coercive methods " . . . " it would be
necessary to accompany them by some offer to
Ulster."

Then began a notable tussle between the Irishman
and the Welshman.

Mr. Lloyd George, Mr. Redmond notes, " argued
strongly in favour of his own proposal, and sought

to lead me to believe that it had the approval of the Cabinet generally."

Mr. Redmond, who had been told the contrary by the Prime Minister, " did not argue the matter " with the Chancellor, " further than to say that I stood absolutely on my memorandum."

Then Mr. Lloyd George threw his colleagues into the scale : " He told me that, under certain circumstances, if no offer were made, Sir Edward Grey, Lord Haldane, Mr. Winston Churchill—and, inferentially, I gathered, himself—might resign, which would mean a general *débâcle*, which would be a very serious thing for Home Rule and for me personally."

To this threat John Redmond was equal :

" I pointed out to him that, so far as I personally was concerned, the consequences would not be nearly so serious as they would be for him personally, that the *débâcle* would mean the end of his career and the end of the Liberal Party for a generation—perhaps, indeed, for ever."[1]

" The end of the Liberal Party "—that indeed Mr. Lloyd George might have faced ; but " the end of his career " ! Before a retort so devastating he appears to have quailed. " He admitted this," says Mr. Redmond grimly. " I think I made an impression on him."

The Irish leader had, indeed, for the moment, made up its mind for the Cabinet.

Next day Mr. Asquith wrote to Redmond a reassuring reply to his memorandum, not indeed quite satisfactory, but promising that there would be no offer to Mr. Bonar Law " at this stage," and on the 27th November, Mr. Birrell—probably sent by

[1] Denis Gwynn, *Life of John Redmond*, p. 238.

Mr. Asquith—saw Mr. Redmond and smoothed down his ruffled hackles : " he discounted a great deal—in fact most " of what Mr. Lloyd George had said, and assured the still suspicious Irishman that " the Cabinet had never even considered the adoption of Mr. Lloyd George's proposal " : that there was " very strong and bitter opposition to it."

Thus the English Ministers propitiated the Irish leader, even to the point of impugning one another's veracity—and giving away the secrets to which they were sworn.

In the meantime the public controversy went on. On the 7th November, Sir Edward Carson was at Dundee. There was a significance in the meeting not lost upon keen politicians, for whereas Mr. Churchill had declined to have Mr. Redmond in his constituency, the President and Chairman and the chief members of Mr. Churchill's Committee were honoured guests (in an opera box) at Carson's meeting in the King's Theatre. " It did not matter," Carson declared, " if he were called a rebel so long as he could go into such a clean Scottish audience and get such a kind reception."

Carson, indeed, seems to have thoroughly enjoyed his situation.

" The speaker " (according to the *Glasgow Herald*) " was obviously stimulated by the fine spirit of the large audience ! . . . There was noted a friendliness almost in the references to the Prime Minister and the First Lord of the Admiralty." Carson, in fact, was trying to divide the Liberals from their Irish allies. He made play with their differences. The Solicitor-General (Sir Stanley Buckmaster) had been prepared for exclusion ; but Mr. Devlin, who had been on that learned gentleman's Yorkshire platform, had said that " he would rather cut off his right hand, or was it his head, than leave Ulster out," and Carson went on to remind his audience that this same Devlin had admitted that " he only wanted to get control under Home Rule of the police and the judiciary . . . to destroy the last link that bound Great Britain and Ireland."

On November 21st, there was a great meeting at Birmingham, at which Austen Chamberlain (who presided) read out a message from his father— " Hold fast and fight hard." Bonar Law modestly described Carson as " the real leader of our fight to-day," and Carson appealed in that great centre of England to the old English spirit : he hoped that in the thrilling and dangerous times before them, " he and they might shake hands across the sea with those men whose only ambition was to remain within the Constitution, and against whom the only charge that could be made was that in all the darkness of past history they had stood by the flag."

There are in those speeches, had we the space to dwell upon them, many passages of dramatic fire, many touches of sardonic humour, as when he claimed that he had the business men of Ireland behind him—all but Lord Pirrie, who had long received his peerage, and who was no doubt, " down in the County of Surrey, with Mr. Lloyd George, mapping out his deer park."

The passage, however, of the greatest interest in that visit to Birmingham was not in public but in private. Edward Carson went to see Joseph Chamberlain, and found the veteran, paralysed, almost speechless, yet still glowing under the ashes of an inward fire. Carson took his hand and bent over him, and the old man contrived to articulate, with a pause between each word :

" Do . . . you . . . know . . . what . . . I . . . would . . . do . . . if . . . I . . . were . . . with . . . you ? "

" No, sir," said Carson.

" I . . . would . . . fight . . . it . . . out . . . to . . . the . . . finish," said Chamberlain.

CHAPTER XVI

THE BRITISH ARMY

Walter Long—F. S. Oliver—The Army—Professor Dicey—Lord Milner—
Military opinion—Sir Henry Wilson.

THERE WERE many Englishmen who thought
with Joseph Chamberlain at that time, that the
Union was worth a fight, even a fight to the finish.
One of the most ardent and implacable was Walter
Long, to whom any talk of negotiation seemed to
hint at some compromise unworthy of true men.
We find him writing from his native Wiltshire on
the 26th November, 1913, asking Carson to allow
his eldest son, Captain Long, D.S.O., Royal Scots
Greys, " to have a little talk with you about Ulster
and the Army—if I may venture to say so, I think it
would not be a waste of your time.

" Asquith," Walter Long went on, " is apparently
determined to force civil war ! We must surely
now make up our minds as to our course, not so
much in the country, this is clear, but in the House :
I hope it will be," Long concluded, " no quarter,
war to the knife against a Parliament not of statesmen but of cold-blooded murderers."

Mr. F. S. Oliver, the accomplished author of
Alexander Hamilton, who might be thought to
represent the well-weighed opinion of more deep-
thinking men, wrote on the 27th November to tell
Carson that " during the last year at least ; and
especially during the last six months, it has seemed

to me that you have done more for peace and a honourable settlement of the present trouble than any man—than any ten men—in politics or out of it."

Oliver had approached the Irish question as a Federalist ; but he no doubt saw by that time that the issues at stake were too deep and too fierce for any such solution. On the 4th December, 1913, he writes again :

"Your view with regard to the effect of 'equality of treatment' on Ulster opinion is naturally very welcome to one of my way of thinking.

"I am very glad of what you said in your speech on this subject last night : also for what you said about the Army. There is a real danger, I think, that the Liberals may succeed—if they are not checked in time—in spreading abroad the idea that Ulster is gambling on Army discontent, and treating it as an asset in the party game. Our amiable opponents are trying this very hard just now, and your words will, I hope, not only discourage them, but impress the country very favourably when they are properly driven home and fully considered."

Carson, as we have seen, had already had a hint from Mr. Walter Long, and no doubt more than a hint from his son, of what was going on in the Army. He had letters besides from officers, both naval and military, offering their services to Ulster ; and always replied to them with the advice that they should stick to their posts. One case, however, was more complicated, and required different treatment. It

happened that a young English officer, Captain
Wilfrid Spender, who had passed through the
Staff College and served on the General Staff in
the War Office, feeling strongly on the subject, had
signed the British Covenant in support of Ulster.
On going to India, he thought it his duty to tell
his commanding officer of this contingent obligation. The question passed as such questions do pass,
from one file to another, until in the end Captain
Spender found himself before the Secretary of State
for War. He had been offered a brilliant appointment by the Military Secretary, and Colonel
Seely congratulated him on the promise of a brilliant
career. The young man expressed himself as delighted ; but had the indiscretion to add that he
hoped the occasion would never arise when he
might find himself called upon to fulfil his pledge
of service to Ulster.

Colonel Seely—it is not surprising—lost his
temper, and the upshot was that Captain Spender,
considering his career at an end, asked permission
to be allowed to retire ; it was refused and he was
told he must resign his commission—which he
felt as a slur on his good name.

In these circumstances, he applied to Carson
for advice. " I ought to add," he wrote, " that
the attitude I have adopted throughout has been
entirely independent of your action, and that
consequently I have no justification in applying
to you, except as an ordinary client." On Carson's
advice, he appealed to the King, was given permission to retire and was put upon the Reserve of
Officers. Moreover, by Carson's good offices, he
was given an appointment on the Staff of the Ulster
Volunteer Force.

That the feeling in the Army was known also to the Government, we find from the interview, of 17th November, 1913, between the Prime Minister and John Redmond :

"... His (Mr. Asquith's) information from the War Office with regard to the attitude of the Army was of a serious character, pointing to the probability of very numerous resignations of commissions of officers in the event of the troops being used to put down an Ulster insurrection. Some of the authorities estimated the number of these resignations as high as 30 per cent. He did not believe in anything like this figure, but he was satisfied that there would be a number of resignations."[1]

Thus there was a certain painful element of likelihood in the tactless and disagreeable comparison drawn by Mr. Bonar Law (at Dublin on the 28th November) between Mr. Asquith and King James II : " King James had behind him," said the Conservative leader, " the letter of the law just as completely as Mr. Asquith has now. . . . In order to carry out his despotic intention the King had the largest Army that had ever been seen in England. What happened ? There was no civil war. There was a revolution, and the King disappeared. Why ? Because his own Army refused to fight for him."

The Liberals, making the most of this indiscretion, accused the Conservative Party of carrying on a propaganda among the officers of the Army, which the Conservatives as hotly denied. " They tell us," said Carson (in that speech to which Fred Oliver referred),[2] " that we are trying to tamper with the Army. It is a foul lie. . . . It would be a bad day

---

[1] Denis Gwynn, *The Life of John Redmond*, p. 236.
[2] At Manchester, 3rd December, 1913.

for the country that the Army, under any circumstances, should refuse to obey the lawful orders of
those who are put in command over them. Of course
they must. . . . No one will blame the Army for
shooting upon Ulstermen ; but the country will
hold the Government that puts forward the Army
responsible."

These " most honest and true words," as he
wrote of them, brought a letter from Professor
Dicey, then an old man. " I have long felt," said
that great authority on our Constitution, " that it
would be a bad day indeed for the country if the
Army were to refuse to obey any lawful orders.
I indeed regretted, to speak quite candidly, that
anything should be said at all about even the possible disloyalty of the Army, for I have always
entertained the strongest conviction that in a
civilised country obedience to lawful orders was
the absolute duty of soldiers and that the British
Army would, in circumstances however painful,
fulfil this duty. . . . It is this which makes me
personally grateful that you, who can speak with
the highest authority, have uttered your opinion
with such outspoken plainness."

Then Dicey went on to discuss the conversations
which we shall have presently to consider :

" I am on the other hand," he wrote, " filled with
fear by the very notion of negotiations, and, above
all, of private negotiations, with the Government.
I have no doubt that Ministers are frightened ; but
I cannot hold that it is the duty of Unionists to
help them out of the scrape into which their
ignorance and their partisanship has led them. You
naturally and rightly fix your mind upon the wrong
with which Ulster is threatened. I must admit that

as naturally, and I hope as rightly, my mind is filled with indignation at the wrong actually being done to the people of the United Kingdom. I hold that the whole spirit of the Constitution is violated by the refusal to dissolve Parliament so as to ascertain the will of the electors with regard to this Home Rule Bill, and with regard to the whole policy of Home Rule. In spite of Asquith's misrepresentations, such a dissolution would be strictly within the meaning, and I venture to say also the spirit, of the Parliament Act, open as that act is to the severest criticism."

This letter, dated the 9th December, 1913, was followed by another on the 15th, which expresses such doubts as many an Englishman must have held : " I entirely feel and share your difficulty," Dicey wrote. " I have long thought over the point you raise ; I have even rather more difficulty than probably you feel as to how an Englishman may, if the Home Rule Act, even without a General Election, should be passed into law, rightly supply money and aid to what would be technically rebellion in Ulster, though I believe it would be rebellion which, on the part of Ulster, would be morally justifiable. I mention this personal scruple because I know it is a duty to be entirely candid with you. We all know that our leader, Mr. Bonar Law, and most Unionists, do not entertain this scruple. I certainly hope to be able to feel with them if ever the crisis arises which makes the question which is before my mind a practical one ; but I have through life so earnestly preached the duty of obedience to law that I do not feel sure what would be my duty in the case I have supposed but which will, I trust, never arise."

Carson had evidently posed the question what was to be done, and may have smiled grimly at the philosophic ease of the reply : " I still hold that the Unionists have not yet done enough to force upon the people of England the absolute necessity for a dissolution of Parliament. The demand is to my mind absolutely just ; it affords the only legal and certain way of avoiding civil war." He to whom the advice was tendered had certainly done all that man could do to bring the issue before the country. Dicey went on to admit as " certain " that Asquith would not advise a dissolution before the Home Rule Bill became law. For that reason there must be " desperate agitation for dissolution in every county and borough . . . petition upon petition . . . the King should be publicly petitioned to dissolve Parliament. . . . I entirely agree that the King can do nothing except on the advice of Ministers. I totally disagree with the doctrine drawn from this principle that he can never dismiss Ministers in order that he may ascertain the will of the nation. Of course, the incoming Ministers must, like Sir Robert Peel, accept responsibility for the change of Ministry. No one need be ashamed of following the principle set by Pitt and Peel." It was an expedient for the rarest occasions ; but the case under consideration was one of them.

Then Dicey went on to discuss through several serried pages the various Parliamentary expedients which might be attempted, ending with the admission that " even the voting for the amendment excluding Ulster is open to some objection, still I doubt not that a Unionist may do this with honour."

It was all very sage and very learned ; but Carson, almost as good a constitutional lawyer as Dicey, knew how futile it all was, without the threat of force behind.

Another letter, of a more practical turn, came from Lord Milner (written from Duke Street on the 9th December, 1913, and marked " very confidential ") :

" MY DEAR CARSON,—It seems an awful thing to suggest, to a man who must be so overwhelmed as you are, but I should immensely value 10 minutes quite straight and confidential talk with you.

" Let me quite briefly explain my position. For all ordinary purposes, I have done with politics. But the business we have been brought face to face with goes far deeper than ordinary party struggles.

" *I am completely in accord with you about Ulster,* and what I want to know is whether there is not something which men like myself, who disbelieve in mere talk at this juncture, can do to help you.

" I don't think the Government are serious in their advances. I think they are just passing the time. If they are not serious, there must very soon, certainly in less than a year, be what would be technically a 'rebellion' in Ulster. It would be a disaster of the first magnitude if that 'rebellion,' which would really be the uprising of unshakable principle and devoted patriotism—of loyalty to the Empire and the Flag—were to fail ! But it must fail unless we can *paralyse the arm* which might be raised to strike you. How are we to do it ? That requires forethought and organisation *over here.* You may say ' Why can't you make a plan for yourselves ? I have surely hay enough on

Qa

my fork.' Quite, quite true. And I don't want to waste your time or add to your burdens in any way. Indeed I think people over here had better act, in appearance at any rate, independently of you. But I, for one, can't even make a plan without knowing a little more than I do of the probable course of affairs on your side. And volumes of correspondence, for which you have no time, would not enlighten me as much as a single interview.

" Please realise (1) that I am speaking entirely for myself (2) that this thing *goes very deep with me.* I can honestly say there is nothing I personally desire except *retirement.* I am getting old, I am not very well, and I am dead sick of party politics. But if I can see my way to being of any real use in this matter, no personal consideration shall be allowed to count."

It would appear that Carson proposed to Milner that he should go to Belfast, since there is a letter, of the 1st January, 1914, declining the invitation, as " for the moment I think I am of more use here. I have got a little bit of a move on, and I don't want to go away from London more than I absolutely must, till I see that this thing has some momentum of its own."

There was a thing of " some momentum " going forward at that time with which these statesmen had nothing or little to do. The Army was thinking. When officers wrote to Carson, as some wrote, offering their services, in case of civil war, he advised them not to consider hypothetical questions; but to keep their commissions. Despite the Liberal accusations, I can find no trace in his correspondence or his speeches of any design to interfere with discipline : he took the simple line that it was the part of the Army to obey, the part of Ulster to resist and the part of the country to intervene. Such in the briefest terms seems to have been his expectation of what would happen. But there were many in the Army and out of it—reckless fellows ! —who thought differently. We get a glimpse into their minds from a passage in one of Tim Healy's letters :

" An Englishman (nephew of a peer) said to me," Healy wrote on January 26th, 1914, " there would be a civil war in England as well as in Ireland, and that Willoughby de Broke and his men would ride up to London and attack Asquith, and that the soldiers would not resist ! I never heard such dire threats."

The nephew of the peer may have been pulling Tim's leg ; but there was, as a fact, little love lost between the Liberal Party of that time and an Army which it pinched in peace and had insulted in war. The Liberal slanders about " methods of barbarism," " hecatombs of slaughtered babes " in South Africa still warmed the ears of the soldiers. But there was a more potent source of trouble in the circumstance that the Army was at that time largely officered by the Irish gentry. It was at once their pride and their livelihood : when the Land Acts deprived them of their functions as landowners, almost their only occupation. From hundreds of old country houses hidden away among the hills and loughs, green pastures and green groves of Ireland, the youth of a fighting stock, generation after generation, went up to Sandhurst and

Woolwich, and thence into every branch of the Army. They went far and rose high—and almost to a man they were Loyalists. Home Rule was not for them a political question ; as in the case of Carson, it touched and revolted an instinct of preservation, a tradition centuries old, something in the blood— even stronger than their ingrained duty of obedience —a matter of life and death. They were everywhere —at Camberley and the War Office as well as in the line. Lord Roberts, whom they venerated and idolised was one of them—the great little veteran was whole-hearted and outspoken for Ulster ; the brilliant and magnetic Henry Wilson was another.

On November 4th, 1913, we find Wilson that day gazetted Major-General, talking the matter over with Sir John French, then Chief of the Imperial General Staff :

" Sir John," the Director of Military Operations notes in his diary, " had a long talk with me about Ulster. He is evidently nervous that we are coming to Civil War, and his attitude appears to be that he will obey the King's orders. He wanted to know what I would do. I told him that I could not fire on the North at the dictation of Redmond, and this is what the whole thing means. England *qua* England is opposed to Home Rule, and England must agree to it before it is carried out. I was much struck by his seriousness. I *cannot* bring myself to believe that Asquith will be so mad as to employ force. It will split the Army and the colonies, as well as the country and the Empire."

If the Chiefs of the War Office were talking thus, it is easy to imagine the talk of the mess-rooms. The Liberal press put it down to the incendiarism of Bonar Law and Carson, and to those social influences which were supposed to radiate from Lansdowne House and Hatfield. As to the former, we have reviewed the evidence ; as to the latter, it is true that the Army, as far as it had any politics, was Conservative, its officers being drawn in the main from the country houses of rural England. Lord Lansdowne and the Cecils—it will be allowed —were too well drilled in the constitutional proprieties to sanction any such propaganda ; but Lord Willoughby de Broke and his fox-hunting friends were probably less restrained. Moreover, the Conservative ladies—as a general rule more agreeable to the military mind than their austerer Liberal sisters—were no doubt talking. Women, as George Meredith said, will be the last things to be civilised by men, and pay but little respect to the law and the Constitution.

There were some officers, as we shall presently see, who would put discipline before everything— much as they might hate their orders ; but the Army was undoubtedly divided in its heart and conscience. As for the rank and file, for their own reasons, they were with their officers. They knew their garrison towns—that in Belfast they were welcome ; that in Dublin, where their flags and their uniforms were apt to be insulted, they had to mind their step.

All these things might be said to flow, according to the point of view, from the propaganda of the Opposition or from the policy of the Government : they were a serious fact, more or less realised by Bonar Law and Carson on the one side and by Asquith and John Redmond on the other.

CHAPTER XVII

MINISTERIAL ALARM

Mr. Asquith is firm—Dublin again—Lord Midleton—The Southern Unionists—Chorus of compromise—Thoughts on Prosecution—Carson at Plymouth—The invitation.

ON THE 14TH OCTOBER, 1913, Mr. Asquith met Mr. Bonar Law in secret at Max Aitken's house ; on 6th November they met again, and parted " in good will but in no very sanguine spirit " ; on 17th November, Mr. Asquith had the interview already recorded with John Redmond, and assured him " that he would under no circumstances make any proposal to the other side, except after the fullest consultation with me."[1] On November 26th, he gave assurance in writing : " There is no question at this stage of making any ' offer ' or proposal to Mr. Bonar Law, though I may think it expedient to finish the conversation with him which was not broken off at our last interview "[2] ; on the 27th November he addressed the National Liberal Federation at Leeds, and made a speech which both Bonar Law and Carson took to be the end of these negotiations. Mr. Asquith was firm ; Mr. Asquith was strong ; a General Election he denounced as " neither constitutionally necessary nor practically expedient." " We are not," he went on, " dissatisfied with the Government of Ireland Bill as it stands ; we are not going to be frightened,

---

[1] Denis Gwynn, *Life of John Redmond*, p. 235.   [2] Ibid., p. 238.

arrested or deflected by menaces of Civil War. We are not going to make any surrender of principle. We mean to see the thing through." He reminded the Army of its duty to obey orders ; he was willing to admit that Sir Edward Carson was a " single-minded man " ; but his attitude was not in the least likely to impress " either the imaginations or the judgements of my fellow countrymen." And again :

" Our attitude in this matter, now or hereafter, has not been and will not be attended by a moment's doubt either as to the duty or as to the power of the State to ensure obedience to the Law of the Land." There was a deprecatory reference to his previous invitation to a " free and unprejudiced interchange from all sides of views and suggestions " ; but " I should be deceiving you and deceiving my-self if I were to say that I see at this moment a prospect of agreement."

Two days later Bonar Law and Carson were in Dublin at what was described as " the most impres-sive and significant demonstration ever held South of the Boyne." The Unionist Societies of Leinster, Munster and Connaught presented Mr. Bonar Law with some forty addresses in the great dining-room of Lord Iveagh's house ; the two leaders were entertained to a luncheon at the famous City and County Conservative Club in Kildare Street, and at night there was a huge meeting at the Theatre Royal with Lord Barrymore in the chair.

The ancient capital and seat of British power in Ireland had reason to be anxious. For months she had been at the mercy of Jim Larkin and his transport workers. At the bidding of " Liberty Hall," the headquarters of his Labour organisation, every trade in the city was liable to be paralysed by a lightning strike, and when W. M. Murphy had organised his fellow-employers to resist, a general and ferocious industrial and class war had brought the city to the verge of anarchy and ruin. Lord Aberdeen reigned supinely and miserably at the Viceregal Lodge ; Dublin Castle was demoralised by Nationalist influence on Liberal policy ; the riots had been handled with characteristic vacil- lation by Mr. Birrell, who had " imprisoned Mr. Larkin to please the Nationalists of Ireland, and released him to please the Socialists of England."

That night the police drew a cordon round the Theatre, where a queue of Unionists stretched for a quarter of a mile nearly to O'Connell Bridge, threatened by mobs of Nationalists and " Larkin- ites," armed with stones, who broke the windows of the tram-cars and jeered at the Loyalists, but did not dare to risk a fight.

It was in such tense circumstances that Bonar Law and Carson gave their reply to the Prime Minister. The former, in his rasping way, made a shrewd enough guess at the situation of the Govern- ment. " There must be," he said, " not only a bar gain with the Nationalists, but some evidence of it in writing which would damn them if ever it came out." He had accepted the offer to go to Ladybank in the belief that Mr. Asquith not only desired a settlement, but had hopes of securing it. After the Leeds speech he thought so no longer. Carson warned Mr. Asquith not to talk about compromise again till he had the consent of Mr. Redmond : " He had far better ' toe the line ' and never take it away."

Then once more he expressed the belief to which

he still clung that Ulster was the key to the situation, that in her resistance lay the hope of safety, not only for herself, but for the South. " If you carry this Home Rule Bill," he said, " you never can enforce it so long as Ulster is firm. Ulster will stand firm to the end."

There were those in the theatre who shouted— " So will Dublin ! " and Carson knew well that there were Loyalists in the South who were prepared to fight, and, if need be, to die for the Union ; but he knew also the weak position of that scattered minority. It is to be remembered that Carson was not, at that time or ever, the accepted leader of the Southern Irish Loyalists. He was, indeed, the Senior Member for Trinity College, Dublin; he was also leader of the Irish Unionist Party in the House of Commons, but that Party was drawn, save for himself and one colleague, from the North of Ireland. A few days before this Dublin meeting, on November 11th, 1913, Lord Midleton had written to him (from Peper Harow, his place in Surrey) :

" In accordance with the feeling expressed that there should be some Committee or delegates representing the South and West of Ireland available for consultation. I saw Barrymore (who is now Chairman of Irish Unionist Alliance)— and he has moved as per enclosed which tells its own tale. *Please return it to me.*

" Lansdowne thinks it will give us what is wanted—a body whom you can invoke at any moment to give an opinion, or who in case of need could come over here to speak with some confidence as the representatives of the South and West.

" It occurred to me that possibly it might be wise, when we are all in Dublin on the 28th, if there were a private meeting with this Committee at which you could put any questions you wished & explain the difficulties of the situation, but this only you can judge.

" It is not very likely that the Cabinet can find any basis for a Conference ; but it would be of great value to the ' Shadow Cabinet,' if they do, to hear definite views from such a body.

" I tried to get a petition against Home Rule signed in Cork City by the 3,000 Unionists they have on the roll, but they in the end decided against it.

" This, in the opinion of several of our colleagues, would have been very useful on platforms.

" It might interest you that at a meeting of representatives from all the 6 Surrey Divisions, the question of any compromise on Home Rule was discussed last week, on the initiative of the Chairman of the evening, H. Samuel, M.P.— There was a most vehement and unanimous consensus against anything of the kind. About 40, including Cave, were present.

" This shows a little the difficulties we might have with our party."

A friendly letter, it may be said ; but it nevertheless suggested that Carson was not the leader of these Southern Unionists ; that they had a separate interest from those of the North, to be represented by a separate organisation, which Carson might consult, but of which he was not invited to be a member.

The difference gained a little in point and

emphasis when the representatives of the North and the South met in Carson's house at Eaton Place about that time to discuss a concert of policy. Before they went upstairs to the drawing-room where Carson awaited them, James Craig asked the representatives of the South if they would join under a common leadership.

They answered that their case was different.

"Yes," argued Craig, "I agree; but Carson, like a good doctor, will give to different patients different prescriptions."

Those Southern Unionists still refusing, they went upstairs together, and after some discussion, which seemed to be leading nowhere, Carson took a used envelope and a pencil from his pocket, saying that he desired to have one or two points clear.

"Is it your decision," he asked the Southern Unionists, "that I am to go on fighting for Ulster?" To this they answered "Yes."

He made his note, and went on—"Will my fight in Ulster interfere in any way with your fight in the South?" he asked them, and they answered "No."

He made another note.

"If I win," he proceeded, "am I to refuse the fruits of victory for Ulster because you have lost?" Here he pointed out that if the Ulstermen were asked to fight only to surrender at the end, it would take the heart out of their movement. And the Southern Loyalists, seeing the logic of the case, answered "No."

Then Carson completed his note, and put the scrap of paper back into his pocket, and from that time on, North and South drew more and more apart, the North marching to victory, the South drifting to destruction.

This, however, is to anticipate : as Carson looked upon that goodly gathering of old friends in the Theatre Royal, he could hardly foresee the full horror of their fate. Yet we gather from his own words that he felt the almost intolerable weight of these gathering burdens : " It sometimes fills me with anxiety so great," he said, " that I wonder if I shall have strength to bear it all." And we see him squaring his shoulders under it : " But I never, I hope, fail in courage, and when I read, day by day, words like Mr. Asquith's, that he will not be intimidated by force, I tell Mr. Asquith that I will not be intimidated by the Government. I have made up my mind long since. The men I have behind me have definitely made up their minds, and as every day brings nearer the climax, they grow the more hardened in their position and the more accustomed to facing the consequences."

This battle of words, covering the intenser struggle of wills, swayed back again from Dublin to England.

Asquith had put his foot down at Leeds ; but his colleagues, with less nerve, insisted on taking a hand in the negotiations : Lord Haldane, the Lord Chancellor, Sir John Simon, who had by that time succeeded Rufus Isaacs as Attorney-General, Mr. Herbert Samuel—they all made speeches, in " a chorus of compromise." Carson laughed at them all. " Every day," he said at Nottingham,[1] " I take up my paper, and I see, ' Behold the door is open.' The next day I see that it is shut. The next day I see it re-opened. The next day I see it slammed, and now it is closing. The open door to what ? I don't want an open door. I want to know what is inside." And at Manchester : " I certainly understood, as

[1] On 5th December, 1913.

a sort of innocent Irishman, that Mr. Asquith, by his speech at Leeds meant to put an end altogether to this idea of compromises. . . . But something has happened. . . . Let them put it down in black and white. We are plain men in Ulster, and we ask for nothing more than to be left alone. Let them put down in black and white the minimum of interference they are prepared to offer. If they don't do that, I would rather see them break off this talk altogether, and let us, if necessary, fight—and fight to a finish."

They had been called " bluffers," Carson went on grimly : " I have often seen one bluffer, or two bluffers ; but I have never seen 90,000 drawn up in one line."

Then Carson proceeded to set forth his own ideas of a settlement :

They had to consider the Union—" essential to the greatness of their country " ;

They had to consider Ulster—" Ulstermen have never shown themselves cowards, and I leave the subject there " ;

They had to consider the Loyalists throughout the rest of Ireland—" while we give prominence to Ulster for what they have done, remember that in the great difficulties and through the great dangers —personal dangers and dangers to property—these men in the South have kept the old flag flying, and they have allowed none to haul it down."

They must have a " national settlement—no settlement which would humiliate or degrade us " ; no treatment " different or exceptional from the treatment offered to any other or all parts of the United Kingdom."

Here Carson laid down in one comprehensive

sentence the principles of a settlement acceptable to both countries.

" We must have preserved to us, what every other citizen has, neither more nor less ; we must have the same protection of the Imperial Parliament, and above all—and it is here our loyalty to you comes in—we must have no Bill or no Act which establishes a foundation for the ultimate separation of your country and ours."

This proposal was made on the 3rd December, 1913 ; obviously distant as its principles were from the course which the Government had been following, it may have seemed to distracted minds to offer at least a hope of compromise. A few days later the Prime Minister at Manchester quoted Carson's conditions and said that he was not in principle inclined to quarrel with them ; he insisted, however, that there must be no surrender of the " essential principles of the Bill." " I am glad to see," said Carson drily, " that he has got back to what has been called his Ladybank form."[1]

There were good reasons for these ministerial vacillations. The Ulster Volunteer Force, " 90,000 in line," was plain for all to see ; they had information besides of five thousand rifles and 95,000 rounds of ammunition smuggled into Ulster ; they had heard from the War Office, what they must have thought even more serious, that anything up to 30 per cent of the Army officers would rather resign their commissions than put down an Ulster insurrection ; they knew also that the Irish Nationalists of the South were also drilling and bringing in arms. Ireland was plainly drifting into anarchy, rebellion and civil war.

[1] At Plymouth, 9th December, 1913.

Mr. Asquith had long been urged to prosecute
Sir Edward Carson; the Liberal press alternated
between jeers at " bluff " and " wooden guns "
and demands that the arch rebel should be put
upon his trial. Mr. J. A. Spender, chief supporter
of the Government in the press, maintained the
view that a " prolonged threat of armed resistance
and open preparation for it " was " deeply de-
moralising," and Mr. Asquith could not, to himself,
deny it. " It would not have been at all difficult,"
he said, long afterwards, " to draw up an indict-
ment, or a series of alternative indictments, in
respect of what had been said and done in Ireland.
The charge or charges could have been framed so
as to be technically watertight, and they " could
have been proved up to the hilt, by clear, and indeed
uncontroverted evidence."

Would an Irish jury convict? was a question
which troubled Mr. Asquith a little ; but what
troubled him more were the political considerations. The Irish Nationalists would not have it :
" We were working through all those eventful years,
in close co-operation and substantial harmony
with the leaders of the Nationalist party. . . . They
were throughout insistent in deprecating criminal
proceedings against the Carsonites, on the ground
that such a step could do no good, and that it
would inevitably secure for the victims an in-
valuable and much coveted place in the annals of
Irish martyrology."[1]

We shall presently have to consider the hypothesis that some of his colleagues proposed to
arrest Carson, with or without the assent of the
Prime Minister ; but Mr. Asquith himself was

[1] *Fifty Years of Parliament,* vol. ii., ch. v, pp. 139–42.

always against it. Long afterwards, when greater
events had reconciled them, he talked this matter
out with Carson and said that he had never intended to prosecute because he feared that he could
not procure a conviction.

" You need have had no fear," said Carson,
" for I should have pleaded guilty."

" Guilty ! " said Mr. Asquith in astonishment.

" Yes," Carson replied, " I should have pleaded
guilty, and I should have said, ' My Lord Judge,
and gentlemen of the Jury : I was born under the
British flag, a loyal subject of His Majesty the King.
So much do I value this birthright that I was even
prepared to rebel in order to defend it. If to fight,
so as to remain, like yourselves, a loyal subject
of His Majesty, be a crime, my Lord, and gentlemen of the Jury, I plead guilty.' And where,"
added Carson, " would you have been then ? "

" That only shows," replied Asquith, " that I
was even wiser in not prosecuting you than I
thought I was."

There was another reason why the Government
hesitated to arrest Carson ; they knew him to be a
restraining influence in Ulster. Thus when Mr.
Birrell was approached by a deputation with the
proposal that if he put Jim Larkin in jail, he should
also imprison Carson, the Chief Secretary replied
by contrasting the state of the two cities. " Belfast,"
he said, " is in peace and calm : nobody's life and
property are in danger."

The Prime Minister, then, did not care or dare
to prosecute; but he had to do something, with his
whole press and party clamouring for action.
As the result of a Cabinet meeting, a Royal Proclamation prohibiting the importation of arms

into Ireland was promulgated in the *London Gazette* of December 5th, 1913.

It was not, considering the state of the case, an impressive demonstration. Carson jeered at it in his Irish way. " Do you think I mind that proclamation," he said, that same night at Nottingham, " No, my lord, you won't gain over the English people to the use of coercion on unarmed people any more than you will on armed." And three days afterwards Carson explained to the people of Plymouth, more in detail, what he thought of this " great proclamation."

" I want to point out to you that a comparatively short time ago there was an Act in force, called the Peace Preservation Act, to regulate in Ireland the whole question of the distribution and the registration of arms.

" When this Government came into power, the Nationalist Party, who keep them in power, said to the Government—' It is contrary to all liberty that there should be in force an Act regulating the distribution of arms in Ireland, and we call upon you to repeal it.'

" And the Government said ' Certainly.'

" That was in the year 1906, and for seven years, at the dictation of the Nationalist Party, they have allowed the Leaguers, the Moonlighters and the Cattle-drivers to arm as much as they please, because their policy was not to stay with England, but to get away from England, and therefore it was right that they should be armed.

" Then they found that we were armed, but our ambition was to stay with England." (Here Plymouth cheered.) " What a disgraceful ambition !

" So the Nationalists came forward and said,

Rc

' We are fully armed in the last six years. Look at these criminals, like Carson, in the North of Ireland. We are told that they are getting in arms, and they are pretending to be drilling. Surely, Mr. Asquith, you are not going to allow this to go on ? '

" ' Certainly not,' he said." . . .

Then Carson turned to matters more serious. " I know well," he said, " that to-morrow, if I desired to do so—which certainly I do not— the men in Belfast and the North of Ireland, pledged to me as they are, and I to them, would take any step that I deliberately asked them.

" Mr. Devlin said last night—whether cynically or sarcastically, or as imputing some sort of cowardice to me—that ' Sir Edward Carson did not want to lead rebellion or a civil war as he called it.' No, Mr. Chairman, I do not, and no man wants to lead a rebellion or a civil war unless he is a knave or a fool.

" But if I am driven to it—if not only my honour is involved, but my civil and religious liberty and that of hundreds and thousands of those who think with me—I declare here that I do not even shrink from the horrors of civil commotion. We will never abandon the essential and elementary rights of citizenship."

And he went on to make what was evidently meant as an offer to the Prime Minister :

" But any offer that is made consistent with these rights, and preserving these rights to us on the basis that I have laid down, I promise to submit to my fellow-countrymen in Ireland, and it will be for them to decide whether the proposals are worth consideration."

Carson, throughout, had been, as Bonar Law had said, the real leader in this great fight for the Union : it is noteworthy that this offer at Plymouth was made on the night of December 8th, 1913 ; on the 10th December Asquith had a last despondent meeting with Bonar Law, and that same day wrote the following letter :

" *Confidential.*   10 Downing Street,
                             " Whitehall, S.W.
                                  " *10th December, 1913.*

" MY DEAR CARSON,—Would it be possible for you to have a little talk with me under conditions of strict confidence ? I would not make the suggestion unless I thought that the public interest justified it.

" I could arrange that there should be no publicity.

                    " Yours very sincerely,
                              " H. H. ASQUITH."

The door which had been opened at Ladybank and closed at Leeds was again ajar. Was there anything inside ?

CHAPTER XVIII

SECRET NEGOTIATIONS

Interviews—Queen Anne's Gate—" Five hundred Ulstermen "—" Not a word of truth "—Suggestions for settlement—The refusal—Beyond doubt.

IT MUST SEEM STRANGE that on the day— December 10th, 1913—he ended with Mr. Bonar Law, that very day Mr. Asquith should have opened with Sir Edward Carson. And such accounts of the interviews as survive do not explain this sudden change from the old love to the new. What we gather is that in his last conversation Mr. Bonar Law was even more despondent than in the first. " He took the gloomiest view," says Mr. Spender, " not only of the extremists, but of the rank and file of both parties." Asquith, we are told further, " broached the Federal Solution "; and Mr. Bonar Law, " now sure that there was no solution that way," held out for " the definite exclusion of the specified area with option to come in later."[1]

It is another curious feature of these conversations that while Mr. Bonar Law continued to press in public for another General Election, he seems to have made but a feeble attempt to persuade Mr. Asquith to that end.

On November 6th, according to Mr. Spender, " Mr. Bonar Law broached the idea of a General Election before the beginning of the next session.

[1] *Life of Lord Oxford and Asquith*, vol. ii., p. 37.

" Asquith thought it the worst possible solution, if an agreed settlement were desired.

" Mr. Bonar Law admitted that the best he hoped for from an election was a balance of parties ; but that, he thought, would make compromise inevitable.

" Asquith rejoined that compromise would be even more difficult after the bad blood of an embittered election."[1]

According to Mr. Redmond—who had it from the Prime Minister—Mr. Bonar Law admitted even more—" that it was the opinion of himself and of all his responsible friends that if a General Election were held, the Government would be again returned to power, but with a reduced majority, and they hoped in these circumstances that the Government would be in a sufficiently chastened mood to agree to a compromise on Home Rule."

To that Mr. Asquith's retort was natural—that " after all the bitterness of the fight, and having gained another victory, the Liberal Party would not tolerate any compromise of any sort or kind."[2]

It is fair to say that we have not Mr. Bonar Law's version of these conversations. The by-elections at that time do not reveal any ground for such prognostications, and an observer as shrewd as he was impartial on this subject, held a different view of the political prospects—Tim Healy wrote to his brother on Christmas Day, 1913 : " I fear Carson's bluff will win, and then the Tories will be in office before twelve months." When we remember, however, that Conservative opinion was still divided over a fiscal issue that united the Liberals, and that,

[1] Ibid., p. 36.
[2] Denis Gwynn, *Life of John Redmond*, p. 234.

on the 11th October, 1913, Mr. Lloyd George had opened his formidable and resounding " land campaign," we find it less difficult to believe that the feet of some of the Conservatives were cold and that Mr. Bonar Law's inveterate gloom intensified their despondency.

In these circumstances the Prime Minister could derive neither comfort nor assistance from the Leader of the Opposition ; but Mr. Bonar Law may have suggested to Mr. Asquith that he should apply to Sir Edward Carson as the true leader of the Unionist cause. So he had called him in public, and so might well call him in private.

This is to speculate : what we have on record is that Bonar Law told Asquith that he could not speak for his " extreme men " either in England or in Ulster ; but that " Carson was quite as anxious for a settlement as he was."[1] What, we may ask, could Asquith hope from such an interview ? He had promised Redmond in writing to make no " offer " or " proposal " at that stage ; he had told him that he was merely seeing Bonar Law to " finish the conversation," yet here he was, a fortnight later, opening another.

There was the same secrecy to be observed in the second negotiation as in the first.

" My dear Carson " (Asquith wrote again on the 15th December, 1913), " Many thanks for your letter. If the day and hour are convenient to you, will you kindly call to-morrow (Tuesday) afternoon at 3.30 at 24 Queen Anne's Gate (Mr. Montagu's house) and ask for me ? Yours ever sincerely, H. H. ASQUITH."

Edwin Montagu, at whose house the assignation

---

[1] Denis Gwynn, *Life of John Redmond*, p. 234.

was made, had been Parliamentary Secretary to the Prime Minister, and might no doubt be trusted with a secret which was not disclosed to John Redmond until the 2nd February following. Asquith then told Redmond that " of the two " (Carson and Bonar Law) " he had found Sir Edward Carson much the most satisfactory to deal with." Mr. Spender tells us that Asquith found Carson " on the whole less pessimistic " than Bonar Law. We are told further that " Sir Edward dwelt on the need of a real settlement which would not be followed by continued agitation " ; and that he also suggested the exclusion of specified Ulster counties "until the Imperial Parliament should otherwise determine in pursuance of some general scheme of devolution."

In the absence of any record, I can only say that in Carson's recollection the conversation was " general," leading nowhere : he does, however, recall one passage, no doubt characteristic.

" I have no doubt, Mr. Prime Minister," said Carson, " you have thought out very carefully what you intend to do, when they resist your Bill in Ulster, and when the first five hundred Ulstermen are shot down in Belfast. . . ."

" My God," said Asquith, jumping up in alarm. " Five hundred ! I tell you that if one Ulsterman was shot in such a quarrel, it would be a disaster of the first magnitude."

Two days later Mr. Asquith wrote again :

" I have thought over our conversation, and it seems to me that, before we meet again, it might facilitate matters if I put down on paper and send you a few rough suggestions. This I hope to do in the course of the next few days. They will be (of course) without prejudice on either side, and I understand that you are, and will be, in close communication with Mr. Bonar Law."

It appears that this crossed a letter from Carson, which, in his sardonic way, may have mentioned the floating rumours of impending arrest as a possible obstacle to a further meeting. Mr. Asquith solicitously reassured him :

"*Confidential.*   10 Downing Street,
                          " Whitehall, S.W.
                          18th December, 1913.

"My dear Carson,—I have just received your letter. I may say at once that there is not a word of truth in the rumour to which you refer. Nor, indeed, so far as I know would there be any legal authority for such a proceeding, if it were contemplated (which it is not) by the Executive.

"I wrote you a line before I got your letter, this morning.

                          " Yours very sincerely,
                          " H. H. Asquith."

Then on the 23rd December, 1913, came the following letter from the same hand, marked " Secret " :

"In pursuance of what I wrote the other day, I now enclose, in the strictest confidence, some ' suggestions ' which have occurred to me. They have not been submitted to my colleagues (though I have talked to one or two of them on the subject) ; and they are entirely unknown to the Nationalist leaders.

"They are, therefore, as you will understand,

not put forward as proposals—which at this stage I have no authority to make—but as opening up the field for practical discussion, and inviting counter-suggestions to be made upon the same terms and in the same spirit.

" If after turning the matter over, you would like to see me and have another talk, I could arrange for an interview, perhaps on Tuesday, or on Friday, of next week.

" All good wishes of the season."

With this letter is enclosed the following note, also in Asquith's own hand :

" *Most Confidential.*   10 Downing Street,
                            " Whitehall, S.W.
" I. *General.*

" 1. Bill to be prefaced by declaration that it is expedient that the Imperial Parliament should, without prejudice to or impairment of its supreme authority, devolve, in the constituent parts of the United Kingdom, the management of local affairs to local bodies.

" 2. Remove from subjects within jurisdiction of Irish legislature and Executive
      (*a*) Post Office
      (*b*) Customs[1]

" 3. Make clear that in all cases where the Irish minority, or any section of it, allege grievance from either legislation or administrative action of new Irish authority, ultimate decision to be with Judge or Judges imperially appointed.

[1] (Compensation for possible loss to Irish Exchequer, in consequence of this change, might be found in the Imperial Exchequer taking a proportion (e.g. one-half) instead of the whole, of the normal increase in Irish revenue, during such time as the Irish account still showed a deficit.)

"II. *Ulster*.

"A ' statutory Ulster ' to be defined for purposes of Act. Its exact geographical boundaries may for the moment stand over.

"In what follows ' *Ulster* '= ' *Statutory Ulster.*'

"1. *Administration*.

"Until Imperial Parliament otherwise provides, in this area :

(*a*) Police—to continue as now.

(*b*) Factory and workshop and Board of Trade Inspection—as now.

(*c*) Education to be under Ulster Board— constituted on same lines as existing authority—responsible to Impl. Executive.

(*d*) Local Govt. Board Administration (if necessary) to be dealt with on the same lines as Education.

(*e*) Patronage (if desired) to be specially provided for.

"2. *Legislation*.

"The area to have the right of representation in the Irish Legislature ; the question of numbers and proportion—as proposed in the Bill—to admit of further consideration.

"Until Imperial Parliament otherwise provides, if majority of representatives of Ulster (as defined) dissent, as regards that area, from any legislation of the Irish legislature :

(*a*) imposing new, or increasing existing, taxation [1]

[1] An alternative suggestion, as regards Finance, would be, that (until otherwise provided) proceeds from " Ulster " of any new or increased taxation imposed by Irish Legislature should be ear-marked to be spent for the benefit of Ulster.

(*b*) affecting religion, or land tenure (outside reserved sphere)

(*c*) affecting education or industrial matters[1]

" Such legislation not to take effect in that area, unless and until submitted to be approved by Impl. Parlt.

" It should in any case be added that as the Impl. Exr. would have to bear the cost of Ulster administration (see above under ' Administration ') the ' transferred sum ' should be reduced by the present costs of those services there. The estimates for the expenditure on Ulster administration would be voted by the Impl. Parlt."

It will be observed that Mr. Asquith made, in this memorandum, a desperate attempt to reconcile two irreconcilable positions—to put Ulster both inside and outside an Irish Parliament, both under and beyond the control of an Irish Government. It is evident that Carson talked the proposals over with Bonar Law, for his reply, written on the 27th December, 1913, is on the notepaper of Max Aitken's house, Cherkley Court, Leatherhead :

" MY DEAR P.M.,—I have seen Mr. Bonar Law & discussed with him the terms of your memorandum—I note that they are not submitted as proposals. So far as I am concerned I cd. not feel justified (& indeed it wd. be useless) in submitting these terms to my colleagues and associates in Ulster, as however guarded, the basis is the inclusion of Ulster in the Irish Parlmt.

" Mr. Bonar Law is also of the opinion that for the same reason he does not think any useful

---

[1] Note.—This is not necessarily an exhaustive enumeration.

purpose would be served in calling his colleagues together to consider them. If under the circumstances you think it is expedient that I shd. again see you, I shall of course do so—but I will be out of town next week tho' I cd. come up to London to see you on Friday if you find that it is convenient."

If the Prime Minister was, as he may well have been, somewhat dashed by this letter, he nevertheless persevered, as we gather from his reply, written on the last day of 1913 :

" I have only just received your letter of the 27th. Notwithstanding its terms, I think it might be well in the general interest that we should have another talk."

And Mr. Asquith went on to propose another meeting at Queen Anne's Gate on the following Friday, which we may suppose took place. That it led nowhere is suggested by a letter from Asquith, evidently in reply to another from Carson of which we have not a copy. It is interesting chiefly as showing how the Liberal statesman hoped to " veil " the figure of compromise, whose shape, were she " naked," would certainly be misliked by Mr. Redmond.

" *Most Confidential.*   10 Downing Street,
                " Whitehall, S.W.
                        " *8 Jan. 1914.*
    " MY DEAR CARSON,—I have your letter of yesterday.
    " I agree that it might be a waste of time, at this stage, to draft anything in the nature of a

detailed scheme of Ulster *Administration* on the basis of ' exclusion.' That was not what I intended to ask of you. Indeed, in my own memorandum I think I indicated in sufficient outline how the purely administrative problems might be dealt with.

" The suggestions in my memm. in regard to *Legislation* for ' statutory Ulster ' were conceived with the double purpose of giving to the Ulster majority the substance of what they claim, while doing as little violence as possible to Nationalist sentiment. They amounted roughly (as we said in conversation) to ' veiled exclusion.'

" If Ulster is to be dealt with separately, while fully conscious of the objections both logical and practical to which the plan is exposed, I thought, personally, that there ought to be at any rate a better chance of an agreed settlement being worked out on those lines than on any other.

" You told me, however, that neither Mr. Bonar Law nor yourself could treat this part of my suggestions as a possible basis or starting point for our present purpose. You could only proceed on the footing of what (by contrast) may be called ' naked exclusion.'

" It was at this point that I wished you to be good enough to go into a little more detail. For ' Exclusion ' may—as you well know—take several different or alternative shapes, and (while the difficulty of coming to agreement upon such a basis may turn out to be insurmountable) it is conceivable that the degree of difficulty, and therefore the chance of success, might vary with the particular form which the proposal assumes.

" I think it would elucidate the position, and

enable both Mr. Bonar Law & yourself on your side, and me on mine, to judge better how far we can fruitfully pursue our communications, if you could let me know what is the precise form of ' exclusion ' which you have in your mind.

" You will agree that it is the Legislation, rather than the Administration, side of the problem which is of paramount importance.

" Believe me,
" Sincerely yours
" H. H. Asquith."

Carson, whose way of thinking was simpler and more direct than the other's, had no use for these sophistications. He put his meaning beyond any doubt in the following reply.

" *vy Confidential*   5 Eaton Place,
" S.W.
" *10 Jan. 14.*

" My dear Prime Minister,—I am in receipt of your letter of the 8th inst :

" I thought that it was always apparent that when the exclusion of Ulster was discussed, I meant that Ulster should remain as at present under the Imp. Parlmt. & that a Dublin Parlmt. should have no legislative powers within the excluded area. Ulster wd. therefore send no members to the Dublin Parlmt., but would continue as at present to send members to the Imp. Parlmt.—

" This would of course involve that the administration of Ulster shd. be under the control of the Imp. Parlmt.

" I do not think I can say anything more specific—

> " I remain
>> " Sincerely yours
>>> " EDWARD CARSON."

Mr. Asquith, at last convinced that Carson would go no further, brought the passage to an end in the following letter.

" *Most Confidential*   10 Downing Street,
> " Whitehall, S.W.

" MY DEAR CARSON,—I received yesterday in the country your letter of the 10th, and I note that you write that you cannot say anything ' more specific ' than what is there stated.

" I am going abroad for a few days to see my wife, and to bring home my little boy. But I hope early next week to have an opportunity of consulting my colleagues in the Cabinet, when I will communicate with you again.

> " Believe me
>> " Sincerely yours
>>> " H. H. ASQUITH."

On the 22nd January, 1914, Mr. Asquith reported to the Cabinet that he had received a letter from Sir Edward Carson " flatly refusing anything short of the exclusion of Ulster."[1]

----

[1] J. A. Spender, *Life of Lord Oxford and Asquith*, vol. ii., p. 37.

CHAPTER XIX

CROSS CURRENTS

Stubborn opinions—Mr. Birrell—An army in being—Appeal to the Throne —Dither of indecision—Oracular words—The Ulster Party—Carson in the House—" Without prejudice "—Lloyd George's plan—Secret conferences.

THUS THESE TWO MEN met and parted—the one to report to his Cabinet, the other to consult with his friends. There had never been any real hope of agreement : Asquith could not yield more than the South would allow, nor Carson more than the North would accept. The main of separation stood between them, and there were strong men to back stubborn principles. What Asquith had to endure from Redmond we shall presently see, and there were Conservatives at least as stiff against any compromise—or even the approaches of negotiation. Before these conversations began Walter Long had written :

" MY DEAR NED,—Many thanks for your letter and for your kind promise to see my son. I will tell him what you are good enough to say.

" I quite agree. I am against a conference and am very glad Asquith killed that idea. I don't believe any arrangement is possible. Both Asquith and Grey declared that it must be a condition that if an arrangement be made, all parties must accept the amended Bill. I don't see how we could ever, in any circumstances, do this.

"I think we ought to have our programme cut and dried and if he declares, as he must, in the House, that force will be used, then I think we must make Government impossible—I believe in this way we could force a dissolution—

"Yours ever,

"W."

This letter, written on the last day of November 1913, already suggests that the great Wiltshire squire would have his friends take all the fences without as much as a look for the landing. On the 1st January, 1914, there is a letter from Bonar Law, carrying that suggestion further :

"MY DEAR CARSON,—I shall be delighted to see you at dinner to-morrow.

"I am getting letters from our people showing great impatience (including one from Long which I shall show you to-morrow) and if you get this note before you see Asquith I think it is really worth while to point out to him that I shall have to make some reference to the negotiations on the 15th, and if there seems to be no prospect of a settlement it will be necessary to say so.

"Yours very sincerely

"A. BONAR LAW."

On the 29th Bonar Law wrote a letter which suggests how little he trusted the Liberals, enclosing another from Asquith.

"It is difficult," said Bonar, "to see what further step we can take, but it is not satisfactory." The letter from the Prime Minister was to apologise for, or rather to explain away, an indiscretion of the

Sa

unfortunate Secretary for Ireland, who never could open his mouth without infuriating the Opposition.

" Mr. Birrell informs me that he had no intention whatever of referring to our communications, and that ' the offers to Ulster ' which he had in mind point only to *public* offers which have been in the course of the autumn and may be hereafter put forward by me.

" I need hardly assure you that I have impressed upon my colleagues the importance of not divulging anything that has taken place between you and me, and the grave impropriety which would be involved in any such breach of confidence."

In the meantime Carson had gone to Belfast, where we find him on the 17th January, 1914, his purpose being to inform and to consult his Ulster friends. He had always told that community to pay less heed to " conversations " than to " preparations " : " I tell you this," he said to them the day after his arrival, " that whether it be in domestic policy or in foreign policy, the golden rule to observe is, ' Let your preparations keep pace with your diplomacy,' and, believe me, the more you are prepared, and the more our people outside are ready, the greater, the stronger, the more potent in these diplomatic relations will be the position of your leaders."

Ulster had not waited for this piece of advice : the Ulster Volunteer Force was by that time 90,000 strong, and well advanced in drill and organisation. In Belfast alone there were four regiments, corresponding with the Parliamentary divisions ; the North, East and South Belfast regiments were each 6,000 strong, and in the Western Division where the Unionists were weaker, they numbered 3,000

Volunteers. On the afternoon of his arrival, although the shipyards were working overtime, all six battalions of the East Belfast regiment mustered for parade and marched out to Ormiston, where their Commanding Officer, Colonel Spencer Chichester, had placed his park at their disposal. Sir Edward Carson and Sir George Richardson were at the saluting base, and as the regiment went by, 3,500 men, in column of route, with the proper complement of officers, chaplains, doctors, ambulance and transport, it was easy to see what a formidable force they represented. They had everything but arms. " The nearer we approach the day of crisis," Carson told them, " the more grow your courage and my courage, your determination and mine." There was a wonderful understanding between him and those mechanics and workmen of the shipyards and engineering shops of East Belfast.

The next day Carson held a meeting with the Ulster Unionist Council behind closed doors ; Lord Londonderry afterwards entertained the whole assembly of 1,000 delegates to one of his great luncheons in Exhibition Hall, and at night there was a great meeting in the Ulster Hall. Neither the business nor the speeches need much detain us. These people had long since made up their minds ; they reaffirmed their resolution " to defeat the present conspiracy " and their confidence in " the wise guidance of Sir Edward Carson, our beloved leader," and they heard from his lips of the failure of the conversations. " I am above all things a man of peace," he said, " but not at any price ; and I know this full well, that there are some things on which there can be no compromise."

Carson by that time had little reason to hope for

any change in Government policy : " the last thing we will allow is an election," John Redmond said a few days later, and Carson already knew the strength of that dictatorship. But he had still hopes of the King, and at that meeting in the Ulster Hall, he made an appeal, humble, passionate (and I suppose unique in our Constitutional history) for help from the Royal hand.

" We will go to the end," he said, " first using every peaceful means.

" We will prostrate ourselves before the throne as loyal citizens, and ask the King to save us.

" We will tell him—' We are loyal and devoted subjects—none more loyal in your Majesty's dominions. When your country had dark days, we were those who never lost confidence, who never refused to stand by you.'

" We will tell him something more. We will tell him that if to-morrow the Kingdom were threatened, our Volunteers would be the very first who would go and assist in repelling the foe.

" We would say this to him—' That has been our history in the past. What is our reward to be in future ? Is our reward to be that we are to be turned outside the United Kingdom ; that we are to be put in a degraded position in the Empire ; and above all that we are to be handed over, bound hand and foot, to those who have ever been your Majesty's enemies and ours ? ' "

" Some of them hope," Tim Healy wrote to his brother on January 26th, 1914, " to get the King to veto the Bill, although this was not the wish of the more responsible. Yet as the time draws near I fancy the extremists' views will prevail. If they can get Lord Lansdowne and Bonar Law so to advise the King, no one can tell the result."[1]

While Carson thus consulted with his friends, Asquith was driven back upon their enemies. On February 2nd, 1914, the Prime Minister saw John Redmond again, informed him of the " obstinacy " of the Unionist leaders, assured him that " he and his colleagues were all firmly opposed to the exclusion of Ulster, or any part of Ulster, even temporarily, and went on to paint the gloomiest picture of the prospects of the Government. There was " a very serious crisis " over the Navy Estimates ; there were fears that the Conservatives would refuse to pass the Army Bill, " until they know how the Army is going to be used in Ulster." As a result of these dangers and forebodings, Mr. Asquith had been driven to the conclusion that he must make some offer to Ulster " of such a character that in the event of their refusal of it—and he thinks at this stage any offer he made short of the exclusion of Ulster would be rejected—it would deprive them of all moral force."

The Prime Minister proceeded to unfold to Mr. Redmond a series of proposals closely resembling those he had laid before Carson, save that the exclusion of the Customs from the Bill was not mentioned.

From his interview " Redmond gathered plainly," says his biographer, " that the pressure which was being brought to bear had intimidated the Prime Minister, and that his apprehension that the King might in the last resort exercise his prerogatives had already convinced him that large concessions must be made."[2]

---

[1] *Letters and Leaders of My Day*, pp. 535-6. In Mr. Healy's opinion, however, as appears on the same page, Carson, so far from being an extremist, was keeping the peace in Ulster.

[2] Denis Gwynn, *Life of John Redmond*, p. 250 *et seq*.

So the tug-of-war went on : Dillon, called in by Redmond, gave it as his opinion that they should let the King act and face the consequences rather than make any concession ; on February 9th, 1914, Birrell told these Irish allies that " great difference of opinion " had been disclosed in the Cabinet ; that Asquith had prepared a general statement as to autonomy in Ulster, he had been overruled for the moment ; but " the Cabinet won't be willing to wait for very long before making up their minds as to what ought to be offered publicly to Ulster." Parliament was about to meet and Redmond used all his power to stop the rot : to make any concessions on the debate in the Address would, he said, be " fatal."

In this dither of indecision Ministers met Parliament on the 10th February, 1914. The Royal speech, it was noted, expressed regret that the " efforts made to arrive at a solution by agreement " had not succeeded, and " my most earnest wish " that " the co-operation and goodwill of men of all parties and creeds " might " heal disunion and lay the foundations of a lasting settlement." " It is said," Tim Healy reported, " the King insisted on the paragraph about ' conciliation ' and that when a Minister objected, His Majesty said, ' It is my speech. Surely I can say this much '—or words to that effect." Many observers rashly assumed that the battle was over and that the Opposition had won. Tim Healy reported that night to his brother that " the ' Party ' (the Irish Nationalists) received the Prime Minister ' without cheers ' when he rose and in silence when he sat down. They were collapsed. . . ." Mr. Asquith in many words said very little, save that the Government regarded it as its

duty " to submit to the House without any avoid-
able delay " suggestions which would certainly be
" honestly put forward " and would be regarded
" by all fair minded men " as " at any rate an
attempt, and a serious attempt " to arrive at an
agreement.

The House sucked such comfort as it could derive
from these oracular words. It had got about,
although Asquith said nothing to justify it, that the
question was settled by the exclusion of Ulster.
" The Irish Party sat silent," Tim Healy noted,
" and Redmond smiled feebly." They were, he
thought, " routed," although in prudence he remembered that " things change continually." As he
was leaving the House he met Carson, " strongly
remonstrated with him on the line he was taking,"
and found him " quite reasonable and good-
natured." Tim gathered that he was trying to get
the best terms for the general body of the Loyalists.
As far as Ulster was concerned, Tim thought the
battle was over.

Carson knew better : he did not speak that night
owing to the pains of a chronic neuritis ; but next
day he pressed the Prime Minister to make known
his terms.

We get pictures of the House in those critical
debates from contemporary journalists : " To the
left of the Speaker is a little group of members who
have the look of business-men and who follow the
debate with an interest almost ferocious. Now and
again one of them interrupts, usually without
humour or originality, but always in dead earnest.
You conclude that the big heavy man, with the
strong Irish accent and the red kindly face must be
the leader of the group. (The journalist is referring

to James Craig.) But it is not so. The logic-chopping has been rather more pronounced than usual, and it has aroused a tall strong-faced man on the Unionist Front Bench, at the very end, whom you had not noticed, with his head sunk deep on his breast. ' Carson's up,' a neighbour whispers, and you do not make any more mistakes as to who, in this connection, is the leader of that tough-looking group just below the Chair."[1]

Carson was up ! The journalist noted the tall, lean body, " the Dantesque character of the face," the " deep sad eyes," the " mysterious brooding air "—" the image which rushes into your mind," he went on, " is that of a tiger or a panther on the point of a spring." And there was certainly something tigerish in that speech on the Address, which began—in a low conversational voice—on " the unparalleled generosity of the speech from the Throne." " ' Grave future difficulties '—what a position for statesmanship to bring this country into ! " The Government had talked of concessions. —" When you talk of ' concessions,' what you really mean is, ' We want to lay down what is the minimum of wrong we can do to Ulster.' " By delaying their task for two years they had made it more difficult.

" You have driven these men into a Covenant for their mutual protection."

Then, with his lowering eyes on the Liberal Benches, Carson raised his voice accusingly : " No doubt you have laughed at their Covenant," he said, " Have a good laugh at it now."

At these words the House was swept as by a storm—with cheers from the Opposition and shrill

[1] *Daily Graphic*, 13th February, 1914.

cries from the Irish Nationalists. " You think," says our journalist, " of Dante, and the Florentine gossips saying that he had seen Hell—for Carson depicted the hell that coercion in Ulster would produce."

Lowering his voice again Carson seemed to plead with the Prime Minister.

Mr. Asquith had said that he did not reject the exclusion of Ulster. He had also said that there was nothing he would not do " consistent with the fundamental principles of the Bill . . . to avoid the terrible calamity of civil war or bloodshed." Why then did he hesitate ?

" I can only say this to the Prime Minister," Carson proceeded. " If the exclusion for that purpose is proposed, it will be my duty to go to Ulster at once, and take counsel with the people there, for I certainly do not mean that Ulster should be any pawn in any political game."

On the other hand—" no matter what the paper safeguards . . . if you tried to compel them to come into a Dublin Parliament, I tell you I shall, regardless of consequences, go on with these people to the end with their policy of resistance."

" Ulster," he said,—" Believe me, whatever way you settle the Irish question, there are only two ways to deal with Ulster. . . .

" She is not a part of the community which can be bought. She will not allow herself to be sold.

" You must either coerce her if you go on, or you must, in the long run, by showing that good government can come under the Home Rule Bill, try and win her over to the case of the rest of Ireland.

" You probably can coerce her, though I doubt it. If you do, what will be the disastrous consequences not only to Ulster, but to this country and the Empire ? "

Then the speech took a turn which surprised as much as it moved the House. Turning to John Redmond, "Will my fellow-countryman, the leader of the Nationalist Party," Carson asked, " have gained anything ?

" I do not suppose he wants to triumph any more than I do. But will he have gained anything if he takes over these people, and then applies for what he used to call—at all events his Party used to call —' the enemies of the people,' to come in and coerce them into obedience ?

" No, sir," he continued, turning again to the Speaker, " one false step taken in relation to Ulster will render for ever impossible a solution of the Irish question.

" You have never tried," Carson went on, addressing the Government once more, " to win over Ulster. You have never tried to understand her position. You have never alleged and never can allege that this Bill gives her one atom of advantage. No, you cannot deny that it takes away many advantages that she has as a constituent part of the United Kingdom. You cannot deny that in the past she has produced the most loyal and law-abiding part of the citizens of Ireland.

" After all that, for these two years, every time we come before you, your only answer to us—the majority of you at all events—was to insult us and make little of us." And turning again upon John Redmond, " I say to the Leader of the Nationalist Party," Carson exclaimed, " if you want Ulster, go and take her, or go and win her. You never wanted her affections. You wanted her taxes."

It was, for a space, as if these two men were wrestling on the floor of that tense and crowded House for the future of Ireland. " I repudiate that statement," Redmond retorted. " No such desire actuates either my colleagues or myself. I care not about the assent of Englishmen. I am fighting this matter out between a fellow-countryman and myself, and I say it was an unworthy thing for him to say that I am animated by these base motives. . . ."

Anxious for peace as Mr. Redmond may have been, the exclusion of Ulster was too big a price to pay for it. No doubt the words used by Carson nineteen months before, and quoted by the Prime Minister in the course of the debate, still rang a warning in the ears of the Nationalist leader. " If Ulster were left out Home Rule would be impossible," Carson had said, " therefore I will vote for leaving it out." Anything short of that Mr. Redmond was willing to consider " in the broadest and friendliest spirit."

The Prime Minister, at least as anxious for peace as Mr. Redmond, was moved by the speech to write a private note ; which might seem a little to mollify the bitterness of the conflict.

" *11th February, 1914.*

" MY DEAR CARSON,—I write, as you know, ' without prejudice ' ; but I should like to tell you that your speech this afternoon impressed me more than anything I have heard in Parliament for many a long day—

" Yours always sincerely,
" H. H. ASQUITH."

Asquith knew, and Carson knew, that a widening gulf divided them ; but it was the general belief in the House that everything had been settled. Even Tim Healy was deceived. " My impression is," he wrote that same night to his brother, " that the exclusion of Ulster will be proposed by the Government and accepted by Redmond."

What deceived that shrewd observer was a speech —" the broadest and the friendliest "—by Mr. Lloyd George. " To-night," Healy observed, " Dillon cheered Lloyd George very pointedly at a passage which showed that this would be the plan. I expect that they are either concealing the situation from Devlin, or that he has not the parliamentary instinct to discern what is being arranged, if he has not also surrendered."

Tim, it will be noted, was rather self-complacent in his sense of mental superiority.

" Lloyd George's speech to-night," he went on, " was delivered after consultation with T. P. He said Carson's speech made a new situation because he referred to Redmond as his ' countryman.' He also buttered Carson enormously.

" I believe," Healy concluded, " all has been arranged behind the scenes. Bonar Law's speech affords proof of this. Last night a press man told me that the Liberals were saying everything had been arranged ; but I told him it was not true. Now I think the other way."[1]

To draw such deductions from the cheers of Dillon or the butter of Lloyd George was hardly worthy of so shrewd an observer. Everything, indeed, had been arranged, but not with Carson, nor

[1] *Letters and Leaders of My Day*, p. 538. The letter quoted is dated 11th February, 1914.

with Bonar Law. Everything had been arranged between Lloyd George and John Redmond. The "enormous buttering" was only part of that arrangement.

Mr. Lloyd George was working for the plan which he had put before the Cabinet in November 1913, and which had been condemned in the Cabinet as unacceptable to the other side.

That, to Mr. Lloyd George, was part of its merit.

With the pride of Machiavelli in the subtlety of his own ideas, he elaborated the scheme in a memorandum to the Cabinet which must have been written directly after the debate just described.

The proposal (of the Government for meeting the case of Ulster) must, he said, have "two essential characteristics":

" (1) It must be an offer the rejection of which would put the other side entirely in the wrong, as far as the British public is concerned; and,

" (2) It must not involve any alteration in the scheme of the Bill; so that if it is rejected, the Unionists cannot say, 'Why you yourselves admitted that your Bill needed amendment.' "[1]

What Mr. Lloyd George proposed, as we have already seen, was to exclude a certain area for a term of years from the operation of the Bill, with automatic inclusion at the end of the period. The Ulster counties were to be given the option to come in; but they were not to be given the option to stay out. When Mr. Lloyd George had first proposed it to the Cabinet, the Cabinet had objected that

[1] This memorandum of Lloyd George's, which was submitted not only to the Cabinet, but to Mr. Redmond, is given in full by Mr. Denis Gwynn, pp. 256 et seq.

" Sir Edward Carson and his friends would never agree to a proposal which would really mean the giving up of the whole principle for which they had been contending " ; but Mr. Lloyd George had insisted on the merits of his scheme—" Men could not possibly go to war to prevent something which was not to occur for five years."

Here then was the ideal political compromise, which could not be accepted by the other side because it took from them " everything for which they had been contending " ; but put them, nevertheless, so " entirely in the wrong, as far as the British public is concerned," that they " could not possibly go to war " to prevent it.

This ingenious plan Mr. Lloyd George urged upon the Irish Nationalists in a series of private conferences. They stood out for a while for the Bill and nothing but the Bill ; Mr. Devlin in particular, as an Ulster Nationalist, and the Head of the Ancient Order of Hibernians, was hot against any compromise which even seemed to deny " the national claim of Ireland." He did not believe in the reality of " the threats of civil war indulged in by Sir Edward Carson and his followers." They were " grotesquely exaggerated " or " absolutely untrue." The real trouble would come in Belfast if the Bill were rejected, as in 1886 and in 1893.

Mr. Lloyd George replied, " from information in the hands of the Ministry," that Mr. Devlin underestimated the danger. That danger the Government were " prepared to face " ; but they must first put " the responsibility " on the other side. He discussed Sir Horace Plunkett's proposal—that Ulster should have the right to vote itself out of Home Rule after ten years—only to claim superior merits for his own.

The Ulstermen, he argued, would have " no excuse for rioting against conditions . . . not yet imposed upon them " and " it will be very difficult for them to get up another such movement as they have organised at such expense during the past couple of years."

We may suppose that Mr. Asquith was drawn rather unwillingly into so disingenuous a scheme, since there is evidence that even while yielding to it, he was still seeking an alternative. It may, of course, have been entirely the influence of the King, who was still using all the Royal influence for settlement ; but at any rate the Prime Minister did make the following " confidential " approach to Sir Edward Carson on the 2nd March, 1914 :

" In consequence of something which the King said to me on Friday night, and of a letter I have received from Lord Stamfordham, in reference to a conversation he had with you on Saturday, I think it may be in the interest of the peace, of which both you and I are desirous, if I could have a little talk with you to-morrow (Tuesday)." And Mr. Asquith proposed, like a secret suitor, " our old trysting-place—24 Queen Anne's Gate as the place of meeting."

What happened at that interview we do not know, nor does it greatly matter. What we do know is that on the very day on which this letter of assignation was written, Mr. Asquith, with Mr. Lloyd George and Mr. Birrell, met Mr. Redmond, Mr. Dillon, Mr. Devlin and Mr. T. P. O'Connor, and plighted his troth anew.

" In their presence," says Mr. Gwynn in his *Life of Redmond*, " the Prime Minister repeated the pledges which had been given by Lloyd George in the previous week, that the proposed concession would be the Government's last word, and as to the procedure to be adopted."[1]

On the 4th March, 1914, Mr. Asquith confirmed the compact in writing, and thereupon Devlin and Jerry MacVeagh hastened over to Ulster, there to obtain the consent of the Bishops of Derry and Raphoe, of Cardinal Logue and of the Ancient Order of Hibernians.

In the following week there were two more secret conferences between the Chancellor of the Exchequer and the leading Irish Nationalists ; by the 7th March, 1914, Mr. Devlin reported all clear in Ulster ; on the 9th March Mr. Asquith moved that " the Bill be now read a second time," and in the course of his speech laid the plan of Mr. Lloyd George, as the policy of the Government, before the House of Commons.

[1] p. 267.

CHAPTER XX

AN OFFER REFUSED

Trick and force—Detective work by Walter Long—Ulster opinions—Mr.
Asquith's offer—Sentence of death with stay of execution.

To REALISE THE TENSE EXPECTATION of that
House of Commons we must remember that all the
preliminaries of the proposals about to be made had
been a close secret. " In these days, when one
cannot write a letter to one's wife without the most
sinister construction being put upon it," the Prime
Minister boasted, " we were able for a number of
weeks, and even months, to carry on in complete
privacy, under the Argus eyes of the whole press of
Great Britain, these confidential communications."[1]

The conversations between Asquith and Bonar
Law, between Asquith and Carson, between Lloyd
George and Redmond, were all behind the back of
that democracy which fondly supposes itself to
govern. By the end of the first week of March 1914,
these negotiations were over : on the one side they
had failed ; on January 22nd, 1914, Asquith reported to the Cabinet, says Mr. Spender, " that he
had received a letter from Sir Edward Carson,
' flatly refusing anything short of the exclusion of
Ulster ' "[2] ; on the other side the bargain was struck
—and put in writing. " We must ask," John Redmond had written, " as a second condition of the
proposal of optional exclusion, that this will be the

[1] *Parl. Deb. Com.*, vol. lviii., c. 79 (10th Feb., 1914).
[2] *Life of Lord Oxford and Asquith*, p. 37.

TC

last word of the Government . . . that on the rejection of this proposal by the Opposition, the Government should pass the Bill as it stands, and face any consequences in Ulster that may ensue." And in a letter of March 4th, 1914, Mr. Asquith had accepted these terms : " We agree that the conditions for which you stipulate are reasonable and proper."[1]

To make an offer such as Ulster must reject ; on the rejection " to face any consequences in Ulster " ; such was the policy of trick and force, which Mr. Asquith unwillingly accepted—the trick from Mr. Lloyd George, the force from Mr. Redmond.

All of this the House of Commons did not know ; half of it Bonar Law and Carson did not know— although they made a shrewd guess. Friends were importunate and contrary in their advice. " My dear Ned," Walter Long wrote on the 6th March, 1914, " I confess I am a little anxious about Monday, as there seems to be a feeling that the proposal will be one which it will be difficult for us to reject. Of course I do not presume for a moment to advise you as to the course you will take. I am prepared, as you know, to back you to the utmost, even though I may, which is most unlikely, disagree in the conclusion arrived at ; but it seems to me that if the proposal is to have a plebiscite in every county, it is wholly impossible.

" I believe the report is correct, as I had strange confirmation of it. I know for a fact that a messenger was sent from the Cabinet the other day to the Irish office for a map which they have there, giving the total population of the Ulster counties, divided into Protestants and Catholics. The fact

[1] Denis Gwynn, *Life of John Redmond*, p. 269.

that the Cabinet wished to see this map points strongly to the conclusion that they have adopted the policy of plebisciting the counties.

" Surely it is an impossible proposal : it means no security for Ulster ; but even if there were some element of safety in it, how is it going to be carried out ? Imagine the hopeless confusion if counties side by side are to be under different forms of Government. You must have a considerable area, and I cannot imagine anything else than the six counties would offer a practical solution.

" I must say," Mr. Long concluded, " that I believe public opinion is now really aroused in the country. There is evidence of this in the rush to sign the Covenant—we are really almost overpowered. I believe people realise now, as they have never done before, the gross injustice to the Unionists of Ireland, are indignant at the proposed betrayal, and will support us in our action. My own conviction is that if no arrangement is arrived at, the Government will try to force their Bill through, and they will find their position in the House of Commons impossible. However, as I have said before, I don't want to bother you when your responsibilities are so heavy. I hope you are better."

Another friend, Joseph Fisher,[1] wrote in the opposite sense—" specially in view of Garvin's wrongheaded shouting about rejection at all costs."

" I am strongly of the opinion," Mr. Fisher went on, " that if Asquith's proffer contains even the germ of immediate exclusion, it ought not to be rejected off-hand. If the *principle* of exclusion by plebiscite is conceded, you have won a very great

---

[1] Ulsterman, journalist and barrister, at one time editor of *Northern Whig*. The letter is written from 3 Essex Court, Temple, and dated 6th March, 1914.

point, and the Devlinites have suffered a severe and possibly fatal set-back. I still have some Nationalist friends and I hear what they say. They have reluctantly and mutinously been coerced into consent, solely on the assurance gathered from utterances like those of the P.M.G., that you and Bonar Law will peremptorily reject the offer, and that then the Bill will be forced through as it stands. If, on the contrary, you keep the matter open over the adjournment, or over Easter, they will be outmanœuvred and will find themselves in the most serious hole they have been in since the split.

" I don't, of course, suggest acceptance. I only recommend that the matter shall be kept open by whatever form of words seems best. It will not do to allow the Government people to say—as they will— that the ' people of Ulster ' had been offered exclusion by popular vote and that you rejected it."

James Craig, upon whose opinion Carson most relied, was at that time in County Down, working steadily in the belief that all those conversations must fail. He had moreover the anxious business of keeping his people under control in the face of a great demonstration the Ulster Nationalists were organising for the 14th March in Derry, " to strengthen the hands of Mr. Redmond and the Irish Party." Redmond, however, wrote to the Roman Catholic Bishop of Derry, to tell him that, " in my judgment it would have exactly the opposite effect," and on the 4th March, Craig wrote to Carson from Craigavon :

" I am able to confirm my telegram of yesterday, that the Derry meeting is off. It is a great relief to us all here.

" I will cross over Sunday night, so as to be present in the House when Asquith makes his statement on Monday. . . . I gather that the Prime Minister will move the Second Reading of the Bill, and, in doing so, reveal his proposals with regard to Ulster. According to the local press, a motion for the adjournment of the debate will then be moved by one of our Front Bench (in order to permit an interval of some weeks during which time you would have an opportunity of consulting the people of Ulster). If I am wrong, of course it alters the suggestion that I feel inclined to make, which is that you or Bonar Law should be prepared to refuse categorically any offer put forward by the Government, bar, of course, total exclusion, and to make it clear, without equivocation, that Ulster will still go steadily ahead with their armed preparations, and, under no circumstances submit. Unless this is done, it will be taken over here, and throughout the country, that the proposals are worthy of consideration, and interest will slacken off, necessitating a rearming of the public at a later date. On the other hand, if it was made quite clear, immediately on the spot, by our leaders that the proposals are unsatisfactory and unacceptable, as I feel confident will be the case, the country during the interregnum will recognise the increased gravity of the situation, and, in my opinion, will support us, as they are in the habit of doing any plucky minority that stands up for its rights.

" I am sure that this consideration has already been present to your mind, but I feel so strongly that a false step now would prejudice us in the eyes of the British public, that I think it only right to let you have my views at once.

" To come to another matter, we must have a cheque for £20,000 here by return of post. There is a big move on into the details of which I need not venture, and it will require the whole of this sum to see us through. Will you, therefore, please sign your name to one of Drummond's cheques, and post it to me c/o Bates, Old Town Hall, where I can get it on Friday morning when I come in to the Committee meeting.

" I am sorry to trouble you, but it has been sprung upon us here in connection with the Special Force the General is now getting well forward.

" There is nothing new except that poor Hacket-Pain got flung off his horse yesterday in Derry. Up to time of writing I have no details, but understand it is not serious.

" Yours ever,

" JAMES CRAIG."

And in a postcript :

" I would be in favour of you or B. L. saying straight out at once that there was no necessity to adjourn the debate ; that you would not recommend Ulster to accept. I am warning Bates to ' stand by ' with regard to a meeting of the Provisional Govt. on Wednesday next.—J. C."

On the 9th March, 1914, Mr. Asquith moved that " the Bill be now read a second time," and in the course of his speech laid the plan of Mr. Lloyd George before the House as the policy of the Government. Seldom had the Commons awaited an announcement in tension so acute. The House was

" packed from wall to wall " ; even gangways and side galleries were full, and there was a knot of Members standing at the Bar. The Ambassadors of the Great Powers, scenting trouble in the wind, were among those who looked on, and every face showed " a strained desire to watch and listen and feel."

It was noted that the Prime Minister had a moderate welcome from his own side, and was received in silence by the Irish Nationalists. Mr. Asquith had a way of bracing his shoulders at a difficult passage, and he braced them several times in the course of his speech. He mentioned the conversations with the Unionist Leaders to deplore their failure : " Although unhappily they did not result in an agreement or even, I am sorry to say, an approach to an agreement, yet they did make all those who took part in them realise more fully, and perhaps more sympathetically, the difficulties which are to be encountered by those who honestly desire a settlement." Of the negotiations with the Irish Nationalists he said nothing at all. Parodying the sententiousness of his own style he introduced the proposals which he had so unwillingly accepted from Mr. Lloyd George as " provisional exclusion by a media between the surrender of principle and the application of force." It was, he said, " the best and indeed the only practical way —at any rate far the simplest and the fairest plan."

Of this proposal, as we already know, he had said to Mr. Redmond : " It was the opinion of the whole Cabinet, and of Mr. Lloyd George himself, that such a suggestion could not form the basis of a settlement, as Sir Edward Carson and his friends could never agree to a proposal which would really mean the giving up of the whole principle for which they had been contending."[1] Nevertheless he recommended it with earnestness, moderation and sincerity, as " a fair and equitable arrangement " —" I see no road to an agreed settlement in which the balance of give-and-take is likely to be more evenly adjusted."

We may spare the reader details of a scheme which was never meant to be accepted, although it may be said that Mr. Long's deduction from the messenger and the map was shown to be sagacious : any county within the province of Ulster—within three months from the date of the passing of the Bill—was to be at liberty to take a poll, and if a bare majority of the electors voted in favour of exclusion, the county was to remain outside the operation of the Act—" for a period " of six years.

It was at this crucial point that Carson interrupted with a question which went to the heart of the matter—" Will the right hon. gentleman say what happens at the end of the six years ? "

" I am coming to that," the Prime Minister replied ; but he seemed so unwilling to come to it that Mr. Bonar Law had to put the decisive question : " Does the right hon. gentleman mean that at the end of the six years the counties which have the option now are not to have it for themselves ? "

" Yes," the Prime Minister replied," they would come in at the end of six years unless the Imperial Parliament otherwise decides."

Mr. Bonar Law's comment was characteristically terse : " If you think it is wrong to compel them to come in to-day," he asked, " how can you think it right to compel them to come in to-morrow ? "

[1] Denis Gwynn, *Life of John Redmond*, p. 235.

And the Unionist Leader went on to describe the offer as it must seem to Ulster. What the Prime Minister really proposed to him was this :

" ' You have by your organisation, extending over two years, placed yourselves in a position of commanding strength.

" ' You have entrenched yourselves in a commanding fortress, and, therefore, I do not ask you to submit now to a Nationalist Parliament.

" ' What I do ask is that you should destroy your organisation, and that you should leave your fortress, and then, when you are weak, you will be compelled to do what to-day, when you are strong, you will not do.' "

The speech of Carson, however, was the crisis of that tense debate. It was made after John Redmond had used words which plainly showed what the Irish Nationalists expected—and what they threatened. If, Redmond had said, the Ulstermen rejected " these far-reaching and generous suggestions," then it was the duty of the majority in that House to place the Bill " without one single unnecessary hour's delay upon the statute book," and to face, " with firmness and with resolution and with all the resources at their command, any movement that may arise to overawe Parliament or subvert the law by the menace of force."

There was an irony, which the House could not miss, in this threat from the Leader of a Party which had long subverted the law to a man who in other times had so stoutly maintained it. But Carson let it go by. He was ill ; he spoke under " great physical difficulties." Faintly at first, but gathering strength as he went, he spoke of the Unionists of the South and West of Ireland :

" We will never agree," he said, " to the sacrifice
of the people of the South and West, whatever
may be the benefits which may be offered to
Ulster."

There was, however, the consideration,—Was this
such an offer as would disarm Ulster, in the sense
that she would no longer resist the Bill by force?
Would it reduce her resistance to constitutional
opposition, " that you may commence your Parliament, wherever it is in Ireland, in peace and
quietness ? " That was a different proposition,
and he admitted some advance in the principle
of exclusion. " But "—and here Carson touched,
whether by knowledge or intuition, the secret
spring of this policy—" there has been added on to
the admission of that principle of exclusion a term
which, I believe, has been added in order that it
may make it impossible for us even to enter into
any such negotiations."

And then in sentences which sounded like strokes
of doom in the ears of that strained assembly :

" So far as Ulster is concerned, be exclusion good
or bad—and I think we are only driven into exclusion from the exigencies of the case and of the
facts—but be exclusion good or bad, Ulster wants
this question settled now and for ever.

" We do not want sentence of death with a stay of
execution for six years."

Then Carson turned to an argument used by the
Prime Minister to recommend the scheme—that it
would offer to Ulster the prospect of reprieve by
one or two General Elections. " You know very
well," he said, " that once your Bill has passed, you
will not get the electors of the country to give their
attention back again on to this question, and your

whole pretence of Parliament intervening is a sham.

" Will you agree," he proceeded to ask, " that they are to stay out until this Parliament otherwise orders ? "

Getting no answer, " If you do not," he said, " you do not really mean this as any safeguard to Ulster."

When Carson went on to say—what we now know to be the truth—that the offer was never meant to be accepted, " and you know never could be accepted," the Liberals raised shouts of injured innocence.

" I know," he proceeded, " very well, that the motto of every Government—it is pasted outside every Department—is ' Peace in our time, O Lord.' But you do not get rid of the difficulty—be it to-day or to-morrow, or a year hence, or be it six years hence. The difficulty will remain, and Ulster will be a physical and geographical fact, and the feelings of loathing and horror of your Bill, the feeling of your threats to these men, which have driven them to combine themselves together in a federation to try and stay in this Parliament, and under this Parliament, that feeling will grow and be taught to their children from generation to generation. Do not tell me that in the North of Ireland they readily forget these things. No sir, the difficulty will not be less after six years, but it will be greater."

Then Carson made an offer to the Government. Let them take the time limit away, and he would go over to Ulster and call a convention. " But with this time limit in, and Ulster ready, as I believe it, for any exigency at the present moment, I shall not go to Ulster."

Thus things were going as the Nationalists

expected, and Carson seemed to know it. " I daresay what I have said is a relief to my Nationalist fellow-countrymen," he exclaimed, " but I cannot help it." Then, with a thought of his friend, Joseph Fisher's advice, he went on : " I have no doubt that if I were playing this game as tactics, if I were agreeable to allow those in Ireland who trust me to be made a pawn in a political game, I would say, ' Well, let us have these things put upon paper, and probably the Nationalists will fall out among themselves.' I would make a pretence that we might accept all this in Ulster ; but I have refused to play this game from the beginning as a game of tactics."

If he had not interpreted Ulster feeling aright, Ulster people were quite independent enough, themselves, without him, to call a convention— " Certainly if they differ from me upon this matter I should, without feeling the slightest bitterness, or that they had treated me in the slightest degree unkindly or ungratefully, step aside as willingly as I step forward to-day to do what they ask."

He turned to the words which John Redmond had used to the House of Commons : " They must assert their authority, they must go straight through with the Bill, and they must employ all the resources of the Government to enforce it against his Ulster fellow-countrymen."

Carson paused. " Men talk very lightly," he said, " about the enforcement of any law. I know something about the difficulty."

Then he appealed from the House to the country : " Are you going to allow the forces of the Crown, which are your forces, and not the forces of any political caucus, to be used to coerce men who have asked for nothing but that they should remain

with you?" Were they going to give up "the right
yourselves to determine what is real liberty"—
and that to a Government which had refused when
asked to appeal to the country?

Thus an offer disingenuously made was indignantly refused, and upon that refusal dire events
followed fast.

CHAPTER XXI

THE PLOT THICKENS

The Machiavellian plan—Sub-Committee of the Cabinet—The presentation—Sir Arthur Paget—Rumours of arrest—Parliamentary " trifling " —War Office plans—Devlin makes a charge—Admiralty orders— Carson at Craigavon.

SOME TIME IN FEBRUARY 1914 Mr. Lloyd George wrote that Machiavellian memorandum in which he proposed "an offer the rejection of which would put the other side entirely in the wrong."

" It would," he argued, " be almost impossible for them " (the Ulster Loyalists) " to justify armed resistance in these counties at the present moment if such an option were given them. For it would be a rebellion not merely in anticipation of some act of oppression which could not possibly occur for x years, but a rebellion in anticipation of the verdict of the British electorate which they themselves have challenged. It would make the course of the Government very much clearer if the Unionists accept the responsibility for rejecting the proposal and countenance resistance."[1]

On the 2nd March, 1914, Mr. Redmond accepted these terms on condition that if they were rejected, " the Government should pass the Bill as it stands and face any consequences in Ulster that may ensue." On the 4th March Mr. Asquith, in writing, accepted Mr. Redmond's terms : " We agree that the conditions for which you stipulate are in the

[1] Denis Gwynn, *Life of John Redmond*, pp. 257–8.

circumstances reasonable and proper." On the 11th March, Mr. Redmond, Mr. Dillon, Mr. Devlin, Mr. O'Connor and Mr. Birrell breakfasted with Mr. Lloyd George. That same day the Cabinet met, and agreed to certain naval and presumably certain military dispositions. It also appointed a sub-committee of the Cabinet to deal with Ulster, to consist of Lord Crewe, Mr. Churchill, Colonel Seely, Mr. Birrell and Sir John Simon—Sir John Simon being then Attorney-General, Mr. Churchill at the Admiralty and Colonel Seely at the War Office.

On the 12th March the sub-committee held its first meeting ; on the 14th the Secretary of State for War sent his letter of instructions to the Commander-in-Chief in Ireland, and on that day, at Bradford, Mr. Churchill made a speech which was like the flash of a sword suddenly drawn and brandished.

If Ulster rejected the Government's offer, said Mr. Churchill, it was because it preferred shooting to voting. If Ulster took any action, the Government would treat it as unprovoked aggression and would deal with it without compunction. The first British soldier or coastguard or constabulary man killed by an Orangeman would arouse an explosion in the country. There were, said the First Lord, " worse things than bloodshed, even on an extended scale," and again : " If every concession that is made is spurned and exploited . . . if all the loose, wanton and reckless chatter we have been forced to listen to these many months is in the end to disclose a sinister and revolutionary purpose ; then I can only say to you, ' Let us go forward together and put these grave matters to the proof.' " This " superb speech," said Mr. Redmond a day or two after, shows that " what is our last word is also the last word of the Government."

It would seem, indeed, that the Government had plucked up courage from these recent events. They had put, as they thought, the Opposition in the wrong with the British public : they had made, with a show of reasonableness, a specious offer which had been brusquely rejected. So staunch a Conservative as Lord Hugh Cecil entertained uncomfortable doubts, not on the case but on its presentation. " I thought your speech very good, if I may say so," he wrote to Carson on the 13th, " but I was a good deal disturbed by the fear that Bonar Law had not been sufficiently conciliatory ; and I still think it would have been better if his speech had been conceived in a more friendly tone. I cannot help fearing that we may incur the reproach of being irreconcilables, which is of all imputations perhaps the most damaging according to English opinion. I had a long conversation with Bonar Law yesterday, and he was, as usual, most kind and indulgent. But I felt all the time that perhaps he did not sufficiently face the fact that in the end our success depends on winning a General Election, and that to do that we must assume an attitude which the ordinary citizen will regard as a reasonable one." Lord Hugh would have had the Opposition at least discuss the proposals, if only to show the weaknesses —" at the same time making it more and more difficult for them to retreat to their old Bill."

These doubts, however, were like feathers in a high wind : the Conservatives were resolved : they would meet menace with defiance.

Lord Willoughby de Broke had been busy among

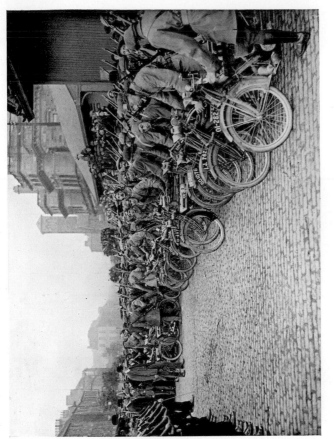

ESCORT FOR SIR EDWARD
awaiting his arrival at Belfast Quay from Liverpool

his friends and day by day new adherents flocked to his standard. On the 28th February, 1914, Lord Milner wrote to Carson of a British declaration in support of the Ulster Convention, which had been signed, among others, by Lord Roberts, the Duke of Portland, Admiral Seymour, Lord Desborough, Lord Lovat, Mr. Rudyard Kipling, the Dean of Canterbury, and Professor Dicey. On the 6th March Mr. Walter Long, President of the Union Defence League, reported (as we have seen) such a rush to sign the Covenant as almost overwhelmed the organisation. On Friday, the 13th March, about a hundred of these stalwarts gave a demonstration of their feelings for Sir Edward Carson. A notable company assembled at the Ritz Hotel and gave him a sword and a beautifully illuminated book of the Covenant—" presented to Edward Carson in the sure confidence that God will defend the right." There were no speeches ; Lord Willoughby de Broke proposed the toasts of the King and of their guest, and Carson, who had a great reception, responded with " No Home Rule."[1]

The Liberals, in press and on platform, tried to raise a laugh at this " elderly barrister " (as Mr. Birrell had called Carson) being given a sword, yet by that time something little less than civil war was in preparation. On the 14th March, 1914, the Secretary of State sent a notable order to the Commander-in-Chief in Ireland. There had been, Colonel Seely wrote, reports of intentions by

---

[1] This, by the way, could hardly have been the occasion of that curious story about the Duke of Norfolk at Blenheim presenting Carson with a golden sword " in appreciation of his strenuous resistance to Rome Rule " (*Life of Redmond*, p. 211). The sword was an infantry sword in a silver scabbard, the presentation not at Blenheim but at the Ritz, nor in 1912, but in 1914, and although there were three Dukes, five Earls, and two Marquises present, the Duke of Norfolk was not among them.

U G

"evil-disposed persons" to raid Government stores of arms and ammunition in various parts of Ireland ; in particular "information shows that Armagh, Omagh, Carrickfergus and Enniskillen are insufficiently guarded."

Sir Arthur Paget, then Commander-in-Chief in Ireland, was an Englishman of great family, an old officer of the Guards, a veteran besides of many Colonial wars ; but, possibly from advancing years, rather infirm of will and indiscreet in speech for such a command in such a crisis. He had probably been a little bemused by the strange language of Colonel Seely, who had summoned him to the War Office in the preceding December, and had assured him that " the Government had no intention of giving outrageous and illegal orders to the troops," and that there would be " no question of enforcing the Home Rule Act on Ulster by force of arms for years to come, and indeed such an event would probably never happen " : but that, on the other hand, action might be " required by H.M. troops in supporting the civil power and in protecting life and property when the police were unable to hold their own."

Before these conversations took place the Chief of the Staff and the Adjutant-General had reported on " a real danger of indiscipline in the Army," due, they said, to the many efforts being made to seduce officers and men from their allegiance ; and Sir Arthur Paget certainly knew of the strong repugnance in his command against the prospect of coercing the North. In a curious speech which he made at the Corinthian Club at Dublin, on the 24th February, 1914, he evidently tried to reconcile both Loyalist opinion in Ireland and his own officers to a disagreeable duty. He had been assured over and over again, he said, that there was no intention, on the part of the Government, to make use of troops in that country, except for one purpose—a very proper purpose—to maintain law and order. They could not be told that too often. His own feelings were very strong on the subject—" It is not think-able—it is not possible—for me to contemplate even being asked to concentrate my men to move against the forces that are (I believe) in being in the North of Ireland." But they had to remember that " we soldiers have to do things that we do not like." The British Army was small ; it was very efficient ; it was in a very high state of discipline ; however distasteful it might be to them they would carry out any orders given to them by the King, " and it may be—God forbid that it may be—my lot to be ordered to move to the North and I regret it. Many officers," thus he rambled on, " —friends of you all—would hate the very idea of moving one mile north of Dublin ; but if that order comes that order must be obeyed, and if that order was not obeyed, it would mean that the Army was not in that state of discipline in which you would wish to see it." He did not for one moment believe—not for a single moment—that there could be any question of such a move being made ; but if it happened, " you must take into consideration what we soldiers are, our training of years, our stern sense of disci-pline, and how vital it is—how important it is—that we should carry out such instructions as we receive. And although you may condemn us for any act of ours, yet at the same time you would say to your-selves, ' Well, after all, they only did their duty.' "

We can almost see the puzzlement and distress

on the old soldier's face in the hesitations of this extraordinary speech, possibly primed thereto by the Secretary of State for War, who had (if we know anything of Colonel Seely) hectored and rallied the Commander-in-Chief in almost this sort of language.

Sir Arthur Paget may have seen the political implications of these orders—that the four towns mentioned made a ring round the Loyalists of Ulster—or he may have considered them merely in their military sense : at all events he replied (on 17th March) that there were already sufficient troops at Enniskillen to guard the depot ; that he was adding a little to the complement at Carrick-fergus ; but that he thought it better to remove the stores than to strengthen the garrisons of Omagh and Armagh, for the reason that any such movement of troops would, " in the present state of the country, create intense excitement in Ulster and possibly precipitate a crisis."

This reply, which suggests that Sir Arthur Paget either did not understand, or did not choose to understand, the object of the Government, crossed a letter from the Secretary of State requesting the Commander-in-Chief to come to London, and fresh orders were sent that the military stores at Omagh and Armagh were not to be removed. On the 18th March Sir Arthur Paget arrived in London and spent all that morning with the sub-committee of the Cabinet and the two Chiefs of the War Office, Sir John French and Sir John Ewart, discussing this urgent affair of Ulster.

The C.I.G.S. gave some account of this discussion to his D.M.O., Sir Henry Wilson, from which it appeared that the politicians wanted to scatter troops all over Ulster " as though it was a Ponty-pool coal-strike." Sir John French objected that " this was opposed to all true strategy," but was told that " the political situation necessitated this dispersion."

Sir Henry Wilson, an Irishman who knew Ireland well, tried to make Sir John understand what these orders meant : " . . . If the Government wanted to crush the North, they would have to mobilise the whole Army . . . even so, I had great doubts whether they could do it . . . there would be a large propor-tion of officers and men who would refuse to coerce Ulster . . . the whole thing was a nightmare to me . . . I could not believe that the Government were so mad as to start this war " ; Sir John French, of a mind both lethargic and opinionated, " seemed surprised at all this," but he was " not impressed."

That night Sir Henry Wilson " dined with Charlie Hunter, where were Milner, Doctor ' Jim ' and Carson," and, it would seem, told them something of what was afoot : " Carson " (he noted in his diary) " says his speech to-morrow on the Vote of Censure will be his last in the House of Commons till after the Ulster question is settled. They all agree the Lords must amend the Army Annual Act."[1]

There had been warnings that the Home Office were preparing warrants for the arrest of the Ulster leaders. Mr. Asquith and his special friends, Lord Crewe and Sir Edward Grey, were believed to be against any such measure ; but it was thought that they would be overborne or outwitted by more headstrong colleagues. Mr. McKenna, the Home Secretary, was supposed to be active in the business,

[1] Callwell, *Sir Henry Wilson*, vol. i., p. 139.

and one night Sir Charles Matthews, the Director of Public Prosecutions, sidled up to Carson as the Benchers were going in to dinner at the Temple. " You will be getting into serious trouble one of these days," he said, and Carson, who knew very well that Matthews would have to prepare any warrants which might be issued, replied with a squeeze of the arm, " It will make no difference between us, old man—you will do your duty and I shall do mine."

On Tuesday, the 17th March, *The Times* printed a paragraph which suggests conflict and compromise on the point : " Sir Edward Carson has arranged to leave London for Ulster on Thursday," it said. " Some anxiety has lately been caused by rumours of intended action on the part of the Government against the Ulster organisation. It is understood that Ministers are not prepared at present to include the leaders of the movement in any action which they may take ; but the tension in Belfast is now so acute that any interference or threat of interference might easily provoke reprisals."

Next day the same newspaper announced that Sir Edward Carson had postponed his departure for Ulster until Friday in order to be present in the House of Commons on Thursday, when he would wind up the debate on the Opposition Vote of Censure. Captain Craig, however, would leave for Ulster on Thursday, and would be Carson's host at Craigavon. Thus the Government had reason to believe that they were well aware of the movements of these two friends. There was what they thought to be trustworthy information that the warrants would be executed either late on Thursday or early on Friday morning. It happened, however, that an

Ulster lady, the wife of a high official, called at 5 Eaton Place, where Carson and Craig were together, and told them that large arrests in which they were to be included were to be made in Ulster, and thereupon Craig resolved to return to Belfast at once, fearing that if these things happened nothing could avert riots upon a great scale. Carson wanted to go with Craig but was persuaded by Bonar Law and Walter Long to remain for the vote of censure.

Carson was in pain on the morning of Thursday, which, to be sure, was more rather than less usual at that time and throughout his life. He rose late and went straight to the House, where Mr. Bonar Law moved a Vote of Censure which was in purport a demand for the formulation of the proposals of the Government.

Mr. Bonar Law, possibly with the counsel of Lord Hugh Cecil in mind, was studiously moderate ; he deplored the language of Mr. Churchill : " There may be," he retorted, " a worse thing than civil war ; but I can hardly imagine anything worse " ; he argued against the limitation to a term of years ; he offered—with the authority of Lord Lansdowne —the passage of the Bill, without impediment, alteration or delay, if only the Government would agree to submit it to a referendum of the people ; he warned the Prime Minister against the employment of the Army : " If it is a question only of disorder, the Army, I am sure, will obey you, and I am sure it ought to obey you ; but, if it is really a question of civil war, soldiers are citizens like the rest of us."

All in vain : Mr. Asquith was reasonable in tone, but adamant in matter. His proposal (he said) gave everything that the Opposition could desire : if they would not consent to the principle, what was the use of entering into detail ? As for the Army— " I very much deprecate the laying down by a statesman of the right hon. gentleman's position of any such doctrine—that it lies in the discretion of those in the service of the King to determine whether or not any particular contingency justifies them in acting as the right hon. gentleman would seem to suggest."

Mr. Bonar Law interrupted to draw a distinction between rebellion and civil war, with special reference to America ; but Mr. Asquith retorted that " the South, as a matter of fact, were always described as rebels."

As to the referendum, the Prime Minister cross-examined the Leader of the Opposition at length on a suggestion which he could not have been seriously considering, and then turning to " the right hon. gentleman the Member for the University of Dublin," he said : " Would Ulster accept the decision ? "

" Does the Prime Minister give a firm offer ? " Carson retorted. " If so I will answer it."

It was not his offer, the Prime Minister replied, and he returned to the offer which he had made— an ample offer, a democratic offer, an offer which adequately safeguarded every interest of Ulster, the only offer which gave real hope of a lasting settlement.

Mr. Asquith was adroit and plausible ; Carson knew the truth and spoke with cold scorn of the speech as " trifling " with the subject. There was, said a Parliamentary correspondent who looked on, " no anger in the voice of Sir Edward Carson. What was in it was a feeling difficult to define but very disturbing. It spoke of a purpose dedicated by honour and duty and therefore fixed and inexorable."

Carson had made up his mind. He turned from the smooth words of the Prime Minister to the rough language of the First Lord.

" I feel," he said, " that I ought not to be here, but in Belfast."

" With your sword drawn ? " a Member interjected, and there was an immediate tumult in the House—like the clash of steel.

" Having been all this time a Government of cowards," Carson exclaimed ; " now they are going to entrench themselves behind His Majesty's troops, and they have been discussing over at the War Office how many they will require and how many they will mobilise." And with growing vehemence : " You may go on with your conferences at the War Office, you can go on calling in your Law Officers for the purpose of telling you when you are within your rights, and when you are not, you can go as far as you like ; but you can never, in the face of these facts, never, never, never, bring this country with you in the belief that what you are doing can ever send a message of peace to Ireland.

" I hate," he continued, " all this talk about the Army being sent to Ulster. Ulster people have always been, and are at this present moment on the best of terms with your Army, and it is the only part of Ireland where that can be said.

" Your Army is welcome there, as is your Fleet, as it was the other day, as much as in any part of the United Kingdom, so much so that you think, before you commence your operations, of removing

the regiments which are there at the present
moment."

It was true ; to the ears of the Secretary of State
for War, startlingly and disturbingly true.

Sir Arthur Paget had been summoned to the War
Office on Tuesday the 17th ; on the 18th his plan
for the guarding of depots had been overridden, and
a very much bigger scheme had been put in its
place. And on that very day, the 19th, when Carson
was taunting the Secretary of State for War, telegrams had gone out from the War Office to send
strong detachments of troops to Omagh, Armagh,
Enniskillen and Carrickfergus. Two hundred were
to be dispatched to Enniskillen, where Paget had
thought 100 sufficient ; his orders to remove stores
from Omagh and Armagh were countermanded ;
100 men were sent to Armagh and 300 sent to
Omagh, and 100 by two cruisers from Kingstown
to Carrickfergus.

Not only so : the Dorset Regiment, then quar-
tered in the Victoria Barracks, Belfast, was ordered
to be moved four miles out to Holywood Barracks,
where the Norfolk Regiment was already stationed.
All stores and ammunition—thirty tons of them—
were to be moved with the regiment, and such was
the haste suggested that, were it thought necessary,
the men were to leave their rifles behind, " after
rendering them useless by removing the bolts."[1]

There were other orders issued that day which
implied larger plans than the guarding of stores
and ammunition. A battalion of infantry was sent
to Dundalk and Newry. At Dundalk, which lay not
in Ulster but in Leinster, there was already a whole
brigade of field artillery—eighteen guns with 530

[1] This seems incredible ; but see White Paper (Cd. 7329), No. VII.

officers and men—at Newry there were neither
men nor stores, only old unoccupied barracks ;
but that place commanded an important railway
junction and an even more important bridgehead.
Newry and Enniskillen, indeed, were the two gates
into Ulster.

To return, however, to the House of Commons.
There had been a fierce passage with Mr. Churchill
over the Bradford speech, and Mr. Devlin, rushing
to the help of the First Lord, in his Celtic charge
threw all cumbersome impedimenta of facts to the
winds.

Carson had said that he was not on the make,
with obvious reference to the rise of the First Lord
in his adopted party.

" When a young lawyer," Devlin retorted, " in a
moment of youthful and generous enthusiasm, pins
his colours to the banner of a great cause for the
sake of all that is good in it, when he becomes an
Irish Home Ruler, and subscribes to the principles
of Home Rule, and when the forces of honour and
justice are beaten, joins the forces of a powerful
enemy—that is what I call a man on the make."

" I wish to say," Carson interrupted, " that the
observation of the hon. member is an infamous lie,
and he knows it."

Winston Churchill, never lacking in magnanimity, rose amid the uproar : " As my name had
been brought in," he said, " may I say that I have
not the slightest personal resentment in respect of
any comments made upon me, and I certainly do
not desire that anyone should take up the cudgels
on my behalf."

At the end of this confused and acrimonious
mêlée, Carson rose and went out. It was observed

that he turned when he got to the side of the Speaker's chair, and, looking down the Chamber, raised his right arm and waved it, " either to salute his friends or in defiance of the House, or both." " I am off to Belfast," he said as he disappeared.

Although the vast majority of the members must have been bewildered by a demonstration of which they did not know the cause, yet there were those on the Government Bench, almost certainly, who saw Carson disappear with that chagrin which the stalker feels when a stag, long sought, leaps up and goes over the crest of the hill into the next glen. But now to follow !

Carson left the House at 5.15, went to the telephone, ordered his servant to meet him at Euston, and then caught the 5.55 for Belfast, with a cheerful farewell to his friend Walter Long, who had gone with him to the railway station.

That night, by another train, Sir Arthur Paget, bemused with many and formidable instructions from the Secretary of State, made for Dublin.

That night also Mr. Churchill and the First Sea Lord (Prince Henry of Battenberg) without summoning the Board telegraphed these notable orders to the Vice-Admiral commanding the Third Battle Squadron then at Arosa Bay :

" Send *Britannia* to Gibraltar and proceed at once with remainder of squadron at ordinary speed to Lamlash. After clearing Ushant you are yourself to proceed in your flagship to Plymouth, handing over command of squadron temporarily to the Rear-Admiral. From Plymouth you are to come to London and report yourself at the

Admiralty, subsequently rejoining the squadron overland at Lamlash, whither your flagship is to proceed in the interval. Report time you expect to arrive in London."

Lamlash is in the Isle of Arran in the Firth of Clyde, over against Belfast.

Still further, and not the least remarkable, on that same day or night Commanding Officer, H.M.S. *Attentive*, is ordered to proceed with consort H.M.S. *Pathfinder* to Kingstown, there to take aboard certain troops for Carrickfergus, to arrive at dawn on Saturday the 21st, after which he is to take his ship to Bangor, County Down, " land yourself in plain clothes, and proceed to Holywood Barracks, and interview General Sir Nevil Macready as to co-operation with military in certain eventualities."

Lamlash, Bangor, Carrickfergus, Holywood, if the reader will refer to his atlas, he will see how these points command and converge upon the City of Belfast, and he will note also how the orders relate to that week-end when Carson and Craig are to be at Craigavon—a notable coincidence in time and place.

These orders will be considered later. In the meantime we must follow Carson to Ulster, where he went, knowing what was threatened, to prevent a clash if he could and at any rate to take what might come to him in the company of his friends. He crossed by S.S. *Heroic* and arrived early on Friday morning, the 20th March, in Belfast Harbour. There on the quay was his good friend James Craig awaiting him, and there also were General Sir George Richardson and his whole Staff, and two companies of the West Belfast Regiment, equipped as for field service, with everything except arms, to serve as a Guard of Honour. Under this escort he moved slowly through thronged and excited streets, wildly cheered as he passed, and so to Craigavon, then under guard, night and day, of two hundred armed men. Thus prepared the two friends awaited the impending event.

CHAPTER XXII

AFFAIR OF THE CURRAGH

Tension in Belfast—Secret reports—The telegram—shadowy movements—
Sir Nevil Macready—Naval plans—Military moves—Officers offered
a choice—Brigadier-General Gough—The Curragh.

SIR EDWARD CARSON found Belfast in a state of
tense excitement. The ominous words of Mr.
Churchill—" Let us go forward and put these grave
matters to the proof "—had seemed to suggest
immediate action. There were flying rumours of
impending arrests. On Thursday it had been
reported that warrants for the seizure of a large
number of officers of the Ulster Volunteer Force
had been issued and that the Government were
" waiting an opportune time to execute them."[1]
Tim Healy, with his ear close to the ground, had
heard something of the same sort. " The retirement
of Carson and his friends to Belfast last week," he
wrote to his brother, " is said to be due to knowledge
of the truth of the rumours of an intention to proceed against them. There had been a conference at
the Irish Office with the Fighting Services and the
Chief Secretary. It is asserted that the decision
arrived at, which determined Carson, was to arrest
him and fifty others, and to raid the offices of the
League in London and in Ireland."
    Whatever might be the truth or falsehood of those

[1] Belfast Correspondent of *The Times*, writing Thursday, 19th March,
1914.

reports, they strongly held and greatly excited the people of Belfast. Their leaders indeed had reason to suspect that trouble might be instigated. They had friends and well-wishers in Ministerial circles who kept them informed of what was under consideration. The historian does not advance the letters of these people as evidence of what actually happened, since he cannot well give the names of the writers, who may have been mistaken or even malicious in what they reported. They are, however, evidence at least of what Carson and Craig were informed as to Ministerial intention, and for that reason I may be allowed to quote from the letter of a member of a household where Ministers were accustomed to meet socially and informally at all hours and discuss matters with considerable freedom.

" Less than a week ago," he wrote (on the 14th January, 1914), " Mr. Asquith, Mr. McKenna and Mr. Pease were there about the same time.

" The plan is to procrastinate until the patience of the hooligan element in Belfast is exhausted and they begin to riot. This is the moment when troops (they have decided which regiments are to be sent) will step in and crush riots and incidentally you and the Loyalists. Mr. Asquith hankers after compromise and is not much in favour of this policy, but is being over-ruled.

" They have agents in Belfast—some pretending to be friendly to your people—who send regular reports and who are to say when it is the right moment to stir up riot. I tried to get hold of one of these reports, but Mr. McKenna never lets them out of his hand and reads them out to the others.

" Mr. Lloyd George is the only one who does not

think things are serious. He said casually over the tea-table, ' Put the Crimes Act in force and the whole thing will fizzle out in a week.' "

And another correspondent wrote, evidently later in the spring of 1919 : " The enemy are evidently planning a coup. I send you this for what it is worth."

"On Monday, the 52 'special service men' in Ulster were summoned by wire to London. They (or 48 of them) did come on Tuesday. . . . Verbal instructions of some kind were given and the men were given lunch and detained until there was just time and no more to catch the train back at Euston. . . . There is I am convinced some concerted plan to provoke a riot, or riots, and then step in with martial law."[1]

Such reports show what Carson had in mind when, on the Friday (20th March, 1914), he made " earnest appeal to all our followers to maintain the same dignified attitude of calm and peace which has hitherto prevailed to the honour and credit of the whole community."

Fortunately by that time the Protestant manhood of Ulster was under good discipline : approximately 110,000 Volunteers had been enrolled ; the whole Province was patrolled and to some extent policed by the force ; they had their friends and agents everywhere ; railways, post office, government offices, customs were all more or less under their influence ; even the police, as we shall presently see, worked with them on terms of guarded friendliness. From the Thursday night onwards over that critical week-end, their motor dispatch riders and

[1] It is fair to add that I can find no confirmation of this story, and it is just possible that the deputation may have consisted of the Liberal Party in Belfast, which at that time numbered about fifty.—I. C.

their signalling corps were busily keeping head-quarters in touch with every part of Ulster. In Belfast part of the Special Emergency Corps of the City Volunteers had been mobilised, and picket companies equipped with bandoliers, haversacks, water-bottles and belts, were told off for duty, out of the public gaze, at various points in and around the city. Thus Friday wore on, a day of tense awaiting. The movements of troops—the evacuation of the Victoria Barracks and the march of the Dorsets with all their stores to Holywood—had their meaning, at which those intent watchers could only guess. Something was afoot, yet nothing happened.

As night drew on the Very lights of the Volunteer pickets flared along the shore road. In Belfast the Emergency Corps kept watch and ward. The police were also out—and in force, either side warily watching the other.

Late on Friday night the Assistant Commissioner[1] was inspecting his posts and chanced to meet Colonel Chichester, who commanded the Volunteers.

" Don't you think," said the policeman with a yawn, " that we might all go to bed ? "

" No," the Colonel replied, " I don't think we can, because we happen to know that you have a certain telegram—and it is upon that information that we are out."

Now it was true that friends of the Volunteers in the post office had supplied them with the copy of a telegram from Dublin Castle to the Police Commandant in Belfast ; but it being in code they could make nothing of it. Chichester's words were a shot in the dark.

---

[1] Afterwards Sir Thomas Smith, K.B.E., Inspector-General, R.I.C., 1920–22.

" Oh," said Smith, " if it is only that, you need not be making all this trouble." And to make good his assurance, he took a decoded copy of the telegram from his pocket. " Here it is," he said, " read it for yourself. There's nothing in it."

All that the telegram said was—" Expect important document to-morrow morning," and this free interchange of intelligence enabled both sides to retire to rest. Nevertheless, as we shall presently see, Mr. Smith blundered in making that disclosure.

Belfast went to sleep ; but the guards at Craigavon kept vigil through the night, while motor-cyclists came and went with orders and information. Nothing, however, happened until dawn, and what happened then only gave distant and uncertain information to the watchers. Two small cruisers stole into the Lough as dawn was breaking and unloaded troops at the old fort of Carrickfergus, on the northern shore ; then one of them crossed the Lough to Bangor—and that was all.

What did those shadowy movements signify? Even now it is impossible to say with certainty, although the orders issued and the arrangements made suggest at least the design of what was intended. Thus we have already quoted the significant directions to the Commanding Officer, H.M.S. *Attentive*—how, after landing the troops at Carrickfergus, at dawn on Saturday the 21st, he was to take his ship to Bangor, County Down—" land yourself in plain clothes and proceed to Holywood Barracks and interview General Sir Nevil Macready as to co-operation with military in certain eventualities."

What were these eventualities ? General Sir Nevil Macready was at that time Director of Personal

Services, that is to say he held a high appointment on the General Staff under Sir John French in Whitehall—what then was he supposed to be doing at Holywood Barracks outside Belfast ? And why should this stealthy assignation be made between him and a naval officer in plain clothes for that Saturday morning ?

On the previous Wednesday, the 18th March, as we learn from the Diaries of Sir Henry Wilson, Sir Nevil Macready attended a conference of the Ulster Committee of the Cabinet and the High Command —Sir John French, Sir John Spencer Ewart (the Adjutant-General) and Sir Arthur Paget. All that was contemplated then—or so Sir John French told Sir Henry Wilson afterwards—was " scattering troops all over Ulster as though it was a Pontypool coal-strike " ; but either that day or the next Sir Nevil Macready received orders which would have taken him to Belfast on that critical week-end, had he not been suddenly indisposed. On Friday the 20th March, after the General Officer Commanding in Ireland had crossed over to Dublin, he received instructions bearing on this subject : It had been decided to appoint an Officer as General Officer Commanding the Belfast District, who was besides to have the powers of a Divisional Magistrate in order to control the Royal Irish Constabulary within the limit of his command : " As you are aware," these instructions continued, " Major-General Sir Nevil Macready has been selected for appointment as General Officer Commanding the Belfast District, but owing to illness cannot take up duties before Monday, the 23rd instant."[1]

Sir Arthur Paget was, therefore, to appoint an

[1] Command Paper, 7329 (1914).

officer to act for Macready between Friday night and Monday morning, and he selected General Friend, his Second-in-Command in Ireland. Now there was at that time a senior military officer, Brigadier-General Count Gleichen, in command at Belfast. Count Gleichen, then, was to be superseded by Sir Nevil Macready, and, when Sir Nevil Macready was delayed, by General Friend. Macready was only to be delayed by one week-end, yet whatever was in hand was considered so important that Count Gleichen was not thought equal to it. The senior officer but one in all Ireland had to be sent to Holywood to take the place of Macready in supreme command of military and police for the week-end Saturday the 21st to Monday the 23rd March, 1914.

Certainly something of first-class importance must have been expected to take place within those two dates. What was it ? Sir Nevil Macready, in his *Annals of an Active Life*, tells us many interesting things about himself and his career—how strongly he felt at that crisis that the first duty of an officer was obedience, what flattering offers were made to him by Colonel Seely, how his special connection with Ireland began in December 1913 ; but on this critical week-end of 21st–23rd March, 1914, he is disappointingly reticent. " King Carson," he says, " was installed in his palace at Craigavon, and I was ordered to go over to Ulster on a not very clearly defined mission," and he adds that if secret orders were indeed given " it is curious that I should not have been informed, as no word reached me of any projected move northwards." He would no doubt have been better informed but for the misfortune of that untimely indisposition.

What we know of a certainty is that Sir Nevil Macready was to be at Holywood that week-end, but that, when his health unexpectedly failed, General Friend was put in his place. He was for certain purposes undisclosed, to supersede Brigadier-General Count Gleichen, and he was also to have special powers over the police. Thus Sir Arthur Paget was notified by the War Office on Friday : " Birrell has issued instructions to Commissioner of Police, Belfast, to take instructions from Officer appointed General Officer Commanding there."

There is a coincidence of time and place which the attentive reader will have noted. Holywood lies within a mile of that " palace of Craigavon " where, as Sir Nevil Macready so wittily says, " King Carson was installed " that week-end. Bangor, to which place the Officer Commanding H.M.S. *Attentive* was to bring his ship on the Saturday morning, lies farther along the southern shore, and Bangor, it may be noted, was further reinforced on the Saturday night by two officers and forty-one men of the Norfolk Regiment, conveyed in a steam pinnace and two long boats from Carrickfergus, which commands Craigavon from the opposite coast. Is it possible that these mysterious dispositions involved a raid on Craigavon, then the headquarters of the Ulster Volunteers, and the arrest of its principal occupants ?

All this is mere surmise, although plausibility will hardly be denied to it. A passage from the Diaries of Sir Henry Wilson throws a less speculative but still doubtful light on the matter. His friend Lieutenant-Colonel A. H. Ollivant, an Officer of the General Staff whom he had lent to the Admiralty two years before, came to see him after luncheon on the 24th March, 1914, and told him what Wilson describes as an amazing story :

" He " (Ollivant) said, as a fact (and I believe him), that Winston had drafted orders to the Third Battle Squadron and two flotillas to go to Lamlash under Lewis Bayley and from there to make a regular Jameson Raid on some Ulster stronghold. This was frustrated by our action in the Army.

Sir Henry Wilson had further information that the receipt of instructions by Vice-Admiral Bayley was delayed for eighteen hours after they reached the 3rd Battle Squadron at Arosa Bay, an accident which may have further dislocated these combined operations. It is, moreover, certain that the Vice-Admiral gave an order for Field Artillery to be got ready at Plymouth to be taken aboard on his way from Arosa Bay to Lamlash, an order explained on the ground that the guns were wanted for shore exercise in the rough weather that was to be expected.

If it be true that there was a design to raid some Ulster stronghold, what stronghold was there in Ulster which would have yielded such rich results in arrested leaders, in captured papers and in psychological effects as that white country house which lay so open between Holywood and Bangor on the southern shore of Belfast Lough ?

When Sir Henry Wilson said that these " drafted orders " were " frustrated by our action in the Army," he was referring to what happened—and did not happen—at Dublin and the Curragh on the Friday and Saturday, the 20th and 21st March, 1914, and if we are to approximate more nearly to the inner meaning of what was done and what was intended, we must turn from Ulster to Leinster.

The General Officer Commanding in Ireland, before he left Whitehall, telegraphed to his head-quarters in Dublin calling a conference of his General Officers—his Chief Officers of the Staff and Commanders of Divisions and Brigades—for 10 a.m. on Friday morning. At least two reports of what happened at that meeting were afterwards published. Sir Arthur Paget's own—a written statement to the War Office dated 2nd April, 1914, after controversy had raged for a fortnight over the affair, has an explanatory, even an exculpatory tone. He speaks of " certain moves of a precaution-ary nature," which the Government believed " would be carried out without resistance," but which Paget feared " would create intense excite-ment " and would set " the country, or if not the country, the press, ablaze on the following day." It is left in Paget's statement uncertain as to how far the choice offered to his officers was his own and how far it was the Secretary of State's idea. We have already seen enough of the General's mode of expression to realise that such misunder-standings were not unnatural. What is certain is that the officers present believed that they were not given an order but asked for a decision ; that they were being put to a test or purge which they in their turn were to put to the officers under them as a preliminary to the issue of orders and the disclosure of plans. Brigadier-General Hubert Gough's report of the interview was made at the time ; it was quoted by Mr. Bonar Law in the House of Commons on the following Monday, without disclaimer or denial by the General Officer Com-manding in Ireland.

" Sir Arthur Paget said that active operations

were to be begun against Ulster ; that he expected the country to be in a blaze by Saturday ; that he had been in close communication with the War Office, and that he had the following instruction from the War Office to convey to the officers :

" Officers domiciled in Ulster would be allowed to disappear and would be reinstated in their position, but they must give their word of honour that they would not fight for Ulster.

" Officers who are not prepared to undertake active operations against Ulster, for conscientious or other scruples, were to send in their resignations, and would be dismissed the Army.

" It was to be fully understood that the officers, brigadiers, and any officers who avoided service on an incorrect plea of domicile in Ulster would be tried by Court Martial."

There can be little doubt of the accuracy of this report, since General Fergusson, who took the opposite view of his duty from General Gough, yet agreed with Gough as to what was offered at the interview. The Divisional Orders issued by General Fergusson state in precise terms the alternatives open to serving officers.

General Gough, in some other notes, reported some further scraps of this remarkable conference. He did not expect any bloodshed, Paget said, " we were too strong. . . ." The Fleet was in Belfast Harbour, and some ships were in Dublin Bay. Nevertheless he was no prophet, and, although he expected no bloodshed, he did expect those officers who embarked with him on this course to go with him to the " bitter end."

Unimpressed by these military assurances, the Brigadier, who belonged to an Irish Loyalist family of the South, asked if the Act of Clemency, as he might call it, which had been extended to officers domiciled in Ulster, could not be stretched to other officers resident in Ireland, whose feelings and sentiments might be no less involved.

The General Officer Commanding in Ireland replied that the condition for officers in Ulster was the last and the only concession that could be granted. Gough, he added, was to expect " no mercy from his old friend at the War Office," meaning, no doubt, Sir John French, and as Gough left the room Paget added, " You need not expect any help from the other side." There would be another conference at two o'clock when he would divulge his " plans " ; if any officers were not prepared to carry out everything that he then ordered, they were not to attend.

This remarkable interview ended, the officers left the room and continued the discussion outside. Fergusson, " white and agitated, with trembling cheeks," argued that the Army must hold together. Rolt expressed a strong aversion from serving against Ulster. Fergusson said he would go and Gough that he would not go.

Then Rolt, under orders from Fergusson, set out for the Curragh to put the alternatives to the officers of his brigade : Gough went in the motor-car with Rolt, but stopped at Kingsbridge to telegraph to his brother " Johnnie " Gough at Alder-shot, and then went to the mess of the 5th Lancers and told the news privately to Colonel Parker, who threw himself on a sofa, exclaiming—" It is monstrous, monstrous—I won't go, I won't."

They then collected the officers of that regiment, or as many as they could find, and put the alternatives before them. " These were big crises," said Gough, " but every man must decide for himself, according to his conscience," and he left the barracks.

In the meantime Sir Arthur Paget was going on with his preparations, and had called another conference—this time of those General Officers who were prepared to serve against Ulster—to expound his plan of campaign, the plan no doubt of the Ulster Committee of the Cabinet, or of its more warlike members.

This higher strategy of the Third Home Rule Bill was never disclosed to a nation which prides itself on governing its own destinies ; although it did become known to the Ulster Unionist Council through a trustworthy channel, and is fully set out in certain papers which, by strange chance, fell into the hands of Sir Edward Carson.

The Third Cavalry Brigade was to move forward and occupy the bridge-heads along the Boyne ; behind it the 5th Division was to advance and consolidate the positions thus occupied, and the 6th Division, stationed in the South of Ireland, was to occupy the places, at the Curragh and Dublin, evacuated by the 5th.

A force of some ten thousand troops was to be moved from Lichfield and Aldershot into Ireland, when the strength of the force engaged in these operations would be about twenty-five thousand, including Artillery, Army Service and Army Medical Corps.

Newry, in advance of Dundalk, was being occupied ; the garrisons at Armagh, Omagh, Carrickfergus and Enniskillen were being strengthened and the Victoria Barracks at Belfast, being untenable, were being evacuated in favour of Holywood. Twelve hundred men were drafted into those various posts in the course of the week-end.

So much for the Army ; but Sir Arthur explained that the object was to blockade Ulster by sea as well as by land, that two small cruisers were already co-operating in the transport of troops ; that two flotillas of destroyers and the 3rd Battle Squadron were on their way to the scene of action.

It was not intended, the General went on to explain, that the Army should begin the fighting. The Belfast Police would receive orders to seize certain concealed depots of arms, and the Old Town Hall, the headquarters of the Unionist organisation. These moves were certain to be resisted ; the Volunteers would attack the police ; the troops round Belfast and a Naval Force would intervene, and the Army would move forward.

Then the General described his conception of the first battle. When the troops had suffered some casualties, he himself would go forward to the " enemy " under a flag of truce and demand a surrender, failing which he would order an assault on the position.

While these directions were being given, Brigadier-General Gough was returning to headquarters to see General Friend and inform him of his decision to resign his commission.

The General, grieved to hear such news, asked Gough if he could not consider the matter as he himself did—that it was his duty to maintain law and order.

" No," said Gough, " if it is law and order now, it may develop into civil war at any moment,

and then it would be much worse—even dis-
honourable—to leave Sir Arthur Paget." It was
better, therefore, and more honourable, to come to
a decision at once.

Gough thought it useless to see the Commander-
in-Chief again ; but asked General Friend to give
Sir Arthur Paget his decision, thanking him at the
same time for " doing his best for us in the matter of
terms at the War Office."

Gough added that he considered himself dismissed
the Service ; but Friend begged him to carry on and
send in his letter of resignation, and he added :
" I have not got a very pleasant job either ; I have
to go to Belfast to-night as Military Governor."

When Gough expressed his belief that twenty
officers of the 5th Lancers would not go, Friend
" seemed surprised and upset and begged me at
once to let him know results soon, as, if there were
many resignations, it might make the Government
alter their policy." With this ray of hope possibly
comforting him a little, General Gough returned to
his own headquarters.

The Curragh, a vast common of springy turf, the
finest ground of exercise for men and guns and
horses in all Ireland, was at that time a great camp
of the British Army—a lively bustling centre of all
arms, radiating its gallant life and consequent
prosperity over the surrounding towns and districts.
And the pride of the Curragh at that time was the
Third Cavalry Brigade, consisting of the 4th Hussars,
the 5th Lancers, the 10th Lancers, the 3rd Brigade
Royal Horse Artillery, the 4th Field Troop and the
3rd Signal Troop Royal Engineers.

To the officers of all these units the Brigadier put the choice at 3.30 that afternoon. He himself, he said, was an Irishman ; his mind was made up and he had resigned his commission. In such a crisis he declined to give advice to anyone ; they must each and all decide for themselves, as their consciences dictated.

It was not an easy choice, for the orders on which it depended had never been disclosed, and while the officers were nearly all against " active service " in Ulster, there were some who thought they ought to know more of the duties proposed.

This seemed to Gough reasonable ; it would at least gain time. Accordingly he wrote to Sir Arthur Paget that his officers wanted further information " before they are called upon at such short notice to take decisions so vitally affecting their whole future." Especially they wanted a clear definition of the terms " duty as ordered " and " active operations in Ulster."

" If such duty consists in the maintenance of order and in the preservation of property, all the officers in this Brigade, including myself, would be prepared to carry out that duty. But if the duty involves the initiation of active military operations against Ulster, the following number of officers would respectfully and under protest prefer to be dismissed."

And the Brigadier proceeded to give the decision of his officers, in numbers, unit by unit.

To that letter no reply was ever given ; but Sir Arthur Paget took action which in the end was decisive.

Possibly Friend suggested it ; at all events the first telegram which the General sent must have rung many bells in the War Office. It baldly announced that the officers of two regiments of Lancers were resigning their commissions and added, " Fear men will refuse to move." And then in a second message the shattering summary of Gough's figures :

> " Regret to report Brigadier and 57 officers, 3rd Cavalry Brigade, prefer to accept dismissal if ordered North."

It was not only the Cavalry which had been immobilised by the test. General Fergusson had involved the Infantry in a similar fate. His Divisional Order of the 20th March makes it clear that in his view the purge had been authorised by Whitehall :

> " In view of the possibility of active operations in Ulster the War Office had authorised the following communication to officers :
> " 1. Officers *whose homes are actually in the Province of Ulster* who wish to do so may apply for permission to be absent from duty during the period of operations and will be allowed to ' disappear ' from Ireland.
> " 2. Any officer who from conscientious or other motives is not prepared to carry out his duty as ordered should say so at once. Such officers *will be at once dismissed the Service*."

In a note General Fergusson added that the words italicised were to be taken " literally and strictly," and expressed the hope that " very few cases would be found of officers who elect to sever their connection with the Service."

Despite this exhortation, and the astonishing

assurance added verbally that the first shot was to come from Ulster, many officers of the line elected to stand by their comrades in the Cavalry.

" I have heard," one journalist wrote, " of many hard cases of officers faced with this painful dilemma. A Quartermaster with thirty-eight years' service, and an officer with thirty years' service, with a private income of only £15 per annum, when suddenly called upon to abandon their prospects in life, unhesitatingly decided to act in concert with their brother officers." One Colonel, evidently a man of plain speech, told his officers that steps had been taken in Ulster " so that any aggression must come from the Ulsterites, and they will have to shed first blood "—a provocation which he described as " hellish." The men were of the same mind as their officers : the cavalry fed and watered their horses, but refused to parade, the infantry left their rifles in their racks ; from Dublin to Cork, officers and men, cavalry, infantry and artillery, with some few exceptions among the officers, were of one mind.

Thus by Friday night the British Army at the Curragh had crumbled in the hands of its Commander-in-Chief. The full effects of the disintegration were not realised till next day, when it became plain to the quick brains of Mr. Churchill and Mr. Lloyd George and the slower mind of Colonel Seely that those combined operations " to anticipate and crush the resistance of Ulster " could not be carried through.

The storm which threatened that white house on the shore of Belfast Lough was destined never to break, save in distant rumble and harmless sheet lightning—over the Boyne.

CHAPTER XXIII

EXPLANATIONS

COLONEL SEELY, with a superabundance of the sort of courage that prompts the bull to charge the gate, precipitately decided on strong measures. Resignations were not to be accepted : officers were to be threatened with courts martial. Brigadier-General Gough was superseded (by Brigadier-General Chetwode) ; and he and his Colonels were to come over at once to the War Office. Confronted with these Draconic instructions, the mind of the General Officer Commanding in Ireland became more divided—and more bemused—than ever. Sir Arthur Paget made one more desperate attempt to reconcile the obstinate scruples of his officers with the imperious orders of the Secretary of State. At eleven o'clock on Saturday morning he held a meeting of his cavalry officers at the Curragh : he himself sat at the only table, and some thirty-five officers, sitting or standing where they could, listened (with well-bred but steely politeness) to what was probably the most remarkable harangue ever delivered by an English Commander-in-Chief to the officers of his Army.

He began in a propitiatory tone : he was their friend, their general and their chief and they must
Xc

trust him : he, for his part, would see that they were not placed in any position to which they might object. He could not imagine why so many officers had resigned, because, though active operations were indeed intended against Ulster, he had no intention of carrying them out.

Only moves had been ordered which were required to protect stores and so forth, and even these were mainly directed against the " Hibernians." In case of a collision with the Ulster Army, he would reverse the ordinary procedure, and go forward with his Generals in front of the firing line : after the first burst of firing, he would hoist the white flag, confer with the Ulster Volunteer leaders, and then go home.

He could reassure them in other ways. He would have a force of from 20,000 to 25,000 men on the Boyne almost at once ; the Navy were to co-operate ; he did not want the Cavalry, except perhaps one regiment, which would act as scouts, for " of course he did not want to march along and bump unexpectedly into a large force of the enemy " ; but they need not fight ; they could hoist the white flag if it came to the pinch ; in the event of a big battle they would be placed on the flank, and need not take part—although, if he were getting the worst of it, he would expect the Cavalry to help him ; he could even arrange for some little disturbance down in the South to which any regiment might be sent which particularly objected to going North.

Finding that these tactical intentions in no way impressed his audience, Sir Arthur Paget tried another line of argument. It was not, he said, a soldier's job to indulge in sickly sentimentality ; he had anticipated only a few resignations on the part

of religious fanatics, and these wholesale resignations would bring disgrace on famous regiments.
As for General Gough and his colonels, they would
be tried by General Court Martial ; the resignations
would not be accepted ; he would march the
Infantry into the Cavalry lines and disarm the
regiments ; if officers refused to go there were worse
things than dismissal, as they would find out.

Then, seeing the steeliness and stoniness rather
increasing than diminishing at these threats, Sir
Arthur tried still another line of approach. His
troops, he said, much to his surprise, had been
received everywhere in Ulster with enthusiasm.
There was not an inch between the two Parties in
Parliament, so near were they to a settlement of the
whole question. Why sacrifice their careers when
the whole thing might be over next day ?

Then, unconscious of his own contradictions, he
proceeded to promise that the Ulstermen would be
forced to fire the first shot. Ulster, indeed, seemed
quiet ; but the Government had made one dangerous move, which he was not at liberty to disclose, but which might cause an immediate rising
in Ulster.

There being still no response, he ended with an
exasperated and illogical objurgation against " those
dirty swine of politicians."

The oration over, one of the senior officers rather
hotly complained of the grave decision demanded,
at short notice, with no apparent cause—" like putting a pistol at one's head." Brigadier-General
Gough remarked that though sentiment might be
a luxury, men had died for it. The General retorted that Gough need expect no mercy, and
Gough replied that he did not ask for mercy.

So ended this extraordinary interview ; and with
it the attempt to march, as King James II had
marched, upon the Boyne.

Four simple soldiers, the Brigadier and his
Cavalry Colonels, set out as ordered for Whitehall,
where they were to make the Secretary of State—
brave man as he was—sorry that he had ever sent
for them. Before they left they elicited from Sir
Charles Fergusson—to whom their final decision
had to be given—the outline of the plan against
Ulster, which was that the Army and the Navy
were to form a blockade and that the police were
to seize important buildings in Belfast.

Meanwhile the rumour of these dire events had
reached London and caused various politicians,
with more or less speed, to reconsider the situation.
Mr. Churchill thought it wise to inform the Prime
Minister that the Third Battle Squadron, and two
flotillas of destroyers from Portsmouth, were on
their way to Lamlash ; what passed at what must
have been an interesting interview is not exactly
known ; but the orders were countermanded
when the Battle Squadron was abreast the
Scillies.

That night Mr. Lloyd George was to have justified
the operations against Ulster to a democratic audience in Huddersfield ; with that agility which made
him great he delivered instead an attack on " the
Aristocracy," which had assumed the " divine
right " previously claimed by the Stuarts to " veto
progressive Bills supported by the Democracy of
this Kingdom," whereby " representative government in this land is at stake."

The Prime Minister, only a day behind his Chancellor, late on Sunday night, authorised *The Times*

to make a statement which discreetly veiled the facts. The movement of troops in Ireland was " purely of a precautionary character " ; so much was obvious to the intelligent observer from the fact that " the disposing of small bodies of troops in Ulster was perfectly useless from a strategic point of view." As for the " so-called naval movements," they consisted in " the use of two small cruisers to convey a detachment of troops to Carrickfergus without the necessity of moving them through the streets of Belfast."

No further movement of troops was in contemplation.

In regard to the " prevalent rumour that warrants are out for the arrest of the Ulster leaders," it " has not and never has had the slightest foundation of fact. . . . The Government has never taken and does not contemplate any such step."

As to the " third misapprehension " at the Curragh, it was due to a " widespread impression " that the Government " contemplate instituting a general inquisition into the intentions of officers in the event of their being asked to take up arms against Ulster. No such action was intended, if only for the reason that the employment of troops against Ulster is a contingency which the Government hope may never arise."

Colonel Seely, in his autobiographical study, *Fear and Be Slain*, gives a modest but thrilling account of himself in various dangers by sea and land ; but is completely silent on what must have been for him the most fearful place of all—when he met the Prime Minister after the news broke over Downing Street. What we gather of the interview is that Mr. Asquith told Colonel Seely to make his peace with the officers from the Curragh on the ground that it was all an " honest misunderstanding."

This was not so easy as might appear : it led in fact to a more tangled imbroglio than at the Curragh. The Brigadier and his Colonels said that they were simple soldiers ; they did not understand politics ; they had been given their choice ; they had accepted dismissal, and if they were to resume their duties it could only be upon terms. Against this attitude, eloquence, exhortations, prayers and menaces broke in vain. The Secretary of State was ready to give every verbal assurance that could be required ; but these simple soldiers insisted that, simple as they were, they would prefer to have it in writing, and so began a series of negotiations which turned upon the terms of a memorandum, " drawn up and carefully revised by the Cabinet," as Mr. Asquith tells us[1] ; but not thought quite sufficiently unambiguous by the Brigadier and his Colonels.

The soldiers were not, possibly, as simple as they seemed ; moreover, they had a counsellor as astute as any statesman, Sir Henry Wilson, who when " Johnnie " Gough came to him from Aldershot with news of his brother, had thrown himself into the affair and advised his comrades upon every step.

On Monday morning Colonel Seely gave his verbal assurance to General Gough that there was no intention to use force to suppress political opposition to the Home Rule Bill. By that time Sir Arthur Paget was with General French at the War Office ; but as their united efforts did not succeed

[1] *Fifty Years of Parliament*, vol. ii., p. 150.

in shaking the four soldiers, the Adjutant-General put the assurance in writing. Colonel Seely had in the meantime gone to the Cabinet and then to the King, who was none too well pleased with these developments in his Army. When the Secretary of State was at the Palace, the memorandum which had been written by Sir John Spencer Ewart came before the Cabinet, which struck out the really operative clauses of the document. Colonel Seely returned ; the Cabinet broke up, and the Secretary of State considered the memorandum in the light of a letter just received from General Gough asking whether the enforcement of law and order meant the enforcement of Home Rule upon Ulster against her will.

Colonel Seely looked round for advice ; the Cabinet had dispersed ; but Lord Morley (and probably, although not certainly, Mr. Churchill) was still in the room. In consultation, with one or both, Colonel Seely reinserted the assurance, and this document, which was initialled by Sir John French and Sir John Spencer Ewart, passed into the possession of the simple soldiers, who returned in triumph to spread the glad news in the Curragh.

The House of Commons met that afternoon in an excitement which Colonel Seely vainly endeavoured to allay. There had, he said, been a misunderstanding of questions put to the officers by the General Officer Commanding the Forces in Ireland. With his approval the officers had now rejoined their units ; the various movements for the protection of stores and arms had been completed, and " all orders issued have been punctually and implicitly obeyed."

Unfortunately for the Secretary of State for War, Mr. Bonar Law had been supplied by Sir Henry Wilson with General Gough's report of the words used by Sir Arthur Paget on Friday morning, and he proceeded in his rasping way to read it to the House. This brought the Prime Minister to his feet ; with that delicacy in the handling of facts which made him justly admired by his colleagues he explained that " a purely protective operation is . . . the simple history of the whole transaction " ; that " General Gough, one of the most distinguished Cavalry leaders of the day, a man of very great and well-deserved influence in the Army, and some of his officers who think with him," had "interpreted the observations and the questions addressed to him by Sir Arthur Paget in a larger and wider sense . . ." ; but were " now satisfied that the Army Council had proceeded in a perfectly correct and proper way."

This presentation of the case did not assuage the rising temper of the Radicals. Not one of their own party, but a Socialist, led the new attack. There was a tradition that John Ward, when he was a navvy, had held up, in some harbour, a coffer-dam upon his stalwart shoulders until his mates scrambled to safety, but in that debate he threw open a sluice-gate which nearly drowned the Government under a turbid flood of Radical fury. " We have here and now unquestionably to decide," he thundered, " whether we are going to maintain . . . civil authority and law within these realms, or whether for the future this House, when elected by the people, must go to a Committee of Officers, and ask that Military Junta . . . whether it is a subject with which they, as the officers of the Army, think that we, as representing the People, are not entitled to interfere."[1]

John Ward, honest fellow and good Englishman as he was, had no deep knowledge either of the laws of his country or the history of its Army. Otherwise he would have known that a soldier cannot plead blind obedience to orders as a defence of the use of arms against the subject : on the contrary, the officer being himself a subject, must always himself, in the last resort, be the judge of whether the order to shoot is reasonable or unreasonable. In a leading case, at Bristol before the Reform Act, an officer who fired upon a mob in obedience to orders was afterwards tried and condemned for " murder " ; another officer who refused to fire on the same occasion was cashiered. Thus the British Officer when called upon to support the civil arm both obeys and disobeys at his peril in an uneasy dilemma between a British jury and an Army Court. Moreover, there is a case in history for the claim of officers to resign rather than serve in a cause of which their conscience disapproves. Sir George Trevelyan says of the American War of Independence, that " not a few officers of every grade . . . flatly refused to serve against the Colonies, and their scruples were respected by their countrymen in general and by the King and his Ministers as well. . . . Some officers retired into private life, others went on half-pay until a European war broke out, when they rejoined the Army, and others accepted commissions in the Militia."

[1] John Ward conveniently ignored the fact that the men were as much implicated as their officers. And not only in the Curragh. According to the *Weekly Dispatch* of the 22nd March, 1914, two companies of the 1st Dorsets threw down their rifles when ordered to march to the neighbourhood of Ormiston, the residence of Colonel Chichester, and one Sergeant is recorded to have exclaimed, " We will have no Home Rule."

If these be called debatable points, it will be allowed—it was admitted by the Secretary of State —that the officers at the Curragh had disobeyed no orders. They had been offered a choice—to obey certain orders not yet put to them or to be dismissed the Service without pension ; they had been offered half an hour to make their decision ; and they had made it. In this there was neither breach of discipline nor defiance of Parliament.

The thin flame of truth, however, was at once blown out by the high wind of politics. " Nothing," Tim Healy wrote to his brother, " struck me more than the extraordinary and historic determination of the Radicals to face the Army crisis at all hazards. . . . We who lived through the Gladstonian epoch are troglodytes compared with the Liberals of to-day. They would rejoice at a crisis with the Army, or with the Ulstermen, and think the Government have gone too far in concession and moderation."[1]

The Prime Minister had the skill to use this enthusiasm to the advantage of the Government. The Secretary of State for War laid his resignation on the altar of constitutional liberties ; it was intended as no more than a ceremonial gesture, and his office would have been immediately restored to him but for the stubbornness of Sir John French and Sir John Spencer Ewart, who refused to play their theatrical parts and insisted upon the reality of their resignations. Then Colonel Seely really went, and the Prime Minister, " in the circumstances, after much consideration, and with not a little reluctance, felt it his duty, for the time at any rate, to assume the office of Secretary of State for

[1] *Letters and Leaders of My Day*, p. 541.

War." The Constitution was saved. "Asquith's device," Tim Healy reported to his brother, "saved them from what appeared to be a hopeless position. ... The Government have emerged with the loss of a few tail feathers."

Such was the so-called "Mutiny" at the Curragh —which was no Mutiny—and its surrounding circumstances. While these events developed Sir Edward Carson and James Craig remained at Craigavon, smiling grimly at the discomfiture of their enemies. "The conclusion I draw from the acts of the Government," said Carson (in a statement which was published on the Monday), "is that in a fit of panic they have made up their mind to attempt two things—one to intimidate and the other to provoke. They will fail in both."

It was an accurate summary of both the intention and the result. From Saturday the 21st March, 1914, onwards, there could be little hope for a policy which rested upon the coercion of Ulster, since the Army in Ireland was immobilised, and in the state of the police (which we must presently consider) the Ulster Volunteers remained—the only effective force.

There was something symbolical of this change in the situation in a curious incident which makes an appropriate end to this chapter. Sir Nevil Macready, recovered from his untimely indisposition, arrived at Holywood on Monday, the 23rd. On the following day he stopped in his motor-car with his aide-de-camp at the gates of Craigavon.

If the guest had come in mufti, like other officers from Holywood when they made a call, it would have caused no remark ; but the uniform, under the grey overcoat of a Major-General, suggested something more than a social occasion, and he was received as ceremoniously as he came. The closed iron gates guarded by two sentries were thrown open ; the sergeant of the guard, an old soldier, gave orders to turn out the guard ; with a buckling of belts the guard clattered out of the lodge and presented arms, looking very like British soldiers in their khaki uniforms, and the Major-General raised his hand to the peak of his gold-edged cap in acknowledgement of their salute."[1]

In his *Annals of An Active Life*, Sir Nevil Macready expatiates on what he calls the " comic side " of the interview : " Mr. Craig . . . received me in a small anteroom and with much solemnity informed me that Sir Edward Carson would see me directly. I did my best to play up to the evident honour that was being done me ; but, unfortunately, for no reason at all, I constantly thought of the Dalai Lama."

The processes of the Major-General's mind are certainly not obvious ; but it may be said that James Craig was also " playing up to the evident honour " of this ceremonial visit ; and when Macready was introduced to the Dalai Lama, Carson played up to it too.

Sir Nevil started the conversation in a guarded way by asking why the Ulstermen should object to the presence of His Majesty's troops in Belfast, and Carson replied that so far from objecting, the Ulstermen were delighted to see His Majesty's uniform at all times ; there was nowhere in the King's dominions where the British soldier was

[1] *See* Percival Phillips's account of this curious episode in the *Daily Express*, February 27th ,1914.

assured of a more cordial welcome than in Belfast.

Sir Nevil, reassured on this point, took his leave : whether he had come out of idle curiosity or as a soldier making a reconnaissance is not clear from his narrative. Sir Edward thought it appropriate to return the visit with the same ceremonial as it had been paid. Lord Castlereagh, then an officer of the Guards, volunteered to play the rôle of Aide-de-Camp, and the two were about to proceed in state to Holywood, when a deputation from the men of the Norfolk Regiment arrived to ask when they might expect Carson as they wanted to turn out a Guard of Honour. With much seriousness Carson thanked them for the compliment ; but begged them not to carry out their intention, and took care not to pass the barracks of the men in approaching the officers' quarters. Unfortunately for the completion of the comedy Sir Nevil Macready was not at home.

A few days later John Ward, by that time champion of the Constitution against the Army, asked the Secretary of State for War about this " official visit " and " the nature of the business transacted upon that occasion." When the Prime Minister asked for notice, Sir Edward Carson interposed with—" I can answer that question, sir." But the question was never answered.

If the historian may be allowed to indulge in the unhistorical luxury of surmise, the object of the visit was not social : if it had been, the General would have gone in mufti. Nor was it (as we gather from the tone of his book) friendly. Sir Nevil Macready had by that time been invested with magisterial powers, and his intention was probably to discover what force would be required to execute warrant of arrest at Craigavon. If, however, that was the idea, Sir Nevil Macready was already too late. After the 20th March, 1914, there was no longer the power in the hands of the Government to coerce Ulster.

CHAPTER XXIV

PREPARATIONS

Bonar's opinion—And Walter Long's—British Covenanters—Carson in the House—And in Ulster—Enter Fred Crawford.

WHILE CARSON remained at Craigavon his friends kept him abreast of events at Westminster. There are, Mr. Bonar Law wrote from the House of Commons on March 24th, 1914, " all sorts of wild rumours about the extent of preparations to invade Ulster, and some of them are so circumstantial that I believe proof will come out that the Government have been lying on a scale which is new even for them. They are, as you will have seen, going to furnish papers to-morrow, and I shall try to see Wilson in the morning and find out to what extent it is false. I should have been very glad to have had you here, and indeed I am not sure that you ought not to come.

" Unfortunately we cannot judge of that until we see the papers they have promised, and it will be too late to wire you to come for the debate which can take place to-morrow on the Consolidated Fund Bill.

" If, however, it looks as if further action can be taken by us I shall at once wire you.

" There is no use telling you what you will have seen in the papers ; but now that the Government have definitely told Gough that he will not be asked to coerce Ulster to accept the Home Rule Bill I really do not know what the Government can do and I think the end is near.

" Balfour, as you would see, made a splendid speech yesterday."

Walter Long, President of the Union Defence League, and busily engaged with the British Covenanters, wrote two days later. He began with a reluctant tribute to " Asquith's skill as a debater, in extricating themselves from what was a very serious and menacing position." There had been " grave and wide discontent " among the supporters of the Government when the House met ; this had been " removed by Asquith's dexterous turning of the debate into channels more favourable to himself ; but to-day, there is a general feeling, as far as I can ascertain, that the position is thoroughly unsatisfactory. . . .

" Everybody is asking questions of all kinds, such as, ' What is Seely's position ? ' . . . Others ask, ' What is the position of Sir John French and Sir John Ewart ? ' Then there are rumours that Lloyd George is very much put out by what has happened and very angry.

" All this," Walter Long went on, " tends to weaken the Government. On the other hand, I am bound to say that I cannot see any immediate chance of dislodging them, as they are impervious to shame and don't seem to care in the least about themselves and their position.

" We are convinced here that (a) warrants were signed for the arrest of political people, such as you and me, and (b) that a deliberate plan was arrived at to attack Ulster on Saturday last with a considerable force. The news that I cabled you to this effect last week came from an absolutely reliable source and is, I know, trustworthy.

" As regards your own particular position, George Gibbs gave a luncheon on Tuesday to the Editors of all the leading London papers, with the exception of *The Times*, to meet Milner and myself. We had a most interesting discussion with thoroughly satisfactory results. The effect of it was this :

" I put the question to them straight : ' Supposing Sir Edward Carson has to move suddenly without notice and adopt the offensive, what will be the attitude of the London press ? '

" They carefully considered the situation and unanimously decided that they would support you whatever you did. As one of them said . . . ' We have absolute confidence in him and shall back him for all we are worth.'

" The conversation then turned upon the provocation going on in Belfast by people of all kinds to tempt our supporters into a row. They all felt that if you could supply them, through one of your officials in Belfast, with some information on this point, it would help them very much. . . . For my part I am convinced that the Government is engaged upon a deliberate attempt to provoke Ulster, and no doubt their efforts will be concentrated in Belfast ; but, of course, it is impossible to produce proof of this, as you will understand.

" George Gibbs gave another luncheon to the Lobby Correspondents yesterday, and the same unanimity was expressed. The only fear, which seems to be shared by a good many people, is that, in consequence of some local trouble, there will be an outbreak and massacre of Roman Catholics in

Yc

the Falls Road District." And Walter Long suggested that to avoid such a catastrophe a cordon might be drawn round that district.

" The number of funkers and ' Constitutionalists,' " Long concluded, " was steadily decreasing " ; public opinion was " hardening and strengthening every day in your support " ; everybody was " full of admiration for the splendid discipline and order maintained in Belfast . . . and there is a universal feeling of complete confidence in you and the others who are working with you."

We get further evidence of the hardening temper of Englishmen at that time in the active recruitment of the British Covenanters. At a meeting in the Caxton Hall on April 3rd, Lord Milner reported that signatures were coming in at the rate of thirty thousand a day.

Carson, who had returned to London, took part in that meeting and also in a greater demonstration which thronged Hyde Park on the following day. " Are you going," he asked the London citizens, " to allow your Army and your Navy to shoot down your own kith and kin ? "

It was a question which many people in England had by that time begun to ask, and for which they were preparing practical answers. While men were signing the Covenant, women were organising hospitals and ambulances and arranging to make over parts of their houses to the Irish Loyalist refugees.

In the meantime, Ministers were stickily disengaging themselves from the mess thay had made of the Curragh and were wavering between the truculence of the Radicals and the timidity of the Whigs. " No orders were issued," Lord Haldane said in the House of Lords, " no orders are likely to be issued, and no orders will be issued for the coercion of Ulster," but in revising the report of his speech for Hansard the Lord Chancellor inserted " immediate " before " coercion." The Prime Minister, who was presenting himself to the electors of East Fife as Secretary of State for War, toyed with " the federal solution " as a way out of his difficulties. " I am not sure," said Sir Edward Grey cloudily in the House of Commons, " whether some proposal might not be made to ensure that in some way, before the six years expire, some federal solution might be arrived at "—and the Secretary of State even hinted at a General Election—" after the Bill had been put upon the Statute Book."

Mr. Redmond, however, dashed any hopes that may have lurked in these ambiguous phrases. He harangued the House of Commons on its " duty to pass this Bill and not to be deterred by threats, by armed threats, of resistance of the law." There might be trouble in Ulster if the Bill were passed ; but he hinted that there might be worse trouble if the Bill were rejected.

This was in the debate on the Second Reading on April 6th, 1914, and Sir Edward Carson was there to reply. There were for him no illusions, nor had there been, he said, " from the moment they elected, a day or two before the Second Reading, to bring about their military evolutions to jump Ulster."

They had failed in that " foolish and criminal " attempt ; it had been followed by " their evasions and alleged misunderstandings, their editings and their mis-statements. . . . Atmospheres and generalities and manœuvres are of no use at this time of day." They " left us unmoved in Ulster."

They had taunted him with breaking the law ; they had said that he ought to be prosecuted.

" Whom do they think they are making a charge against when they say that ? " he asked scornfully, turning to the Labour benches, " Is it against me or is it against the Government ? "

The Prime Minister had confessed that he never had behind him the authority of the people to use force in Ulster, which was why, " for two and a half years he has let us go on without interruption in our preparations to carry out our determination that we will resist by force."

Carson ended his speech with an appeal for the alternative to force : let the Government and the Nationalists remove by their faith the mountains of doubt and suspicion ; let them show to Ulster the advantages of the new system over the old ; but he knew well enough that such appeals were in vain. He had already seen sufficiently far into the secrets of the Cabinet to realise that the only argument which counted in such a struggle was the strength to resist, and he spent Easter Week of 1914 reviewing the Ulster Volunteers, by that time, as described by a Military Correspondent, " a democratic organisation on a full military basis," with the *esprit de corps* of regular troops, and all the auxiliaries of a regular army—ambulance, engineers, transport and signalling corps.

On Easter Monday we find Carson addressing the South Antrim Regiment, 2,800 strong, in the grounds of Antrim Castle. They were, he told them, soldiers of the King as much as the Regular Army ; they would, at any moment, be willing to tender their services to His Majesty. For the rest, they were an Army of peace asking nothing but to be left alone, " and we tell the men who come to take away from us what we have that we will never submit to it as long as we have a single man left."

An Army of peace ready to die to the last man— it was a boast both Irish and true. The great Volunteer Force encamped that Easter week in every park in Ulster, had hammered itself into excellent trim and was wholly devoted to its cause and its leader. It had arms not a few : many of the men owned their own rifles and revolvers ; it had even a few machine-guns ; but one thing chiefly it lacked— a uniform supply of rifles and ammunition.

It was this preoccupation above all else that filled the minds of Craig and his Committee and the Staff of his Army that Easter week-end. They had risked a great sum on one venture, and one man ; they had received nerve-racking reports ; they had even heard that their argosy was captured— although they could not be sure—they knew that squadrons of destroyers had been mobilised and were scouring the North Sea ; they had sent a warning to their man to go back—even to sink his cargo in the German ocean—but they could not be sure that the message had reached him ; they were stretched on tenterhooks with the anxieties of this protracted adventure on which the fate of Ulster seemed to depend.

On the night of Tuesday, the 14th of April, James Craig, Sir Edward Carson and their Committee were sitting round the hospitable dinner-table at Craigavon debating these perplexing uncertainties, when the host withdrew in response to a message.

In the hall an angry little man, haggard, pale, unkempt, with wild reddish hair, in clothes which looked as if they had not been taken off for weeks, was demanding furiously to see Carson.

" I will shake hands with no one," he shouted at James Craig. " You promised our fellows not wooden guns, but real guns."

Then Craig put a great arm round the shoulder of the little man, as if he were quietening a child. " Come on, Fred," he answered, " everything will be all right."

Thus they entered the dining-room together, Craig and Crawford the gun-runner, with such a tale as it requires a new chapter to tell.

CHAPTER XXV

GUN-RUNNING

The gun-runner—Crawford meets Carson—The *Fanny*—The Harbour-Master of Dagelycke—Spender sends a telegram—Herr Schmidt—Carson decides—The *Mountjoy II*.

THE ULSTER LOYALISTS never had any intention to raid the Government arsenals for arms, not being that sort of people, yet were practical enough to feel the disadvantage of fighting without rifles, and bought them where they could. At that very time there was a great law case in motion between the Crown and a Belfast firm of gunsmiths, over the seizure of arms, and with the case hanging over them, the Headquarters Staff of the Ulster Volunteers turned an active mind to gun-running. Captain Spender, Assistant Quartermaster-General and therefore responsible for equipment, was vehement on the point. With the support of James Craig and Sir George Richardson, he put up a scheme for the landing of arms at Larne ; but he had not gone far before he found that someone else had been at work independently on a similar scheme—Fred Crawford.

A Crawford, in 1638, had signed the Solemn League and Covenant in his own blood, and in 1912 Fred Crawford followed the example of his ancestor. The grim ritual suggests the breed and the man : a fierce bright fanatical fellow with a spark of Celtic fire in the Lowland Scottish flint. Wholly devoted to his faith and his city, he had besides the characteristic technical equipment : he had been a premium apprentice in the shipbuilding yard of Harland & Wolff and had served as an engineer in the White Star line before settling down to his father's little engineering business in Belfast.

Crawford belonged to the people. As a child he had heard the whisper go round that the native Irish would make a bloody business of Belfast when Mr. Gladstone gave them Home Rule : his first memories were of those ferocious riots between Falls Road and Shankhill Road. As a boy he had led his district in games that resembled war : in 1892 he formed a secret society called Young Ulster, with an oath of loyalty to the Queen, to the end of fighting Home Rule, a condition of membership being to possess one of three weapons—a revolver, a Martini-Henry rifle or a cavalry Winchester carbine, with 100 rounds of ammunition. The flower of young Belfast joined Crawford in this adventure ; as the Arms Act was in force they filled their cartridge shells in hay lofts, and melted down their lead into bullet moulds in the furnaces which heated certain Presbyterian churches round about Belfast. Scouts kept watch and ward : the cry of an owl gave warning of the police.

Such was the youth of Fred Crawford : Lord Ranfurly, as much a fanatic as himself, provided him with shooting ranges and training camps in his park. In 1894, when feeling ran as high as in 1914, Crawford unfolded to Ranfurly the following plan. Mr. Gladstone was accustomed to take the air on the sea-front at Brighton : to run in with a pinnace from a ship in the roads ; to kidnap the old gentleman ; to transfer him out of sight of land to a fast steam yacht ; to convey him to an island in the

Pacific and there to provide him with Homer and the Bible, paper for writing and an axe for felling palms, until a change of Government should avert the danger of Home Rule—was it not a likely scheme for the salvation of Ulster? Young Fred was bitterly disappointed when Lord Ranfurly refused to risk £10,000 on the venture.

The danger of the Second Home Rule Bill faded out of most minds with the defeat of the Administration ; but Crawford remembered, and when another Liberal Government was returned in 1905, he set about his own preparations for the arming of his people. To that end he advertised for " 10,000 rifles and one million rounds of small arms ammunition " in the French, Belgian, Italian, German and Austrian newspapers, and building on the knowledge thus acquired, he became expert in that Continental traffic in arms which had for its centre the free port of Hamburg. When the Ulster Volunteer Force was organised in 1912, he had already been an officer in the Militia Artillery for nearly twenty years, and with his knowledge it seemed natural that he should be made Director of Ordnance on the Headquarters Staff. Nevertheless some of the more staid members of the Standing Committee of the Ulster Unionist Council, of which he was also a member, found his enthusiasm for the practical argument of cold steel a trifle disconcerting. A collection of rifles, with bayonets, which he laid before the Committee as samples of what might be procured from the Continent, brought home to some of the members for the first time the logical end of the enterprise on which they were engaged.

Crawford tried many ways to bring his arms

into Ulster. He was for trade purposes "John Washington Graham, G.P.O. Box 2758A, New York City, U.S.A."; to heighten the illusion he insisted on receiving his own "rake-off" when he bought machine-guns "for Mexico" from Vickers, and he very nearly spent seven years in a fortress over some tests of machine-guns in Germany. He had at one time a depot in Hammersmith disguised as an antique furniture store; but Scotland Yard, getting wind of these activities, seized a consignment of between six and seven thousand Italian rifles. This and other losses convinced Crawford that to avoid the risks of storage and transfer he must bring arms into Ulster in a vessel of his own. With that end in view, he set out for Hamburg, and there with a Jew named Schmidt—whom he knew and had reason to trust—negotiated for the purchase of fifteen thousand Austrian and five thousand German army rifles, with bayonets, slings and a supply of standard Mannlicher cartridges. There were besides ten thousand Italian rifles in store on his account.

This large transaction entailed several journeys between Belfast and Hamburg, and so it happened that in the beginning of February 1914, Crawford was in London on his way to Germany. Although he had the authority of James Craig and his Committee to accept the offer, he suspected that some of the members had little liking for the business, and it was partly to get the support and countenance of their leader that Crawford paid a call on Sir Edward Carson at 5 Eaton Place.

Crawford has given his own account of that strange interview between the gun-runner and the statesman, at that time engaged in vain negotiation with the Prime Minister. Each was serving the cause of the Union after his own fashion, and it may have seemed to Carson that Crawford's way was the more hopeful.

Crawford told his leader that as far as he was concerned, once in Hamburg, he was committed : there could be no turning back ; he would accept no cancellation, and he asked Carson if he was willing to back him to the end.

" We were alone," Crawford reports. " Sir Edward was sitting opposite to me.

" When I had finished, his face was stern and grim ; . . . he rose to his full height, looking me in the eye ; he advanced to where I was sitting and stared down at me, shook his clenched fist in my face and said in a steady determined voice which thrilled me . . . ' Crawford, I'll see you through this business if I should have to go to prison for it.'

" I rose from my chair. I held out my hand and said : ' Sir Edward, that is all I want. I leave to-night ; good-bye.' "

To pack thirty thousand rifles and three million rounds of ammunition was no slight affair, especially as Crawford insisted on their being made up in small parcels of five rifles each, with bayonets, slings and five hundred rounds—packages weighing some 75 lb. apiece, which, he foresaw, would be handy in the business of a night landing on the coast of Ulster. While this work was going forward Crawford, with the help of a friend, was finding a suitable vessel. This friend, Captain Andrew Agnew, one of the skippers of the Antrim Iron Ore Company, was (like himself) a hard-bitten fellow, with nothing to learn of the tramps, harbours and coastwise traffic of the North Sea.

By the middle of March they had bought the *Fanny*, a steamer of eight knots and 484 tons burthen, which had just run into Bergen with coals from Newcastle. This little tramp, which remained in the nominal possession of her Norwegian captain and was still manned by her Norwegian crew, was brought by Agnew to a rendezvous between the Danish Islands of Langeland and Fünen. Meanwhile, Crawford had his packages loaded into a lighter which was tugged down the Elbe, and through the Kiel Canal.

It is not to be supposed that the comings and goings of Crawford and so large a transaction in arms in such a port as Hamburg had gone altogether without notice, but if the German authorities knew they made no sign. At Kiel three men were found to have cross-questioned the lightermen and the skipper of the tug ; but they were thought to be Mexicans who had a professional interest in contraband arms, the more as an agent of ex-President Castro was at that time buying in Germany, and one of his lighters was lying at Nordenham with 300 tons of his stuff for transhipment to a fast steamer. A German official who wanted to inspect Crawford's cargo was bought off with a 100 mark note, and the tug with lighter in tow made her way across Kiel Bay to Langeland, where Crawford was duly met by Agnew in the *Fanny* at their rendezvous outside the harbour of Dagelycke.

The weather being calm, Crawford proposed to steam out to sea before transferring the arms from lighter to ship-hold ; but when the Norwegian captain assured him that he had often transferred cargo at that spot, they began the operation in a channel between the islands. And then indeed their troubles began. For in the afternoon—it was Monday the 30th March, 1914—the harbourmaster of Dagelycke came aboard and began to pry into their cargo. According to the manifest the *Fanny* was bound for Iceland, which was unfortunate, as Iceland was under the King of Denmark and the Icelanders had no lawful reason to be importing rifles. The harbourmaster was not satisfied with the assurance that the lighter *Karl Kiehn* carried only general cargo ; he pried into one case and found rifles : all the cases being of the same appearance, there could be but one conclusion. A bribe, tactfully described as a fine, was firmly refused. The harbourmaster was civil but obdurate : he would refer the matter to Copenhagen ; no doubt everything was in order, in which case the papers would be returned next morning at Rudköbing ; but the papers of both ships he must have. He left with the papers in his possession : a ship without papers is a ship in chains.

Crawford had reason to despair ; but maintained his courage. He kept the lightermen at work, pressing them on with it, so that by midnight the whole cargo was transferred from barge to hold. Then, as he believed, in reply to his prayers—for the little man was on his knees—a miracle happened : a heavy squall laden with a driving mist blinded the channel, and through this Egyptian darkness the *Fanny* groped her way out to sea.

She was off ; but she was like a pirate ship—sailing without papers. While still in the Cattegat they transformed the *Fanny* into something as different from her old self as paint and canvas could make her. But the news was out. *The Times* of the 1st April had the story from its Berlin correspondent, who had it from Copenhagen—the whole story of the *Fanny* and the lighter and the tug and the harbour-master of Dagelycke and the ship's papers, and the rifles, and the " two English-speaking persons on board the Norwegian steamer," and the sailing without papers. " It is assumed that the rifles are destined for Ulster," the German telegrams said ; but the Hamburg correspondent added the story of the ex-President of Mexico, and the whole thing was headed in painfully prominent type :

GUNS TRANSHIPPED IN THE BALTIC
CARSON OR CASTRO

The reader of *The Times* might take his choice ; but for Craigavon there remained no doubt, and the depressing certainty was confirmed day by day in telegrams which seemed to focus the light of the whole world upon the *Fanny*. Denials from Berlin were balanced by affirmations from Copenhagen. Thomsen, a Customs official, who had watched the *Fanny* for two days while she waited for the lighter, was certain there were 30,000 rifles on board—and two English-speaking gentlemen. The *Fanny*, besides, had touched near Stavanger on the Monday night and had " secretly " landed a sick steward, who said she was destined " for Ireland."

There could be little hope of getting the vessel through the searchlight of publicity and the screen of gunboats, cruisers and destroyers in the North Sea and the Irish Channel.

Such was the general decision ; the only thing to do was to get the rifles back into Hamburg and wait until the scare died down. Then they might at least save the cargo, in which £70,000 of Ulster's good money were invested. Captain Spender was detailed to send a telegram from the G.P.O. Dublin to this effect.

Spender went upon his mission sorrowfully : coming out of the post office he was confirmed in his gloom by a newspaper placard :

ULSTER'S MYSTERY ARM-SHIP CAPTURED

He returned to Craigavon in the depth of despair to find Craig, Carson, Richardson and Hacket-Payne discussing the disaster with the Committee. " See what your mad plans have brought us to," one of the Committee said to him as he entered ; but Craig took him by the arm into dinner, with a cheery, " Come and have a meal ! " And Carson said, " Now we must begin all over again, like a general after a defeat—we must have a new plan ! "

Spender, not a little comforted, found a telegram from London awaiting him : someone from Germany had arrived and wanted to see him as soon as possible. At last there must be news from Crawford. Spender took the first boat for London, and there found, not Crawford, but Schmidt.

This German-Jew trafficker in contraband arms gave Spender some further comfort. The *Fanny* was not captured : she was somewhere in the North Sea, and would no doubt keep the rendezvous which Crawford had made with Spender—Loch Laxford off the West coast of Sutherland. Spender, still thinking it impossible that Crawford could get through to Belfast, deemed it a wise precaution to make a formal sale of arms and ship back to Schmidt, and the two set off together to take delivery in the North of Scotland.

They were sportsmen going salmon-fishing : that

must be the tale. They had no rods, and Herr
Schmidt was arrayed for the noble sport in a black
frock-coat, cashmere trousers and patent-leather
boots. But they made their way from London to
Largs and from Largs to Rhiconich Inn, where
Spender passed four days in conspiratorial seclusion,
going out every evening at dusk to the bay where
the *Fanny* was to make the nocturnal rendezvous,
and returning weary with watching every morning
at dawn. Schmidt was spared these vigils by the
necessity of returning to London to get the docu-
ments of transfer put in order. After some four of
these increasingly hopeless dawns Spender returned
wearily to Belfast to find the whole position
completely, almost miraculously changed.

The *Fanny*, transmogrified and rechristened the
Doreen, had crossed the North Sea ; on 7th April
Crawford had sent Agnew ashore at Yarmouth with
orders to go to Belfast, get another steamer and
bring it back to a rendezvous at Lundy Island.
Then he beat down the English Channel in such
a gale of wind as he had seldom faced. In that storm
he fell desperately ill and looked so like dying that
the Norwegian skipper would have put into Dun-
kirk to find a doctor ; but Crawford, staggering to
his feet, put a pistol to the captain's head and made
him turn out to sea again. So, in sad case and sore
perplexed, he worked round into the Bristol Channel
and hung about there between Cardiff and St. Ives
for two days and nights, expecting every hour to
be accosted by one of His Majesty's gunboats, until
at last, at 5 a.m. on Monday morning, a passing
steamer gave the expected signal. It was Agnew in
one of Sam Kelly's coal-steamers, the *Balmerino*.
Agnew brought with him a messenger from the

North who put into his hands a message, unsigned and typewritten : " Owing to great changes since you left, and altered circumstances, the Committee think it would be unwise to bring the cargo here at present, and instruct you to proceed to the Baltic and cruise there for three months keeping in touch with the Committee or else to store the goods at Hamburg till required." Crawford, who knew nothing of the telegrams in the press and the mobilisation of the fleet, fell into such a towering rage over this letter as lasted until he reached Belfast. Rather than obey instructions so pusillanimous he would run the *Doreen* ashore at high water on the coast of County Down and leave it to his countrymen to salve the cargo.

Muttering such threats and imprecations, the gun-runner left the ship and set out by himself for Belfast. He arrived at Craigavon, as we have already seen, on the evening of Tuesday the 14th April, and with James Craig's friendly arm round his shoulder was brought into the room where Carson sat with the Committee.

Carson began by asking Crawford to give an outline of what had happened since they last met in London, and this Crawford proceeded to do, ending up with a strong argument for his plan of transhipping the arms to some vessel well known on the coast and landing the arms at Larne.

The Committee were divided ; some, taking their ground on the instructions already sent, were for dumping the guns overboard in the open sea, or for sending them back to Hamburg ; others were for a cruise in the Baltic until the vigilance of the authorities should be relaxed. To all this Crawford replied hotly that neither he nor his friend, Andrew Agnew,

Zc

in charge of the ship in his absence, would move her, save for one purpose only—to land the arms on the Ulster coast.

The feeling of the meeting was against the gun-runner, or so Crawford felt, but he was sure of Carson. " I knew my man and never mistrusted him," he wrote afterwards ; " he and James Craig would back me up against the whole Committee if necessary."

He was right. Very quietly the Chairman gave a summary of the arguments, as if he had been a judge weighing the *pros* and *cons* of a case. Crawford, he said, in the face of many difficulties, had brought the arms almost to their door. After doing so much, he could surely be trusted to do the rest. Crawford had proposed Larne : that point could be left for further consideration ; but as to the ship which Crawford required for transhipment from the suspicious-looking *Fanny* alias *Doreen*, he understood that there was a vessel unloading coal in Belfast, and he proposed she should be bought and handed over.

Carson's little speech settled the doubts of the Committee ; they crowded round congratulating the gun-runner on what he had done and wishing him well in what he still had to do ; the collier *Clydevalley*, at that moment in Glasgow with a cargo of coal for Belfast, was bought by Kelly ; she picked up Crawford on the sands of Llandudno on the night of the 17th ; after a desperately anxious search, the two vessels came together in a bay of the Welsh coast ; the cargo was transhipped ; the much-enduring *Fanny* steamed off to her home waters of the Baltic ; the *Clydevalley* went boldly into Belfast Lough with still another name painted (on canvas) in white letters on a black ground at bows and stern, the name of the vessel that had broken the Londonderry boom, a name historic in Ulster : the *Mountjoy*.

At 10.30 on the night of the 24th April, 1914, the *Mountjoy II* came alongside the landing-stage at Larne and began the work of unloading her cargo of arms.

CHAPTER XXVI

ATTEMPTS AT SETTLEMENT

Secret intelligence—Unloading—The Prime Minister—Churchill's appeal—
His Majesty's laws—Formula-hunting—The Irish Volunteers—Storm
in the House.

ON THE NIGHT of the 24th April, 1914, the
Customs Officers of Belfast were deeply interested
in the behaviour of a tramp steamer, which came
dodging up Channel in a most suspicious manner,
and in a large wagon which came down to the docks
as if to receive her cargo. As they proceeded to
examine her, all kinds of teasing obstacles were
placed in their way : the ship's papers could not be
found ; the skipper's keys were missing : when at
last, after a wasted night, they were produced and
the hatches were opened—there was only coal.

In the meanwhile there were well-concerted
preparations at Larne, at Bangor and at Donaghadee. One coast guardsman of the last-named port,
perceiving what was afoot, mounted his bicycle and
rode so hard uphill, that he dropped dead outside
the door of the post office. If the faithful fellow
had reached his destination it would have made no
difference, for the telegraph wires had been earthed
by the Volunteers.

Fifty thousand men had been mobilised for the
night's work, so discreetly that Sir Nevil Macready
himself knew nothing of it until the morning. " As
the secret had been kept," he says in his book, " no
extraordinary measures had been taken either by

troops or police." The real military commander in Belfast that night was Roberts's old friend, the Indian veteran, Sir George Richardson, who worked while Macready slept.

James Craig, who knew everybody and everything in Ulster, was his friend and adviser : these two had overlooked nothing. When Smith, the Police Commissioner, had rashly shown Colonel Chichester the text of the decoded telegram—so that they might all get to sleep—the clue had been used to decipher the Government code, and thenceforward everything that went between Dublin Castle and Belfast was known at Craigavon. As for Macready's Intelligence, Craig treated it with good-natured contempt. Once, when ringing up Richardson, he heard a voice at the Exchange : " Quick, Mary, give me the pencil. Craig and Richardson are going to have a conversation." " Wait a bit, Richardson," said Craig, " till the girl has got her pencil from Mary."

For the general apathy on his own side Macready blames Mr. Birrell, and the Liberal policy of drift. The Liberal Administration had, indeed, discouraged and betrayed the police under the pressure of the Nationalists until there was no initiative left in that once magnificent corps. Macready records an interchange on the subject between Mr. Churchill and Mr. Birrell. " It could hardly be expected," said the Chief Secretary, " that the poor police, scattered about in such packets, and spending their time fishing, would take the risk of tackling armed disturbers of the peace." Churchill burst out, in evident annoyance, with a rebuke which " made no impression on that light-hearted statesman."[1]

[1] Macready, *Annals of an Active Life*, pp. 178–9.

This betrayal of the Police, in the event, was avenged upon the Liberal Government.

The Volunteers had it all their own way. At Larne a strong cordon surrounded the town and five hundred motor-cars awaited the cargo, Sir William Adair and Captain Spender (back from the North of Scotland) superintending operations. The *Mountjoy II* was unloaded on both sides, partly on to the quay and partly into a motor-boat which took her portion to Donaghadee. When this boat came into the little harbour, she found another vessel lying alongside the single crane, and a crusty old skipper below who refused to budge at that time of night.

" There's something special on," James Craig, who was in charge at Donaghadee, shouted into the companion-way, " if you move up you can charge your own demurrages."

" That's spoken like a gentleman," said the skipper, and then as he came on deck, and saw the aspect of affairs : " Can I gi'e ye a hand ? "

The whole community was in it heart and soul, every man doing his appointed task : a corps of motor-cyclists kept touch with every point in the system of distribution : at every cross-roads sentinels were ready to direct the motor-cars and vans, which carried Crawford's well-calculated bundles throughout the length and breadth of Ulster. At the risk of their lives—not knowing at what moment they might be ambushed and shot—small parties of the volunteers distributed the weapons among their friends in the wildest parts of Nationalist Ulster—in South Armagh, South Tyrone, Donegal, Monaghan and Cavan, without losing a gun. There were no mistakes ; but one ardent spirit remained unsatisfied.

" She's all right," said the Rev. John McDermott, ex-Moderator of the General Assembly, " she's all right " (" she " being the rifle) ; " but I would like another hundred cartridges."

At five o'clock in the morning, the *Mountjoy II*, having discharged the main part of her cargo at Larne, went across to Bangor where she unloaded what remained in broad daylight. Then Crawford and Agnew, who had superintended all this stevedoring, set out to sea again. Her brave adventure done, the old collier, stripped of the canvas which carried her romantic name, jolted down the Irish Sea in her pristine dinginess—like Cinderella going home from the ball. Crawford landed at Rosslare and made his way to Hamburg ; Agnew took the *Clydevalley* to a rendezvous with the *Fanny* in the Baltic, and brought back the Ulstermen of her crew. There were no loose ends to this adventure.

" If it had not been for the splendid position you took up," Crawford afterwards wrote to Carson, " this work never could have been carried through." But Carson—and Lord Londonderry—had by that time gone over to London, there to await the news. When Craig, following Carson, arrived at Eaton Place, he found Lord Roberts rubbing his hands before the fire in the dining-room.

" I could not have done it better myself," the old soldier remarked as he left the house.

On May 1st, 1914, Sir George Richardson wrote this letter :

" MY DEAR SIR EDWARD,—A friend of mine going to London to-night has kindly promised to leave this at your house.

" I wired to you on Saturday morning 25th. I

knew you would be anxious to hear. Craig was employed elsewhere, working like a black.

" That night arms were concealed all over Ulster.

" Since then, we have been removing them by night to pockets nearer Home. All dangerous localities have now been relieved, and issues will be completed in a day or two.

" The ' Coup ' was really successful in every detail. Nothing went wrong. Not a rifle or one round of ammunition astray.

" The ' Mausers ' are little beauties, being fascinating weapons—and very popular.

" You did splendid service for us on the 29th and 30th. I hope you may be spared for many years of health and happiness, as the fruit of your labour.

" Belfast is very steady, and very pleased with itself.

" After the incident of the 24th they will do anything.

" The best of Good Luck
                    " Yours sincerely,
                            " GEO. RICHARDSON."

There was cause for these congratulations. If we consider these two groups of events of the Curragh and Larne in March and April 1914, it will be seen that *before* them the British Government was armed and the Loyalists of Ulster were unarmed, and that *after* them the British Government was disarmed and the Ulster Loyalists were armed.

We do not know if the Prime Minister realised this uncomfortable change in the situation as he faced the House of Commons on the Monday after.

Over against him sat his grim antagonists, Carson and Craig, as if challenging him to action ; around him and below the gangway tiers of angry Liberals and furious Irish Nationalists, and on the paper a clear recital of the events of the previous Friday night and Saturday morning, ending with the question put by Mr. Lough—What steps did His Majesty's Government propose to take in the matter ?

None knew better than Mr. Asquith that the time for taking steps was over. Yet, squaring his shoulders as his manner was in a desperate case, he put a bold front on his dilemma : " Well sir," he said, " in view of this grave and unprecedented outrage, the House may be assured that His Majesty's Government will take, without delay, appropriate steps to vindicate the authority of the law and protect officers and servants of the King and His Majesty's subjects in the exercise of their duties and in the enjoyment of their legal rights."

By that time it had become clear that Colonel Seely's explanations of what had happened and what had not happened in March, were more modest than veracious, and next day the Opposition pressed for a " full and impartial enquiry " into the " Naval and Military movements recently contemplated by the Government against Ulster." Then followed another debate in which the magnificent audacity of Mr. Churchill well, in their tight corner, served the Government. Sweeping away all the apologies and inconsistencies and " honest misapprehensions " in which Colonel Seely had involved the Government, as " out of date " and superannuated by subsequent events, he demanded to know who were the Opposition, " fresh from their exploits in Ireland," to ask for a judicial enquiry into the conduct of those responsible for the maintenance of law and order. Here, indeed, was a vote of censure by the criminal classes on the police. True, the police had not arrested the criminals—leniency was the only accusation he was not prepared to answer—but there was, nevertheless, the Treason Felony Act ; the long preparations for rebellion, the planning of military operations against the organised government of the King ; the arming of 100,000 men with rifles and ammunition to shoot down the King's servants ! In these circumstances the Government had a perfect right to put 40,000 or 50,000 men into Ulster ; to use the Fleet in support of the Army ; to begin the arrest of leaders, the seizure of arms, and the general prevention of drilling. To what pretty pass had they come, when they were told that British troops might not march about the United Kingdom in any way they chose !

For the last two years they had been forced to listen to a drone of threats of civil war with the most blood-curdling accompaniments and consequences.

Did they really think that if a civil war came, it was to be a war in which only one side was to take action ?

Did they really believe that it was all going to be dashing exploits and brilliant dramatic gun-running coups on the side of rebellion, and nothing but fiendish plots on the part of the Government ?

" I wish to make it perfectly clear," Mr. Churchill continued, gathering the cheers of his party about him like the folds of a toga, "that if rebellion comes we shall put it down, and if it comes to civil war, we shall do our best to conquer in the civil war.

But there will be neither rebellion nor civil war unless it is of your making."

These words spoken, the First Lord turned to the foreign aspect of this domestic broil. "Of course," he said prophetically, "foreign countries never really understand us in these islands. They do not know what we know, that at a touch of external difficulties or menace, all these fierce internal controversies would disappear for the time being, and we should be brought into line and into time."

Were men so constituted that they could only lay aside their own domestic quarrels "under the impulse of what I will call a higher principle of hatred"? Here Mr. Churchill made direct appeal to the antagonist whom he had threatened a few minutes before with the Treason Felony Act. The Member for Trinity College, he said, was running great risks—none could deny it—in strife. "Why will he not run some risks for peace? The key is in his hands now." Let him ask for the amendments to safeguard the dignity and interests of Protestant Ulster and promise in return to use his influence and goodwill to make Ireland an integral unit in a federal system. In that case all those "hideous and hateful moves and counter-moves" would give place to a "clear and bright prospect which . . . would save these islands from evils for which our children would certainly otherwise hold us accountable."

This passage, read, as was noted, from a type-written paper, staggered the supporters of the Government, who saw in it a white flag—an appeal for parley. The Radicals hung their heads, angrily muttering of betrayal and surrender; the Irish Nationalists were furious. "But this carefully prepared peroration," says the biographer of John Redmond, " revealed once and for all that the Government's only intention was to find some means of escaping from its responsibilities. That night Redmond wrote an indignant protest to Asquith ; but his former authority with the Government had been shattered."[1]

It was on the following day that Carson replied to these menaces and appeals. For the former, he had weighed all the consequences : neither he nor his friends in Ulster had " negligently or inconsiderately entered upon their course."

As to the statute about treason-felony which the First Lord had read to the House—" Does he not think that I know all these laws ? Does he think that I have not considered them ? " What besides was the use of saying, " We will send 40,000 troops against you to put you down " ? He would be sorry to think that the British Army and the British Navy were not strong enough to put down a community such as was in Ulster. But were they to conquer her " because she is trying to preserve what not one of you would give up " ?

For what had happened on the Friday before— " You need not drag it out of me. I take full responsibility." Yet he was not the cause of it. It was the people themselves who were determined not to submit.

Then Carson came to the proposals to parley. " Nobody," he said, " supposes that at my age I prefer strife to peace." Let the Government take the limitation of six years away and put instead, " Until this Parliament shall otherwise determine." He touched on the proposals for federation with

[1] Denis Gwynn, *The Life of John Redmond,* p. 306.

which the air was at that moment thick. He would be prepared, he said, to see " Ireland as an integral unit in the federal scheme," but that " depends upon goodwill and can never be brought about by force." For himself, all he wanted was " loyally to carry out the promises I have made to those who trust me, and to get for them such terms as will preserve for them their dignity, and their civil and religious freedom."

Carson, as we have seen over and over again, had no faith in half measures between Union and separation, and if he supported the exclusion of Ulster from the Home Rule Bill it was only as a means to wreck that measure. He still hoped and fought for a General Election—victory and Union. He was being overborne, nevertheless, by events and by men.

It was, by the way, to this time Colonel Repington referred when he said in his diary that the arrest of Carson had been stopped by the personal intervention of the King. The legend is picturesque : " Had a talk with Carson about the Ulster business. He told me how near we were to an explosion, that the Government had determined to arrest the chief leaders, that he had arranged to send the word HX over the wire to Belfast, and this was to be the signal for the seizure of the Customs all over Ulster. He called to see the King, and told Stamfordham exactly what was going to happen, and the arrest of the leaders was promptly stopped."[1]

---

[1] *The First World War*, vol. i., p. 69. This gossip was finally set at rest in 1920 with the exchange of the following notes. " The whole statement is untrue, as also the question of the telegrams . . . a garbled narrative of a matter with which the King had nothing to do, and mixes up matters which had no relation to each other." Carson to Repington.—" I fully accept your assurance that my entry is incorrect."—Repington to Carson (4.11.20).

The Provisional Government of Ulster certainly did consider the seizure not only of the Customs but of all public offices in Ulster : as we shall see later in this story ; but the time had not arrived. Nor did Carson ever " call to see the King," nor did the King ever intervene to prevent the arrest of a subject who defied his Government, and could say like honest Kent :

> *My life I never held but as a pawn*
> *To wage against thy enemies, nor fear to lose it,*
> *Thy safety being the motive.*

If the Government were divided on this matter, their own prudence must have counselled them that to arrest Carson would remove the strongest influence for peace in Ulster ; their own common sense that it was impossible at once to negotiate with Carson and imprison him. Time and opportunity had been allowed to slip : even a Government cannot recover the past.

The clock

> *Rapide avec sa voix*
> *D'insecte, Maintenant dit, je suis*
> *Autrefois.*

The negotiations were nevertheless reopened. Mr. F. S. Oliver, inspired by the example of his hero, Alexander Hamilton, had been canvassing a federal system which might settle Ireland as an incident in a general distribution of government. That incorrigible formula-hunter, Mr. Lionel Curtis, was more busily engaged in formulating bases of discussion, after the " Round Table " style, proposing an Irish National Convention to settle the federal difficulty, reconciling every difficulty with an ingenious compromise, taking into account every-thing—except human nature.

Ulster was to be excluded ; but the exclusion was to be revised by the Convention, while the Commission was to develop legislatures for England, Scotland and Wales. Ulster was not to be coerced into the Irish unit ; but was not to be allowed either to govern herself unless by permission of the rest of Ireland or to enter into any other subdivision of the British Isles, and the promoters hopefully assumed that the Irish Convention would agree upon a scheme to unite Ireland ; that the Commission would agree upon a scheme to separate England, Scotland and Wales ; that Ulster would agree to leave the one and cleave to the other, and that Parliament would agree to give the force of law to the whole arrangement.

Mr. Curtis, as indomitable as Don Quixote, was helped in this crusade by his hopeful squire, Mr. Edward Grigg. Carson, although he could hardly have hoped much from them, was willing to accept their ingenious arrangements as a basis of discussion ; by April 23rd they reported that Mr. Lloyd George had been brought into their promising negotiations ; on the 25th Lord Lansdowne, in a letter to Carson, gives his doubts after a long conversation with this " very useful set of young men." The scheme was very clever, but probably unworkable ; he was not prepared to say that he thought it statesmanlike or likely to stand the test of time :

" If, however, we can obtain, as a preliminary, the firm exclusion of the six counties and the

deletion of the anti-federal clauses of the Home
Rule Bill, much will have been achieved ; and if
such an offer were to be made to us, I do not see
how either you or we could afford to turn it down
after what we have said in public. I should like to
add a stipulation, that clauses should be added to
the Bill for the protection of Unionists outside
Ulster."

The young men were persistent ; by May 4th they
had seen Bonar Law and arranged for a conference
—next day—with the Prime Minister at the old
secret trysting-place in Queen Anne's Gate. A note
of May 4th from Asquith to Carson suggests that
the Prime Minister had no scruple about conferring
with the author of a " grave and unprecedented
outrage " :

"MY DEAR CARSON,—Many thanks for your
letter and enclosure. I have telegraphed to
General Macready to let me know upon what
information the apprehensions of the Irish military
authorities were founded, and I will let you know
the result.

" I am hoping to meet you at 24 Queen Anne's
Gate to-morrow (Tuesday) morning.
" Yours sincerely,
" H. H. ASQUITH."

What happened at that meeting may be gathered
from the event. Carson had been coached by his
new allies to press upon the Government the necessity, as a condition precedent to further negotiations, of persuading the Nationalists to make
the same advance as he had made himself, i.e.
to accept the scheme as a basis of discussion.

But Redmond by that time was in no mood, nor had he any longer the power, to make further concessions. For him, too, the clock, " *avec sa voix d'insecte* " had said " *autrefois.*" His people, always ready for intrigue and revolt, were threatening mutiny. Sinn Fein had been for some time in progress : the Irish Volunteers, which at the beginning of the year had been barely 10,000 strong had grown to 100,000 by the middle of May, of whom one-third were in Ulster. Professor MacNeill, an innocent enthusiast for the dead Celtic culture in which he was a scholar, was the titular head of a movement the real direction of which was more sinister and occult. Sir Roger Casement, Bulmer Hobson, P. H. Pearse, Darrell Figgis—these and others, whose affiliations touched Germany on the East and the Fenian Clan-na-Gael of America on the West, aspired to take the destinies of Ireland out of the hands of the Nationalist Party. They were preparing to import arms without the knowledge of Redmond, and were determined that those who provided the arms should control the force, whoever might be appointed to the Provisional Committee. Devlin and Dillon were deep in suspicious and angry negotiation with MacNeill ; but could come to no terms in the control of those forces which threatened to supersede and to destroy the Irish Nationalist Party. In such a dilemma Redmond could ill afford to listen to any new proposals from Asquith : he could only threaten the Prime Minister with a political crisis if he did not stick to his bargain.

There were also on the other side men who suspected any approach as a betrayal of their cause. Walter Long, among the most vehement, wrote to Carson on the 9th May, 1914 :

AAc

" My dear Ned,—I am greatly alarmed about this movement for federalism, and the conversations—a very bad effect is being created. I find it in my collection of funds very severely and I am sure that it is doing us great harm in the constituencies. People say, ' Redmond is the only strong man who knows his own mind and won't budge.'

" Yours ever,
" W."

Carson, strong in his organised resistance yet knowing all that resistance meant, could afford to smile at such little barbs of friendship. Only a fool, he had said some time before, would fight were accommodation possible. But was it ?

The Government might have stretched a point and agreed to the exclusion of Ulster without a date ; but they were held as in a vice to their bargains by the Irish Nationalists. On the 12th May fierce debate raged in the House of Commons over points of procedure. Mr. Asquith had announced that an amending Bill would be introduced in the House of Lords, and the Leader of the Opposition demanded to know what that Bill contained before the House of Commons gave the original Bill its third reading. They must know, he pointed out, how the Bill was to be amended before they read it a third time. That was the only natural course, the obvious course, the proper course. Why had they not adopted it ? " The right hon. gentleman has not told us but I think we can guess. The hon. and learned gentleman (Mr. Redmond) has made it a point that the Bill has to go through as it stands, and the Government obey him."

This was Mr. Bonar Law's pungent way of putting things : no doubt the Prime Minister refused to make disclosure of the Amending terms because he still hoped, with Mr. Redmond's consent, still further to amend them. But Redmond was in no mood for concession, and, when the case was again raised on the 21st May, Mr. Asquith was in no better position. He still refused to disclose his terms ; Mr. Bonar Law accused him of treating the House with contempt, and the Conservatives shouted " Adjourn ! Adjourn ! " until at last the Speaker, out of all patience, asked the Leader of the Opposition whether the unruly scene had his " assent and approval."

" I would not presume to criticise what you consider your duty, sir," Mr. Bonar Law retorted, " but I know mine, and that it is not to answer any such question."

The temper of the House, as much as the attitude of the Irish members, seemed to forbid any hope of peace.

CHAPTER XXVII

CRITICAL DAYS

Secret societies—Growing danger—Further approaches—Carson stands fast—The Amending Bill—" No hopes of peace."

THROUGH the months of May, June and July 1914, Ireland seethed and simmered like a pot which at any moment might boil over. In the North the Ulster Volunteer Force, Carson exhorting, Craig directing, maintained its orderly rule : in the South ill-disciplined levies of the Irish Nationalist Volunteers threatened private revenge and public anarchy.

These latter had sprung up, as we have seen, in defiance of John Redmond, of John Dillon and of the Irish Nationalist Party. It is commonly supposed that they owed their origin to that Celtic enthusiast, Professor Eoin MacNeill, who had an idea of reviving Henry Grattan's Irish Volunteers. He was, indeed, the innocent figurehead, but behind him were more dangerous men. The Irish both of Ireland and America have always been hag-ridden by secret societies, and several of these fought darkly for the control of the volunteers. There were the United Irish League, the Irish Republican Brotherhood, the Ancient Order of the Hibernians, all Societies strong both in the United States and in Ireland. Joseph Devlin was the head of the Hibernians in Ireland ; but the American Branch of the Order disputed his sway, and their agent,

Matthew Cannings, was sent over to secure control,
Devlin being thought too mild a man to manage
such a movement. The I.R.B., which contained the
most desperate men of all—the Invincibles, the
Molly Maguires, the remnants of the Fenians and
the Moonlighters—watched and profited by these
dissensions. Quietly joining the Irish Hibernians,
they contrived to secure executive positions in the
various branches, and everywhere made the order
more restless and more extreme. It was in fact a
committee substantially composed of the Irish
Republican Brotherhood which started the Irish
National Volunteers. It was, moreover, the
Irish Republican Brotherhood which stood behind
Sinn Fein.

The oath of this formidable society—" I will do
my utmost to establish the National Independence
of Ireland, and that I will bear true allegiance to
the Supreme Council of the Irish Republican
Brotherhood and Government of the Irish Re-
public," etc.—did not admit of those constitutional
compromises with which John Redmond hoped to
satisfy his people. The whole movement involved
a threat both to his policy and his party ; but, after
secretly circularising the Roman Catholic Church
in a vain endeavour to put it down, he found the
thing too strong for him, and consented to appear
to be the leader of an army which he could neither
control nor suppress.

The Ancient Order of Hibernians had by that
time become a recognised Society under Mr. Lloyd
George's Insurance Act, and the agents of both the
Order and the Brotherhood cunningly used the
means and the patronage given to them under that
act to extend their organisation and confirm their

power. They levied besides a weekly charge of a few pence a week on members of the Force and drew large funds from the bitter enemies of England in the United States, who promised them besides a plentiful supply of arms and ammunition.

At the beginning of 1914 those Irish Volunteers were of no great strength. According to a careful estimate, in February of that year their total strength was less than five thousand ; but they grew rapidly in the months which followed, so that by the middle of May—or so it is stated by Mr. Denis Gwynn—they were over 100,000 strong, of whom one-third were in Ulster and one-third in Leinster. They were recruited chiefly from the farmers' sons and labourers in the country districts and the corner-boys of the towns. At first a few regular officers, chiefly Colonel Maurice Moore, who had commanded the Connaught Rangers, took a hand in the organisation, " foolishly believing that the movement was consistent with loyalty to the British connection " ; the drilling was done chiefly by old soldiers of the Irish regiments and ex-sergeants, principally of the Munster Fusiliers and the Connaught Rangers, but the Volunteers were little amenable to discipline : they hated and affected to despise those old professional soldiers who gave them orders, and sulkily clamoured for arms before they knew well how to use them. " The cavalry in this town," says one report, " consists of three very drunken car drivers on hired car horses . . . one of the instructors is a militia private and a notorious blackguard and drunkard." " All the drunken ne'er-do-weel ex-soldiers about here," said another report, " are earning £1 a week for drilling." " There was a rendezvous of the Irish

Volunteers at Multyfarnham on Sunday evening,"
one of Carson's friends wrote to him, " being within
the *bona fide* limit. Of the Ballinalach fifty, which is
beyond the three-mile limit, fifteen were not drunk.
They dismissed one of the drill inspectors, who was
blind drunk. It is chiefly the loafers who have joined
on in West Meath." From Carrick-on-Shannon it was
reported that " Volunteers are largely corner-boys,
and gravest fears are felt of their running amuck " ;
in Galway the Volunteers had not taken on well,
but a large number of rifles and ammunition had
been smuggled in ; in Athenry and Croughwell the
Volunteers were in two camps, well armed with
shotguns, revolvers and numerous rifles, " and
police expect that on first available opportunity
they will open fire on each other " ; in Tralee there
were 1,500, " all controlled by ex-army men and
rank and file respectable, but good percentage of
corner-boys " ; in County Clare, which was
" nominally quiet, in reality seething with lawlessness," there were corps in every town and village,
and " firearms are used on the slightest provocation " ; in Limerick, " men better drilled and
equipped than any other centre visited . . . a good
many rifles." In Wexford " drilling done amongst
themselves ; ex-soldiers dismissed as at New Ross."
Where the leaders of the Corps were members of
the Ancient Order of Hibernians, the men were
kept under better control but the organisation was
by so much the more formidable.

Decent people in the South of whatever party
saw with alarm the growth of this ill-disciplined
and ill-regulated force which they had reason to
fear would rule the country under Home Rule.
" The farmers," says one report, " regard the

movement with the utmost concern and would be delighted if it were stopped." " You have thousands of Roman Catholics with you in spirit," one of Carson's friends wrote from Newtown Forbes, " and a great many of the tenant proprietors through the country are in wholesome fear this accursed Bill will become law, no matter what creed they profess."

" I have at last got an answer to your perpetual query ' What good will Home Rule do anyone ? ' " another old friend wrote to Carson.

" I was in Co. Westmeath last week, and went with my brother-in-law to see a neighbouring farmer who was once a prominent Leaguer, but has bought out his farm and now breeds excellent pedigree stock and goes in for up-to-date farming methods.

" After seeing the cattle, the Colonel said to him, ' Well, Killiaghan, now that you have got Home Rule what good will it do you ? '

" ' Well, Colonel,' he said, ' I never got such a start in my life as when I seen we had got it in the papers. It came as a great surprise to us all.'

" ' Yes, but what good will it do you ? '

" ' Well, I can't rightly tell. They say there will be great things ; I don't know meself what they are. But sure enough it will be a good thing for us all to be done looking for it anyway.' "

Even the Roman Catholic priests grew nervous of an issue which threatened the peace and order of the countryside. " Nine-tenths of the ' Healy-ite ' priests in County Louth," a letter-writer reported, " and two-thirds of the ' Redmondite ' priests " were against Home Rule, although one of the most notable had joined the Volunteers, and a Protestant clergyman, who found himself in a railway-carriage-ful of priests—and was himself mistaken for one—heard from them that they were going to a private meeting to " arrange some plan for the defeat of this Home Rule Bill." Feeling, however, ran differently in different localities. " It has all turned into a Papist *v*. Protestant affair down here," a correspondent wrote from New Ross. " The priests are ravening for our blood ; but they ain't going to get it."

If the Roman Catholics, much more the Protest-ants had reason to fear these preparations. On the 15th June it was reported in Dundalk that the various lodges of the A.O.H. and I.N.L. had been instructed to prepare complete confiscation lists of all Protestants and of any Roman Catholics who were known to be Unionists : they were to lose their farms, estates, and businesses when Home Rule came. In Athenry, " the old practice of digging graves near residences of unpopular persons is being revived." In Enniscorthy, " Protestants are apprehensive of reprisals and have made arrange-ments to concentrate at a defensible centre." In Sligo " the Unionists are strong and an ex-cellent organisation for mutual protection exists. The scheme will consist in concentrating on de-fensible centres in the event of trouble. Unionists have been driven to take these steps by the certainty that any rising in Ulster would be followed by immediate reprisals. In the town of Sligo there is a dangerous mob." What increased these anxieties was the demoralisation of the police : officers re-luctant to prosecute ; rank and file nursing griev-ances ; some of the Head Constables and sergeants in suspicious contact with the Ancient Order of

Hibernians, and many of the younger men resigning and emigrating. If Home Rule came, as this devoted minority could plainly foresee, nothing stood between them and the sinister power of an armed mob. Short of an attack, they would be defenceless, without power or influence, prospective victims of the rapacity of their neighbours, to be squeezed out of their livelihood and habitation.

The Loyalists of the South, as we have seen, had long ago acquiesced in the policy of Ulster. A Commissioner of the Irish Unionist Alliance who visited the counties of Cork, Kerry, Limerick, Clare, Galway, Roscommon and Mayo during April and May 1914, and interviewed officials, constabulary officers, resident magistrates, land agents, solicitors, merchants, and his own friends, may here be cited on this point. After describing the fate which the Minority feared, " I now come," he continued, " to what might be expected if a compromise was agreed to under which Ulster would be excluded. There have been some statements made by certain Loyalists in the South and West of Ireland that such a compromise would be looked upon as an act of treachery and betrayal. I could find no such feeling existing amongst the intelligent and sensible Loyalists. On the contrary, while they naturally hold that their interests would be best served by destroying the Bill *in toto*, if this be impossible, and if the only possible alternative to complete Home Rule is the exclusion of Ulster, then they would be far safer under such an arrangement than under full Home Rule."

And the Commissioner proceeds to give his reason :

" A Redmondite Executive, governing only Nationalist Ireland, would never cease to covet the inclusion of Ulster. Its policy would be to show Ulster that it was tolerant and just to the Loyalist minority. This minority would have a guarantee in the independence of Ulster that they could not be openly ill-treated."

Yet although the Southern Loyalists knew all this, although they knew besides that with Carson it was a desperate expedient calculated to " wreck the Home Rule Bill," the visible approach of a hideous danger was too much for the nerve of some of them. These saw themselves deserted—exposed to robbery and murder—while Ulster found a selfish safety in exclusion, and although they had never accepted the leadership of Carson they reproached him for his policy.

Thus his old friend Lord Ashtown (writing from Woodlawn House, Co. Galway, on the 2nd May, 1914) :

" Thanks for yours. As far as I can make out, is not the offer the exclusion of Ulster till there is a Federal Settlement and then Ireland is to be one unit ? Does not this mean the exclusion of Ulster till Federalism comes ? Does not this mean the throwing of the Southern Unionists to the wolves ? . . . The Unionists round here are not satisfied. I had six letters this morning. One stated plainly that, ' it seems Ulster, Carson, Bonar Law, and Balfour mean to hand us over to the Nationalists. . . . All politicians are d——d rogues'—I quote in full; I was nearly leaving out the last part. As for civil war in Ulster there can be none *unless* the Government send troops there.

They *dare* not start civil war. I am much more afraid of the Bill passing and being put on the statute book and the Government going to the country. I suppose if the Unionists came in they would repeal it? Then the fun would start in the South. There would be murders and houghing of cattle, etc."

There would be no trouble if the Bill was not passed; " They want to understand there will be no consent to Home Rule in any form at all." After thanking God that Balfour was no longer the leader of the Unionist Party, the old man ended with the appeal, " Don't agree to a compromise that will hand us over to the Nationalists ! "

Lord Arran, in a letter to *The Times*, compared the Ulster Unionists to " the stronger element of a crew of a leaking ship, who, feeling themselves sufficiently strong to force their way to the boats, decide to cease manning the pumps and to save themselves, leaving women and children to their fate."

As we have seen, the Unionists of the South had never accepted Carson as their Leader ; but they nevertheless kept in touch with him through one of their committees formed for that purpose, and under the direction of Lord Midleton and Lord Barrymore they resolved and agitated against the Conservative policy on the Amending Bill. In particular, the Committee " desired to place on record their deliberate and unanimous conviction that the exclusion of any part of Ireland would gravely aggravate the menace of the Home Rule Bill to the future safety and contentment of the Irish people." Carson, who sympathised with their fears, whatever he may have thought of their logic, assured them that he would do nothing without consulting them and that there was no danger of any compromise, as the Government would not come to terms with Ulster unless Redmond consented, which consent he thought " highly improbable."

These meetings could suggest nothing practical : no safeguard, no amendment could help them : if the Bill passed they were doomed—like tainted wethers of the flock, meetest for death. They still fixed their hopes on the rejection of the Bill, and were nervous of any amendment which might seem to give colour to the idea that there was any weakening or compromise on the principle of the Bill. On the 14th May Midleton wrote to Carson on these doubts and fears and reported the "unanimous opinion" of " men representing practically all parts of the South and West " that if the Home Rule Bill fell through at the last moment, " although there might be some trouble with mobs in places like Limerick and Sligo . . . it was impossible to get the mass of the people to show any interest in the rejection of the Bill."

And on the 27th June, Midleton wrote again, enclosing more notes of meetings in Dublin :

" The utmost loyalty and confidence was shown by all present with regard to yourself, and they were most unwilling to take any course which could in any degree militate against your operations. But there is undoubtedly very great uneasiness amongst them, and I feel myself some doubt whether, if the result should be contrary to your expectations and some agreement is

come to on the Ulster amendment, if nothing
is done for the South, they will not ultimately
feel that they have lost their opportunity."

Carson, no doubt, smiled ruefully at these re-
proaches expressed or implied. He had worked
harder than any to defeat Home Rule ; he had
organised resistance where resistance was possible.
He had taken his line about the exclusion of Ulster
in order, as he said, to " wreck the Home Rule
Bill " ; he was committed to it, and must follow
it out, as upon the whole the best in the desperate
circumstances of a case almost beyond his endeavours
and his prayers. As to negotiations, he was strong
enough to neglect no opportunity : he might be
trusted to follow his ruling principle in law :
" never to settle unless he could get better terms
by settling than by fighting the case to the end."
Negotiations, secret and fruitless, had been taken
up again. We get a hint of the course they were
taking from an undated letter of the Prime
Minister's :

" MY DEAR CARSON,—When we met the other
day you said you were having a map prepared
with reference to the delimitation of Ulster
areas.

" I don't know whether it is now ready, and
if so whether you would allow me in confidence
to see it ? "

A postscript helps us to date the letter: "I see
that my late lady friends are transferring their
attention to you ! " One of these lady friends, the
militant Mrs. Drummond, had paid her attentions
to Carson at his doorstep on the 13th May. On the

14th—probably on the day that this letter was written—the Prime Minister had to receive a deputation of Liberal Members with Neil Primrose at their head, angrily wanting to know why he was not prosecuting the gun-runners of Ulster. Mr. Asquith told them, with becoming firmness, that the Government " would not go back on its decision not to institute proceedings."

On the 23rd, despite this friendly consideration, Carson is at Ipswich making a speech said to be decisive in the defeat of Mr. Masterman, a minor member of the Government whom Carson described as " a beautiful soul thirsting for blood." On the 2nd June, and again on the 13th, Asquith is asking for the map and promising to " send you any we have as soon as I get back to London."

The lawyers of Mr. Asquith's Cabinet seem to have been far at that moment from any thoughts of prosecuting the man whom in public they so roundly denounced. " My dear Carson," Sir John Simon wrote to him on May 28th, 1914, " I should be so proud and pleased if—for old sake's sake—you found it possible to come to my King's Birthday dinner on June 22. . . . I appreciate that you may possibly feel a difficulty (though I trust not) and if you came you would add greatly to my pleasure. . . . My own feeling of gratitude and devotion to you for all you did for me never will be altered, whatever happens." Sir John was then Attorney-General.

Mr. Asquith was evidently endeavouring to get the Irishmen down to the details of this forlorn hope : he had been supplied with maps by Mr. Redmond. Thus Edward Sanderson, who was in the secret, reported to Lady Londonderry on the 26th May : " . . . all arrangements changed and I hear this morning that Ipswich did it." A map had been prepared and sent over to the Cabinet setting forth the rural districts in Ulster which are predominantly Protestant.

" It brings in a good slice of Donegal and excludes bits of Armagh and Fermanagh. They wanted me to tell them who were the most prominent people to discuss boundaries with.

" I have written to R. and told him that Birrell had much better keep out of Ulster as the people had placed the matter in the hands of their leaders and would probably refuse to discuss anything with him, and then wish him a speedy journey to the hinterland of Hades."

There was little either of hope or substance in these negotiations, and Carson never relaxed in his main design to force a General Election and to maintain the front of resistance in Ulster. On the 20th May, he spoke at a great meeting in the Queen's Hall, passionately pleading that faith in King and Constitution could be no treason ; on the 29th at Mountain Ash he addressed the Covenanters of Wales on the blessings of " that message of peace, the Third Home Rule Bill "—" fourteen battleships about Belfast Lough, police drafted in from all parts of Ireland, soldiers confined to their barracks, and the Lord Mayor keeping the peace of Belfast, not through the troops but through the Ulster Volunteers."

All these activities, public and private, brought Carson volumes of advice from friends, and especially from Walter Long, at that time recruiting his health at Schinznach-les-Bains : " If we can avoid a row in Ulster," Long wrote on the 28th of May,

" and force the Government to begin, I believe we shall sweep the country and be able to do as we like. I am only afraid of two things : 1. A premature row in Ulster ; 2. Rejection by the Lords of the Amending Bill if latter has been accepted by Ulster. Save these and conversations—from which may the Lord deliver us !—I believe that election must come in July at latest and that we shall win.

" You have done wonders," he added, " if the Empire is saved it will be through you," and again on the 30th Long wrote congratulating Carson on his speech at Mountain Ash : " You put the case of the King splendidly. . . . If you stick to ' Ulster as a whole and no time limit,' I think we are safe, as I feel sure Asquith will never consent to this : or rather he won't be let."

Over Whitsuntide Carson was in Ulster, at that time like a military camp. " No matter in what direction one walked," the correspondent of the *Morning Post* reported, " one met soldierly men, mostly clad in the now familiar khaki, marching and counter-marching." " I think," said Carson, addressing the West Belfast Regiment on the 6th June, " I recognise some of the cargo of the *Mountjoy*. . . . I rely on you to keep your arms with a view of keeping the peace."

On the 20th June, Carson spoke at great meetings in Lancashire, and referred to the Amending Bill— " a Bill to amend a Bill that is still a Bill "—as merely repeating the offer of the 9th March " which I called, and call again, a hypocritical sham. . . . We are to be sentenced to death, but they are not to pull the rope round our necks till six years are expired. . . . I would rather be hanged to-day."

The Amending Bill, which was introduced in the House of Lords on the 23rd June, fulfilled this ominous description ; but Lord Crewe left one door open : he invited amendments to the Amending Bill, and we find Carson's sarcastic comment in a speech at Herne Hill on the 5th July. " They bring it in," he said, " in this kind of way : ' We know that you have rejected, four months ago, the offer we make you in it ; but that is the only offer we can make for the moment. But if you will try to put something better into it, then we will go to Mr. Redmond, and we will say—" For God's sake, John, come to our rescue, John ! " ' "

In this speech also Carson used definite terms about the exclusion of Ulster : " Let us have done," he said, " with six-year limits ; let us have done with county limits, as if men in one county are going to abandon men in another county just because there may be a majority here or a majority there."

He would never, he said, settle behind the backs of the people of Ulster. Whatever proposals were made, if he thought them worth it, and not till then, he would take them over to the people of Ulster " and they shall decide whether they will accept them or not."

On the 8th July, the Amending Bill was amended by the Opposition in the House of Lords : for county option and the time limit the permanent exclusion of the whole Province of Ulster was substituted. By Friday, the 10th, Carson was again in Ulster, received like a king, by vast crowds which lined the shore and packed every ship, barge, hulk and dock-side between Carrickfergus and Donegal Quay. " Sir Edward ! " " Sir Edward ! " they shouted. " No Home Rule ! No Surrender ! "

That day the Standing Committee of the Ulster Unionist Council, met as the Ulster Provisional Government, resolved " to press on with the completion of our arrangements to resist by every means in our power every attempt which may be made to impose the authority of any Home Rule Parliament on Ulster." Carson, who presided, stood at the head of a Provisional Government, with such authority as could be derived from a people united and armed, ready to take over, " in trust for His Majesty the King " (as they always said) every court and office of the Crown in Northern Ireland. " At an hour's notice," said the correspondent of the *Morning Post*, " Sir Edward Carson can call into being a situation which will bring back to a British Cabinet the disasters created by the revolt of the American Colonies."

To that end all the plans were laid, everything in order, after the business-like method of Ulster. Next day Carson was at Larne, reviewing the local force of volunteers and publicly thanking Fred Crawford, who happened to be there, for providing them with arms. " The lesson of that night," said Carson, " has taught you what discipline means : it has taught you what can be achieved, not by any rowdy spirit or rowdy element, but by carefully thought-out plans and by obedience to orders."

In that speech Carson used grave words. " I see no hopes of peace," he said, " I see nothing at present but darkness and shadows . . . we must be ready. In my own opinion the great climax and the great crisis of our fate, and the fate of our country, cannot be delayed for many weeks . . . unless something happens—when we shall have once more to assert the manhood of our race."

" Unless something happens "—much was about to happen ! The Baron Hermann von Rütti of the Bavarian Chancellery was even then in Ireland, on the pretext of a mission to study agriculture, but incidentally gathering the impression that Ulster really did intend to fight. And certain German newspaper correspondents, who watched these parades with keen yet misapprehending eyes, pressed round Carson, expecting to hear threats of rebellion. When Carson spoke to them instead of Ulster's loyalty to King and Constitution, they asked him to explain the apparent paradox of armed force. " To make you understand," said Carson, " I should have to tell you the history of the past four hundred years."

CHAPTER XXVIII

THE EDGE OF WAR

Carson in Ulster—James Lowther—The time limit—Asquith, Lloyd George and Redmond—The Palace conference—It breaks down—Dublin Bay—Craig's plans—The Germans intervene.

SIR EDWARD CARSON, although he did not know it, had come almost to the end of his sojourning in Ulster. If he had known, it would have grieved him, for he had come to love " the black North," both country and people, who, on their side, trusted— even adored—their " leader." " Sir Edward," a red-haired giant, who had shouldered his way up to him, shouted in his ear after one of his meetings, " are ye a good hater ? " " I am," said Carson looking him in the eye. " Then gie me a grip o' your han', man ! " They could hate, these people, and the measure of their hatreds was the measure of their love.

Not only the men and women but the children came near to worshipping him. A Belfast clergyman, inspecting a boys' school, asked the question : " Can any of you tell me who is the Supreme Being ? " With one accord they cried " Carson "—all except one little lad who timidly suggested a more orthodox hypothesis. " Ah, you Papist ! " they shouted at the apostate.

Carson was Irish enough and man enough to relish this adoration : his own nature, despite his learning in the law, remained elementally simple ;

there was a side to his character little suspected by his staid friends in the Temple. At Homburg for example, after midnight, when the natives were all asleep, the ex-Law Officer of the Crown, and a friend after his own heart, discerning that the shop signs could be taken down, rearranged them, with startling results. The zest of the schoolboy remained in this " elderly barrister," whose richly humorous Irish nature enjoyed every point and every turn of his Ulster progresses.

There were besides those dearest friends, the Craigs, and Craigavon, which he came to call his home, where he could shake off all his cares. There were so many other friends besides : F. E. Smith was frequently with him, the good-natured subject of continual banter. The genial Lord Londonderry, who had been Lord Lieutenant of Ireland, Carson and Craig, his dear friends, always treated with a certain respectful deference. " Come and play billiards, Sea," said F. E. Smith one night, using a diminutive of Seaham by which Londonderry was only known to old Etonian friends. " I didn't know, Lord Londonderry," said Carson ceremoniously, " that F. E. had been to school with you." But the rebuke left F. E. entirely unmoved. Mount Stewart was another house which was hardly less a home to Carson : its mistress, Lady Londonderry, was at her wittiest and best when he was there.

The dreaded " twal'th " of July, 1914, safely over, Carson returned to re-enter the negotiations of which he knew there could be only one result. On the 8th July the Amending Bill had itself been amended by the Opposition in the House of Lords : for the County Option and Time Limit proposed by the Government the permanent exclusion of the

whole Province of Ulster—the " clean cut " as
Balfour called it—had been substituted. Would the
Government accept the change ? If they did, as
Carson saw, they must differ with John Redmond.

Of persuading Redmond to some concession Mr.
Asquith must still have had hopes, for on the 2nd
July we find the Prime Minister writing to Carson :

> " I am sorry that there has been so much delay
> in getting hold of these maps.
>
> " I fear they will add little or nothing to your
> information.
>
> " To avoid misunderstanding, I should point
> out that they were not prepared by or for the
> Government, but as suggestions by outside per-
> sons, whose opinions were entitled to consider-
> ation.
>
> " In each case the suggested area of exclusion
> cuts county boundaries.
>
> " From every point of view the County Tyrone
> seems to present the greatest difficulties."

The " outside persons," no doubt, were Redmond,
Dillon, and possibly, as it was an Ulster question,
Devlin.

In these attempts Mr. Asquith did not stand
alone : the Speaker of the House of Commons took
a hand.

"If you think," James Lowther[1] wrote to Carson
on the 24th June, 1914, " that any good purpose
would be served, in bringing about an arrangement
on the Irish question, by a meeting between yourself and Redmond, I should be very glad to place
my services and the use of my library at your

[1] Afterwards Viscount Ullswater.

disposal. My library is neutral ground and remote from the public eye, and as to myself I would either be present at, or absent from, your meeting as you think best."

Mr. Lowther added that he was writing a similar letter to Redmond, and an assurance that the matter would be kept " absolutely confidential." For on the 16th June Lord Crewe had referred in the House of Lords to negotiations between the Prime Minister and Sir Edward Carson. The latter protesting against such a breach of confidence, Lord Crewe replied, admitting the " private and informal nature of all the proceedings," and his knowledge that " the recent interchanges between you and the Prime Minister did not amount to much."[1] Mr. Asquith, in an undated private letter, added his regrets. The incident, nevertheless, may have left Carson with a sense of the need for wariness in these matters. Mr. Lowther's assurance may have been in sly reference to this untoward incident.

That the replies were not encouraging appears in a second letter to Carson from Lowther (of the 26th June) : " I fear that a meeting between you and Redmond, at the present moment, would not, from the contents of your letter, appear to be of any use ; but Redmond says, in his reply to me, that he is quite ready to accept my suggestion if you think it would be in any way useful.

" I gather from him, however, that he is not prepared to accept the exclusion of Ulster as a basis for negotiations ; but is ready to discuss any other proposals."

Yet on the 29th Mr. Lowther wrote again—snatching at a straw :

[1] See Hansard, Lords, 23rd June, 1914.

" THE TWAL'TH " OF JULY

Carson in Belfast

" . . . It seems to me that the exclusion of Ulster must be, as you say, the basis on which any attempt to arrive at a settlement must be founded.

" I notice that in your letter you put the word Ulster between inverted commas, and I think I remember hearing you use the expression ' Statutory Ulster ' as being something distinct from the province of Ulster, as shown in the maps. The question, therefore, is, what do you mean by Ulster and what would Redmond mean by Ulster?

" Don't you think that by a meeting we might so far clear the air as to be able to arrive at some understanding as to what counties and cities might eventually become statutory Ulster ?

" I feel pretty sure that I could persuade Redmond to discuss this with you in confidence.

" What do you think ? Will you try it ? If so, if you will fix any day except Wednesday morning (when I am giving evidence before a Committee) I will communicate again with Redmond and hold myself at your service.

" We could leave over the question of the time limit and other matters for future discussion, either here or elsewhere."

Carson appears to have replied that the time limit must take precedence of any question of territorial adjustment, for on the 2nd July Lowther wrote again asking if he might refer the point to the Prime Minister, " as that appears to be a matter to which it is indispensable that he shall assent, and I have reason also to think that he would be quite prepared to modify or change that limitation of six years."

This reference brought a letter from Asquith to Carson. On the 6th July, 1914, the Prime Minister wrote : " The map shall be sent to you. The Speaker has shown me your letter. I think it might be well if you and I could have a short talk before you leave for Ireland. Could this be arranged ? "

Whether arranged or not it came to nothing. On the 10th July T. P. O'Connor sent an urgent letter to Redmond, then at Eastbourne, " reporting the result of an hour's conversation with L. G." Mr. Lloyd George, it appears, had " his suspicions " of the Prime Minister, which were " shared " by that Father Confessor of the Liberal Party, Mr. J. A. Spender of the *Westminster Gazette*, who had dined with Mr. Asquith a few nights before and had been " surprised and a little alarmed by Asquith's confident anticipation that settlement would be arrived at." Mr. Lloyd George, always the loyal colleague, reported these suspicions to T. P., insisting at the same time on the " absolute and urgent necessity " of Redmond seeing Asquith. Such ominous preliminaries prepare us for the interview which took place on the 13th July between Asquith, Birrell, Redmond and Dillon.

The Prime Minister seems to have been uneasily conscious that his confidence had been betrayed : " He desired to state most emphatically that any idea that he had come to any definite conclusion on any points in controversy was quite wrong," and he desired the Irishmen to dismiss that idea from their minds, " no matter from what quarter, direct or indirect, the information reached us." Did he suspect the source of the intrigue ? It is impossible to say.

Mr. Asquith then plunged into the problem of the exclusion of Ulster ; but his exposition was stonily received. The Nationalists remarked that it would be " fatal " for Mr. Asquith to give any hint of

possible concessions on the Second Reading unless a
settlement had been reached ; the Prime Minister
anxiously assured them of " his desire to keep in
daily touch with us " : " No large concessions," he
promised them, " would be agreed to without the
fullest discussion with us and consideration of all
that we had to say."

Then, like a heavy whip suddenly brought out
and flourished, came Redmond's last word : " I
intimated to the Prime Minister that it was quite
conceivable that he might announce concessions . . .
which would render it absolutely necessary for us
to vote against the Bill, and I pointed out the consequences which were bound to follow, amongst
other things, that a very large proportion of the
Liberal Party would vote with us, as also the Labour
Party, and that he might be forced to rely on Tory
votes to carry his Bill."

On the 16th July there was another interview to
the same effect. Mr. Redmond repeated his threat :
" The great bulk of the Liberal Party and the whole
of the Labour Party would vote with me." The
Prime Minister admitted that such a position
" would certainly be an intolerable one for the
Government, and he did not believe that it could
or would be allowed by them to arise." And he
ended by making complete submission : " He did
not press me in any way to agree to any further concessions, and indicated clearly that he would act in
conjunction and in consultation with us in every
step that he would take."[1] Mr. Asquith might have
exclaimed with Dr. Faustus : " I writ them a Bill
with mine own blood ; the date is expired ; the time
will come and he will fetch me."

[1] Denis Gwynn, *The Life of John Redmond*, pp. 334-5.

Carson had told Lord Midleton that, " The Government will not come to terms with Ulster unless Redmond consents, and that agreement is in these circumstances highly improbable " ; he was right, and there was nothing for it but to go forward with the preparations for resistance. On 3rd July Sir Henry Wilson notes in his diary a conversation with Lord Milner : " He told me that unless Asquith agreed to the Lords' amendment, and he does not think that there is a chance of it as Redmond won't allow it, Carson will set up a provisional government and will take over such Government offices as he can without bloodshed. This will bring matters to a head."[1]

That the Ulster Loyalists intended to take over the Government, if they were put to it, is certain ; what date they were to choose remained their secret. Milner told Wilson that he was " altogether against Ulster waiting any longer to suit Asquith's convenience " ; but Milner was not in command, and both Carson and Craig, with cooler heads, must have seen the danger of premature action. Redmond, from his point of view, saw it also. On the 15th May, 1914, he had written to Mr. Birrell :

" Conceivably they might occupy some public offices, such as the Post Office and the Customs Office ; but even in the event of such action we believe it would be quite possible for the Government to put an end to the movement without a single drop of blood being shed. The port would be closed, and all postal and telegraphic communication with Belfast could be prevented.

" If this were done the provisional government

[1] *Field-Marshal Sir Henry Wilson*, vol. i., p. 148.

would crumble to pieces in ridicule after a very short time."

Mr. Asquith may have thought so too, or pretended so to think.

" In a mixed company," Lord Londonderry wrote to Carson on the 17th July, 1914, " a reliable person told me that Asquith hopes, and has said so, that you will set up the provisional government as he says ' it cannot last a week and Ulster will look ridiculous ' as the Customs could not be collected. I thought I ought to tell you as I think the information is correct."

While these things hung in the balance, there were others who took a hand in those desperate eleventh-hour attempts at a settlement. Lord Murray of Elibank, returned from Bogota, busied himself with both sides ; but despite an incorrigible optimism succeeded not at all.

There was, however, still one with more authority who might succeed where others failed : both sides in their perplexity turned to the King. In his speech at Mountain Ash, Carson, in his simple way, had put the dilemma of the Crown :

" What advice," he asked, " will Mr. Asquith give the King ?

" Is he going to tell the King : ' Sir, you are to sign this Bill with the certainty that some of your Majesty's most loyal subjects in the North of Ireland will have to be coerced by Your Majesty's troops ' ?

" Is he going to say to the King : 'We do not know whether the country wishes you to sign this or not, but we are prepared to tell you to sign it even if the country is against the Bill ' ? "

And again on the 5th July at Herne Hill he had put these difficulties not only of the Prime Minister in advising but of the King in considering the advice. The Bill having been passed, His Majesty's Ministers would ask the King to sign the Bill, and being upright, honest and straightforward men, they would tell him the whole truth :

" ' Sir, you must remember that we have already told you, and you have put it in your gracious speech from the Throne, that if you do sign it there would be serious commotion, civil commotion, in the North of Ireland, and we also told you and advised you, and you graciously put it in your speech, that if you do not sign it there would be civil commotion in the South and West of Ireland,' and then they will say: 'We honestly must confess to you that that is the condition to which Your Majesty's trusted Ministers have brought the country.'

" But His Majesty might very well ask: 'What about the Ulster Volunteers ? '

" Well, I suppose he would be told: 'Don't be afraid of them because they have got volunteers in the South and West.' And then I can imagine the gracious reply of the King : 'But is not this a message of peace ? ' "

Carson, it is plain, was appealing, desperately, passionately, to his King on behalf of those loyal subjects of Ulster.

" Why should he sign it ? " someone shouted.

" That," said Carson, " is what I am always being asked as I walk through the streets of Belfast.

" Men come up to me and say: 'Sir Edward, we have always been loyal to the King ; we are devoted to his person and dynasty ; we have been faithful subjects of the United Kingdom, and the King will never sign the Bill.' "

" When I tell them, ' Your King is a constitutional monarch and will act on the advice of his Ministers,' they shake their heads and say : 'He is the King : we are true to the King, and he will be true to us.' "

Mr. Asquith also was a subject—in trouble no less than the troubles of the subject in Belfast, and on the 18th July, in his desperation, he too turned to the King, begging His Majesty to " intervene before the crisis becomes more acute." The crisis, indeed, was not merely in Ulster : it was in Europe : on the 28th June the Archduke Franz Ferdinand had been murdered at Sarajevo ; in the middle of July things already looked like war.

On the 20th July, instead of introducing the Amending Bill in the House of Commons the Prime Minister announced that the King had called a conference at Buckingham Palace. Next day it met, the Government represented by the Prime Minister and Mr. Lloyd George ; the Conservatives by Lord Lansdowne and Mr. Bonar Law ; the Nationalists by Mr. Redmond and Mr. Dillon, and the Ulster Unionists by Sir Edward Carson and James Craig. The King impressed his anxiety upon them : " For months we have watched with deep misgivings the course of events in Ireland. The trend has been surely and steadily towards an appeal to force, and to-day the cry of civil war is on the lips of the most responsible and sober-minded of my people."

Then, with an expression of his feelings for Ireland, and a prayer for their guidance, His Majesty left them to their deliberations, the Speaker taking his place in the chair.

It is a common belief that the Buckingham Palace

Conference came so near to a peace that only Tyrone divided the parties : as a matter of fact, there was never any approach to agreement.

The Nationalists stood on the terms of the Amending Bill : they would concede nothing more. The Unionists stood for the " clean cut," that is to say, the exclusion of the Province of Ulster without a time limit. Carson, as we have seen, had adopted that course as his deliberate policy, hoping thereby to wreck the Home Rule Bill, and even when that hope faded out the policy remained, as, on the whole, the less disastrous alternative. If he had had any doubts of the feelings of Ulster a sheaf of exhortatory telegrams would have removed them, as, for example :

> " To Sir Edward Carson, Conference Room, Buckingham Palace. Act the patriot. Do not play the part of the harlot against whom Solomon decided."

The Unionists proposed to discuss the Time Limit, which they took to be fatal to any prospect of settlement : the Nationalists objecting, that issue was postponed. The exclusion of the whole Province was proposed ; but it was rejected by the Nationalists. Then the Unionists proposed that the six counties, which now make Northern Ireland, should vote as one unit, for or against exclusion ; but the Nationalists stood firmly on voting by counties. Redmond said he was prepared to make large concessions to calm Protestant fears if only the Unionists would accept the principle of the Bill on the basis of a United Ireland. Ulster refused to consider any such compromise.

It was Asquith who tried to concentrate the dispute on local issues. He first proposed that certain areas of Ulster, South Down, South Fermanagh, South Armagh, and North Tyrone, should go with Southern Ireland, and then proposed arbitration in the case of County Tyrone ; but these expedients were never accepted either by the Nationalists or Unionists.

The spirit of these negotiations is suggested in a letter of the 21st July, 1914, to Carson from his friend Alexander McDowell :

" The statement made in the English papers as to Tyrone being the bone of contention has enabled one to see very clearly the opinion of the bulk of the people here. It is decisive against giving up any portion of Tyrone. The question of Down apparently has not got out ; but the feeling about Tyrone is so strong that any partition of Down would certainly not be agreed to.

" I had a visit to-day from a very leading Home Ruler to ask me to use my influence to get the clean cut idea abandoned. He said he was authorised to say that if it were, and the principle of Home Rule accepted, they would consent to Ulster having twice the number of representatives provided for by the Bill and that the Government was prepared to give more money to be tied up in any way we thought right and for any purpose. He spoke of the bitter feeling which separation would cause, the glorious future before the country if we were all united, and all the other usual cooing-dove arguments which on occasions like this are made use of. I thought it best not to
Cca

argue but simply told him his party had sinned
away their day of grace, that you had announced
the decision of the party here, and that if they
really wanted peace and were in earnest in their
desire to win Ulster ultimately they would accede
at once to your demand, that this holding out
only confirmed Ulstermen in their view that they
want to force them into chains, and that view
only stiffened Ulster resistance. Evidently from
this gentleman's demeanour there is consternation
in the Nationalist camp. . . . We are pressing on
our preparations on the basis of the Conference
proving abortive."

Thus these two embattled opposites stood out
against any agreement. Carson, who had proposed,
possibly with some secret misgivings, the solution of
the clean cut, gave it as his opinion, long afterwards,
that if Redmond had accepted that offer, he would
thereby have won Ireland for Home Rule, since
the Protestant Minority would not have been
strong enough permanently to hold the whole
Province of Ulster.

After four days of this sort of fencing, the Conference broke down, " being unable to agree either
in principle or in detail."

On the 24th July the Prime Minister, Mr. Birrell
and Mr. Lloyd George met John Redmond and
John Dillon ; and could think of no better expedient
than to send General Macready back to Belfast with
instructions to do nothing : even if the Provisional
Government were proclaimed the Cabinet proposed
to await the consequential orders which might be
issued by Carson before determining upon their
next move. " A more thoroughly unsatisfactory

position for any soldier," said Macready ruefully, " it is hard to imagine."[1]

While Macready awaited the " bloody tragedy " which he feared from the action of the " fanatical enthusiasts " of Ulster, it came suddenly, where it might have been expected, in the more impulsive South. The Nationalist Volunteers had resolved to emulate Ulster with a landing of arms ; but did not imitate the Ulstermen's discretion. The rifles were landed in Dublin Bay in broad daylight on Sunday the 20th July, and seven hundred Irish volunteers marched back towards Dublin with the weapons on their shoulders. Mr. Harrel, Assistant Commissioner of Police, called out both police and military ; the King's Own Scottish Borderers blocked the entrance to the Dublin Road ; some of the volunteers were disarmed, others escaped, under cover of their front rank, into the open country. The soldiers returning to barracks were pelted with stones by the city mob, and in the mêlée some of the soldiers firing without orders, three of the crowd were killed and thirty-eight injured. True to its traditions, the Liberal Government humiliated the police and punished Mr. Harrel.

In the meantime Ulster was going steadily forward with her preparations. On the 15th July Craig had written to Carson concerning an impending purchase of ammunition which would require a large sum of money. According to the situation Carson was to telegraph either " Go ahead " or " Hold back in the meantime." On the 29th July this question—and something more important— was still pending.

" I have got your letter," Craig wrote to Carson,

[1] *Annals of an Active Life,* vol. i., p. 194.

" and you may take it that immediately you signify by the pre-arranged code that we are to go ahead, everything prepared will be carried out to the letter unless in the meantime you suggest any modification. All difficulties have been overcome, and we are in a very strong position."

It looks from this letter as if nothing less than the establishment of the Provisional Government was under consideration, not as an eventual but as an immediate measure, and with the object of forcing a crisis—and a General Election—upon the British Government.

" We have decided," Craig continued, " that when you come over next this place (Craigavon) will be converted into the old camp again, the Committee and Headquarters having approved. The old Town Hall will be adequately guarded, and everybody will take steps for personal protection, alongside which there will be of necessity a partial mobilisation so as to create an atmosphere over as large an area as possible."

So far, then, Craig is absorbed in the preliminaries of this coup which he is organising ; but another crisis intrudes upon his plans and finds a place in his letter :

" The important aspect to be considered by you," he proceeds, " in treating with the Government—if they approach you again—is with regard to officers and men of the Reserve, who would, in the ordinary course, be called upon by the Government in view of the European situation. . . ."

Here Craig referred to a memorandum enclosed which showed that some sixty officers holding important commands and staff appointments in the Ulster Volunteer Force were liable to be called up

either from the reserve of officers or in the Special
Reserve and Territorial Force ; a large number of
the men were in a similar position.

" I cannot help thinking," he proceeded, " that
the danger to the peace of Ulster would be intensely
aggravated if all these men were withdrawn, because, instead of a properly organised Force, some
districts would be left without their proper military
commanders. I look on it somehow like this. If the
Government for the sake of peace will offer the
' clean cut ' or the six counties with an adjustment
of boundaries, we on our part would not only instantly free the officers named on the list, but could
promise that law and order would be maintained
in the Province without the presence of any troops
whatever. On the other hand, if an unsatisfactory
plan is forced upon us, then, without a doubt, they
will have to face considerable civil disturbance.
You will know how to make the best of this in any
conversations with the other side. . . .

" Needless to say, if you require any of us over at
short notice, you have only to send a wire. I am not
crossing to-night because I gather from your letter
that the debate will be adjourned till next week, and
there is necessarily so much work here that loafing
about the House of Commons is more than I can
stand.

" Nothing more at present. Bertie McCalmont
takes this over, and if you have anything important
to communicate Cambray will find a messenger. All
well and ready for the fray."

All was ready for the fray, but it was not to be in
Ulster ! If the strong and obstinate mind of Craig
entertained for a moment the idea of bargaining with the Government over the Reserves, he

dismissed it, as we see in the following telegram sent
by Craig to Carson on the 30th July, 1914. After
acknowledging a letter from Carson it proceeds :

"If Government offer unacceptable, am of
opinion you should to-day, openly, on highest
patriotic grounds, take the initiative in suggesting
that the Home Rule question be postponed. You
doing so in the House in first instance will be fully
understood here and appeal to the loyalty of the
people. Offer Government our officers, men and
arms generously to see the matter through. Much
better that than have the matter squeezed out of
you ' in camera ' and easier for you to explain to
people here."

In a letter written that same day in explanation
of his telegram Craig said :

"Not only do I consider the offer, at great sacrifice on the part of Ulster, to postpone the whole
matter a most patriotic and generous suggestion ;
but looking at it from the other point of view, it
may very greatly disconcert the Coalition, especially the Nationalists. They would find it extremely awkward to follow on with a similar offer
from their side, and surely the country would be
able to read between the lines and store up that
much to our credit when the issue is finally fought
out."

Then his obstinate mind recurred to the " action of
drastic character" which they were prepared to take
and of his arrangements to hold meetings in Glasgow and other seaports, the object of which meetings
suggests that Craig anticipated nothing less than a

blockade. Glasgow was to send " a shipload of whatever necessaries we may requisition . . . according to the General's dispositions they will be able to decide what supplies are most necessary, i.e. flour, meal, tinned beef, tea, sugar, etc. It occurred to me that this would be about the most tangible way of showing sympathy with Ulster, especially if shipping was interfered with by the Government." Lord Milner and his League of Covenanters might organise something similar in the English ports : " There is no doubt the further afield the heather is fired the better for our purpose. I can only say in conclusion," Craig ended, "that whatever you decide upon, immediately or in the future, will find us absolutely ready here, so do not allow any thought of want of preparations to weigh with you for a moment."

This letter of July 30th, 1914, suggests the dramatically close coincidence of those two crises. The two furies of domestic and of foreign war were running neck and neck. The Amending Bill was to be debated in the House of Commons that same day, and it is likely that Carson had Craig's telegram in his pocket when he went to consult with Bonar Law upon what was best to be done. Weighing the one crisis against the other, they came to a momentous decision. That day, as he records in his Diary, the Prime Minister was " sitting in the Cabinet room with a map of Ulster and a lot of statistics about populations and religions, endeavouring to get into something like shape my speech on the Amending Bill," when a telephone message came through from Bonar Law " asking me to go and see him at his Kensington abode." The sorely-harassed Minister got into Bonar Law's car and was taken to the house where he found the two men together. Bonar Law proposed that they should postpone the Second Reading of the Amending Bill so as not to " weaken our influence in the world for peace." " Carson said that at first he had thought it impossible to agree, as it would strain still further the well-known and much-tried patience of Ulstermen ; but he had come to see that it was now a patriotic duty."

Mr. Asquith began by welcoming a proposal which, after consulting his colleagues, and Mr. Redmond, he accepted. Thus these inveterate antagonists, obeying the common instinct of the British race, formed front to meet a foreign foe.

INDEX

INDEX

DDc

INDEX

INDEX

437

Ireland, prosperity under the Union, 28
— rebellion (53rd) of *1798*, 13, 14
— religious, social, and racial divisions, 10–11
— secret and terrorist societies, 13–14, 388–9
— separation of Northern and Southern Loyalists, 251
Irish House of Commons, Bill to reform, *1783*, 13
— burnt down, *1793*, 13
Irish in United States, Clan-na-Gael, 30
Irish Legislature, loyal to England, 14
Irish Loyalists, extreme nervousness, *Summer 1914*, 394–6
Irish Nationalists, after Curragh and gun-running, 379–80
— after 1910 Election, 22
— and King's Speech, *10.2.13*, 278–9
— anger at Duke of Norfolk, *1912*, 129–30
— as buffer Party, 18
— attack on Sir Horace Plunkett, 29
— attitude to Churchill's Belfast meeting, *1912*, 89
— determination to include Ulster, 80
— effect of Lord Loreburn's letter, 200
— ill-disciplined attacks, 388
— on People's Budget, 19
— opposition to separation of Ulster, 164
— relation to United Irish League, 28
— strength at Westminster, *1910*, 57
— to support Government, *1910*, 42
Irish, native, attitude to House of Lords, 56–7
Irish Parliamentary Party, 29
Irish Republican Brotherhood, 388
— Oath, 389
Irish Unionist Alliance, 222, 249, 394
Irish Volunteers, convention of, *1783*, 13
— growth of, 385, 390–1
— gun-running, *20.7.14*, 419
Isaacs, Godfrey, and Marconi case, 173, 174 *et seq.*, 184
Isaacs, Harry, 179
Isaacs, Sir Rufus, *see* Reading, Lord
Iveagh, Lord, 247

JAMES I, and Ulster, 68
James II, compared to Asquith by Bonar Law, 237
John, Mr., explanation of Lloyd George's Marconi transactions, 181

Karl Kiehn, lighter with arms for Ulster, 365
Kelly, Sam, owner of the *Balmerino*, 368
Kilkeel, Carson's meeting, *Sept. 1913*, 206
Kilmorey, Lord, 206
Kinloch-Cooke, Sir Clement, 113
Kipling, Rudyard, on "sale" of Southern Loyalists, 105
— supporter of Ulster Convention, *Feb. 1914*, 305

LABOUR PARTY, after *1910* election, 22
— strength of, *1910*, 57
Ladybank, Fife, Asquith's meeting, *25.10.13*, 224
Lagan Force, of Irish Rebellion, *1641–2*, 70
Lamlash, 317, 340
Lancashire, Carson's meetings, *20.6.14*, 401
Land League, 77
Lansbury, George, on Marconi rumours, 175
Lansdowne, 5th Marquess of, and Lionel Curtis, "negotiations," *25.4.14*, 383
— at Buckingham Palace Conference, *21.7.14*, 415 *et seq.*
— attitude to creation of Peers, *1911*, 60
— attitude to Irish question, *1910*, 47
— attitude to separation, *Oct. 1913*, 220 *et seq.*
— in Bonar Law's reports to Carson, 211–2
— on Lord Loreburn's letter, *11.9.13*, 195
— on Royal intervention, *Sept. 1913*, 202
— on Southern Loyalists, 249
— supporter of Carson, 52
Larkin, Jim, Labour leader in Dublin, *1913*, 247–8, 256
Larne, Carson's meeting, *11.7.14*, 403